THE DIVINE WITHIN

BOOKS BY ALDOUS HUXLEY

Novels
The Genius and the Goddess
Ape and Essence
Time Must Have a Stop
After Many a Summer Dies
    the Swan
Eyeless in Gaza
Point Counter Point
Those Barren Leaves
Antic Hay
Crome Yellow
Brave New World
Island

Essays and Belles Lettres
Brave New World Revisited
Tomorrow and Tomorrow
    and Tomorrow
Heaven and Hell
The Doors of Perception
The Devils of Loudun
Themes and Variations
Ends and Means
Texts and Pretexts
The Olive Tree
Music at Night
Vulgarity in Literature
Do What You Will
Proper Studies
Jesting Pilate
Along the Road
On the Margin

Essays New and Old
The Art of Seeing
The Perennial Philosophy
Science, Liberty and Peace

Short Stories
Collected Short Stories
Brief Candles
Two or Three Graces
Limbo
Little Mexican
Mortal Coils

Biography
Grey Eminence

Poetry
The Cicadas
Leda

Travel
Beyond the Mexique Bay

Drama
Mortal Coils—A Play
The World of Light
The Discovery, Adapted from
    Francis Sheridan

Selected Works
Rotunda
The World of Aldous Huxley

THE DIVINE WITHIN

SELECTED WRITINGS ON ENLIGHTENMENT

ALDOUS HUXLEY

EDITED BY JACQUELINE HAZARD BRIDGEMAN
INTRODUCTION BY HUSTON SMITH

HARPER**PERENNIAL** ● MODERN**CLASSICS**

NEW YORK ● LONDON ● TORONTO ● SYDNEY ● NEW DELHI ● AUCKLAND

HARPER**PERENNIAL** ● MODERN**CLASSICS**

Originally published under the title *Huxley and God: Essays* in 1992 by HarperSanFrancisco, a division of HarperCollins Publishers.

P.S.™ is a trademark of HarperCollins Publishers.

HarperCollins books may be purchased for educational, business, or sales promotional use. For information, please e-mail the Special Markets Department at SPsales@harpercollins.com.

FIRST HARPER PERENNIAL MODERN CLASSICS EDITION PUBLISHED 2013.

Library of Congress Cataloging-in-Publication Data [for the original 1992 edition]

Huxley, Aldous, 1894–1963
Huxley and God : essays / Aldous Huxley ; edited by Jacqueline Hazard Bridgeman ; introduction by Huston Smith.
p. cm.
Originally published: San Francisco : HarperSanFrancisco, c1992.
Includes bibliographical references.
ISBN 0-8245-2252-4
1. Religion   I. Hazard, Jacqueline.   II. Title.
BL50.H88 2003
200-dc21
2002155675

Page 306 constitutes a continuation of the copyright page.

ISBN-13: 9780062236814

ISBN-10: 0062236814

23 24 25 26 27 LBC 16 15 14 13 12

CONTENTS

CONTENTS

PREFACE

"Officially an agnostic," Aldous Huxley was to declare in 1926, "but [he demurred] when in propitious emotional circumstances with certain landscapes, works of art, . . . certain people, I know that 'God's in His heaven and all's right with the world.'"

The above passage, from an essay written when the author was thirty years old, clearly shows that he entertained ambivalent feelings about religion and God. The intuitive versus the rational. Huxley's "mystic germ," as William James called his own inner voice, apparent here, lay dormant for many years.

In his novels and essays of the 1920s, Huxley was scathingly skeptical of religion and its "life-retreating" pious aspirants. His gods were "life, love, sex." Religion that negated this trilogy, he scorned. He abhorred the views of Swift, Pascal, Beaudelaire, Proust, and even St. Francis of Assisi! According to Huxley, they were "life-haters."

Huxley's earliest mentors were the passionate "life-affirmers"—Robert Burns, D. H. Lawrence, and William Blake. In his words, he was a "life-worshipper." His God was the God of Life. He believed in the diversity of the human persona; all desires served but tempered by reason. The moderation that Aristotle preached. The philosophy of the Golden Mean. It was, as Huxley wrote, a matter of "the equilibrium of balanced excesses." As with the Greeks he advocated the worship of many gods—celebrating all aspects of human life. One could live with this "celebration of excesses," as he called it, by using discrimination and balance and simply good manners; an impossibly fragile concept for all but the intellectual and moral nobility of persons such as Huxley himself.

Over the next twenty years, his hedonistic attitude began to recede, and his "mystic germ" began to mature. Pluralism gave way to monism as seen in *The Perennial Philosophy* (1944), a documentation of the common doctrine in all major religions: that the truth is universal, that God is One.

By the 1940s Aldous Huxley was labeled a "mystic." It is an accurate description if one understands mysticism as William Blake defines it, "The self at one with God," and by Plotinus's description of spiritual ecstasy, "The flight of the alone to the Alone."

Mysticism is often understood by bad poets to mean the mysterious and by sophistic savants as "humans becoming God." The word's literal definition is "intimate union of the soul with God through contemplation and love."

The pronouncement that Aldous Huxley unabashedly believed in God may startle the current generation of young people charmed by *Brave New World* (1932), which has been a favorite with the fiercely dedicated college agnostics who never bothered to read any of the author's later novels.

That Aldous Huxley intuitively knew the reality of God—or "The Divine Ground of Our Being" or J. D. Salinger's "Fat Lady" or George Lucas's "The Force" or Bill Wilson's "Higher Power" or Emerson's "Divine Spark"—is beautifully expressed in these essays.

Originally printed in the bi-monthly magazine *Vedanta and the West* between the years of 1941 to 1960, the essays are here published in book form for the first time. *Vedanta and the West,* now extinct, was published by the Vedanta Society of Southern California from 1941 to 1970 with a modest circulation of under a thousand subscribers. Its celebrated array of editors were Aldous Huxley, Christopher Isherwood, John Van Druten, Gerald Heard, and Swami Prabhavananda, who headed the organization. Among the magazine's illustrious contributors were the likes of India's Nehru, Rabbi Asher Block, U Thant, Somerset Maugham, Arnold Toynebee, Vincent Sheean, Tagore, Alan Watts, and Dr. Joseph Kaplan, chairman of the physics department at UCLA.

In the twenty years that the author was associated with the Vedanta Center, he contributed over forty articles to the magazine. We have chosen the more representative of this output. These essays are new to the general reading public. For thirty years they lay lost in the files of the Vedanta Society. A few of the articles eventually became portions of the novels Huxley was writing at the time, most importantly *Time Must Have a Stop* (1945), Huxley's own favorite work.

Huxley remained a devotee of Prabhavananda, a monk of the highly respected Ramakrishna Order of India, and during this period was eventually initiated by him. But there came a rift between guru and disciple when the author began experimenting with mescaline and LSD as tools toward enlightenment. Prabhavananda was adamantly opposed to the use of drugs, and drugs used as a short cut to spiritual awareness. Huxley's guru claimed that drugs were a deterrent to spiritual growth—if you were a fool when you entered the drug-induced visionary state, you remained a fool when you returned to normal consciousness. Whereas a genuine spiritual experience would leave one transformed and enlightened as witnessed in the lives of the great saints and spiritual geniuses.

Eventually, Huxley was drawn to Krishnamurti, who espoused freedom from any prophet or path and was closer to Zen than Vedanta.

Even though he drifted away from the Vedanta Society, Huxley continued to supply the magazine with essays. His admiration for Swami Prabhavananda never wavered. He delivered his last lecture, titled "Symbol and Immediate Experience," in 1960, three years before his death.

Jacqueline Hazard Bridgeman

INTRODUCTION

From the time that I first met Aldous Huxley when I was twenty-eight until he died seventeen years later, he was important to me not only as a writer but as a friend and mentor. So before I proceed to the main object of this introduction, which is to situate the essays of this book in the context of Huxley's literary career, I shall insert a memorial that, on the twenty-fifth anniversary of Huxley's death, I wrote for the *Los Angeles Times*.

There was a moment in the 1950s when there was talk of pooling the talents of Aldous Huxley, Igor Stravinsky, and Martha Graham to turn *The Tibetan Book of the Dead* into a ballet with Greek chorus.

That moment passed, but when Aldous Huxley died a quarter-century ago this week, it was the words of that Tibetan manual that were read into his ear by his prior request: "Now there is approaching that clear white light of the Void. Do not be afraid. *Do not be afraid*. It is your friend. Go fearlessly into that Light of the Void" (abridged).

It was likewise of the Void that Huxley spoke most during my first meeting with him in 1947. He and his wife, Maria, were at their cabin hide-away in the Mojave Desert, and Aldous took me for a long walk through its scrubby stretches.

He loved the desert, he told me, for its symbolic power. Its emptiness emptied his mind. "The boundlessness of its sands [I paraphrase] spreads a mantle of sameness—hence unity—over the world's multiplicity in the way snow does. The Nothingness to which the Desert Fathers were drawn is not a blank negation. It is a no-thing-ness in which everything is so interfused that divisions are transcended. Pure light contains all the frequencies of the rainbow, but undemarcated. The Void is the vacuum-plenum complex, grasped by its vacuum pole."

Years later, when I helped to bring Huxley to the Massachusetts Institute of Technology for the 1960 fall semester, the audience for his public lectures grew until by midpoint in the series the Boston Police Department had to augment its force on Wednesday evenings to manage traffic that backed up from Cambridge across the Charles River. When I alluded to this as a tribute, Huxley characteristically disclaimed it. "It's because I've been around so long," he said. "I've become like Anne Hathaway's Cottage. If I lived to be a hundred I shall be like Stonehenge."

He didn't live to be a hundred, and when he died, at the age of sixty-nine, the world lost an exceptionally creative intelligence. Most obviously, it lost an encyclopedic mind. When a leading newspaper decided that the Fourteenth Edition of the Encyclopedia Britannica should be brought under review, no one was surprised when Huxley was asked to do the job. (He found it inferior to the Eleventh Edition.)

More impressive than the range of the man's mind, however, was its sympathy and interest. Few major intelligences since William James have been as open. Huxley's regard for mysticism was well known by dint of being almost notorious. What some overlooked was his equal interest in the workaday world and its exigencies: peace, the population explosion, and conservation of our natural resources. To those who, greedy for transcendence, deprecated the mundane, he advised that we "make the best of both worlds." To their opposites, the positivists, his message was the same but worded differently: "Fair enough; one world at a time. But not half a world."

His wit was playful and incisive. Alan Watts happened to pass through Cambridge during Huxley's MIT term, and when I discovered that these two articulate Californian Englishmen had not met, I arranged a supper to introduce them. Alan had to leave early for a lecture somewhere, and when Huxley and I resumed our seats, there was a pause during which I could almost hear him sorting things out. Then his verdict. "What a curious man! Half monk, half race-track operator." When I later reported this assessment to Alan, he loved it and acknowledged its accuracy.

It wasn't Huxley's wit alone, of course, that powered his talk—he was a master conversationalist generally. His imposing height and magnificent profile contributed, but it was the way he used words to shape ideas that accounted for the magic. I have been in restaurants where surrounding tables fell silent as their occupants strained to eavesdrop. I seldom left his presence without feeling recharged, as if some new corner of the world—if not new vistas of being—had opened for me.

Accepting the fact that "truth lies at the bottom of a very muddy well," he descended: to ESP and LSD and to "sight without glasses." But never as embattled renegade; rather, the drive of his investigative mind led him to the interstices between the pigeonholes of established knowledge. If toward the end he lost his reputation with highbrows, it was not for his omnivorous interests, but because he wasn't content simply to do what he could do well. His competence bored him. So the master of words moved on to what eludes words, remarking over his shoulder that "language is a device for taking the mystery out of reality." Not needing triumph, adulation, or disciples, he could bypass them for truth.

He could bypass them because he had so little egoism. A supreme unpretentiousness characterized him to the end, which came on the same day as John F. Kennedy's assassination. "It's rather embarassing," he said, "to have been concerned with the human problem all one's life and to find that one has little more to offer by way of advice than, Try to be a little kinder." If, as he had earlier observed, the central technique for man to learn is "the art of obtaining freedom from the fundamental human disability of egoism," Huxley achieved that freedom.

But that was not his supreme achievement, for his personal problem was not pride but pessimism. "Did anything more than usually disastrous happen last night?" he asked one morning as he approached the breakfast table where I was glancing at the newspaper. And underlying the world's disasters was its vanity, the seeming meaninglessness of it all—"tomorrow, tomorrow, and tomorrow creeps in this petty pace from day to day." His final victory, therefore, lay not in emerging selfless but in winning through to equanimity—an evenness of spirit and generalized good cheer. Thereby the line he used to close perhaps his best novel, *Point Counter Point* (1928), became the appropriate epitaph for his own life's journey. "Oh such is the Kingdom of Heaven."

Said this time without sarcasm.

Huxley's first book, *The Burning Wheel* (1916), a collection of poems, was published when he was twenty. In the forty-nine years that followed, he published over thirty books—novels, poetry, collections of short stories, and treatises on social and philosophic subjects. No other author of his period put himself more lucidly on record. The *New Yorker* styled him "one of the few English-speaking novelists who actually appears to be decently educated," and it was true, for throughout his life, even after his eyesight was impaired, he read voraciously. This equipped him with a vast store of knowledge to draw upon as well as a huge vocabulary, which he used with economy and precision. Few prose stylists of his day approached him.

The question for this introduction is where God figured in his life and work.

We can see clearly from Aldous Huxley's earliest books that religion fascinated him from the start. This is not to say that he approved. In his early novels he misses few opportunities to ridicule Christianity and oriental mysticism alike, while at the same time being unable, it would seem, to get them off his mind. *Antic Hay* (1923) is typical here. An important character in the novel, the fierce, bearded Coleman, is so adroit at finding ways and opportunities to blaspheme that his conversation sounds like an endless black mass. Even when he is engaged in seduction, he delays his triumph briefly to ask the lady, "Do you believe in God?" When she answers, "Not m-much," he goes on to say,

> I pity you. You must find existence dreadfully dull. As soon as you do, everything becomes a thousand times life-size. . . . It's only when you believe in God, and especially in hell, that you can really begin enjoying life.

It was not common in the Roaring Twenties for religion to figure as prominently in novels as it did in Huxley's. The way that he represented religion shows him to be sharply at odds with himself on the subject. His conscious mind could see no meaning in life, but intuitively he rebelled against the emptiness of such an outlook. His loathing for the futile sensuality of his characters raises passages in *Antic Hay* (and to a lesser extent *Chrome Yellow*) to levels of prophetic grandeur. As one reviewer observed, "The more he hates, the more lucid his style becomes." Never has the modern atrophy and perversion of the human spirit been etched with more surgical exactness.

In the three years between *Antic Hay* and his next book, a collection of essays gathered under the title *Jesting Pilate* (1926), Huxley's psychological struggle becomes explicit. The whole of *Jesting Pilate* is a sustained witness to Huxley's turmoil and inner confusion at this stage. He tells us that mysticism is bunk, but he cannot conceal the fact that something in him draws him strongly toward it. His mind fights to damp down and resist a strong, opposing intuition.

The conflict reaches its climax in *Point Counter Point* (1928). In this story, most of the characters are caught up in the familiar Huxlian quest for happiness, particularly sexual happiness. But the reader closes the book feeling that virtually everyone has reached a dead end.

This, then, was the Huxley of the late 1920s: a man who theoretically advocated the balanced, well-rounded life that the Greeks supposedly espoused. *Brave New World* (1932) changed nothing on that front. A masterpiece of satire, it was witty. Huxley was letting the issue of how life should be lived idle while he thought through—and put permanently behind him—the seductive prospect that it be lived scientifically. Whatever the road he would subsequently travel, it would not be the superhighway to a technological utopia. A letter that he wrote to Chad Walsh of Beloit College shows that even while he was publicly siding with the Greeks, the mystics continued to engage him.

> My preoccupation with the subject of mysticism—an interest partly positive, partly negative; a fascination that was also hostile—dates back to my youth. The title of my first volume of undergraduate verse, *The Burning Wheel,* is derived from Boehme, whom I read while still at Oxford. In a later novel, *Point Counter Point,* there are episodes in which something in the nature of a mystical experience is interpreted in terms of Leuba's explaining-away hypothesis. The negative interest became positive in the early Thirties, not as the result of any single event so much as because all the rest—art, science, literature, the pleasures of thought and sensation— came to seem (as patriotism came to seem to Nurse Cavell) "not enough." One reaches a point where one says, even of Beethoven, even of Shakespeare, "Is this all?"

After *Eyeless in Gaza* (1936), a novel dealing with the conflict between the intellectual and the sexual and its resolution through mysticism, Huxley's mystical commitment never wavered. Indeed, uncharitable critics would all but dismiss his subsequent novels as mystical tracts with thin storyline veneers. *After Many a Summer*

Dies the Swan (1939) has Mr. Propter, Huxley's spokes-
man, summarize the book's thesis as follows:

> Good manifests itself only on the animal level and
> on the level of eternity. Knowing that, you'll real-
> ize that the best you can do on the human level is
> preventive. You can see that purely human activi-
> ties don't interfere too much with the manifesta-
> tion of good on the other levels. That's all. . . . The
> realists who have studied the nature of the world
> know that an exclusively humanistic attitude to-
> ward life is always fatal, and that all strictly human
> activities must therefore be made instrumental to
> animal and spiritual good. They know, in other
> words, that men's business is to make the human
> world safe for animals and spirits.

Compared with *Many a Summer,* which contains elements of Gothic grotesqueness, Huxley's next novel,
Time Must Have a Stop (1945), is sweetness and light. His
insight into human foibles is as keen as ever, but now
he pities rather than despises the characters who typify
values he considers false and futile. The reigning compassion of the book suggests that its author's conversion
is spreading from his head to his heart, transforming his
attitudes and responses.

In *The Perennial Philosophy* (1944), an anthology of
mystical writing of the last twenty-five centuries, Huxley
provides us with the most systematic statement of his ma-

ture outlook. Its running commentary deals with many of the social implications of Huxley's metaphysics.

One last point deserves mention before I let Huxley speak for himself. That the essays in this book initially appeared in *Vedanta and the West* does not show that Huxley's mysticism was oriental. It does, however, suggest that the mystical register of religion—the only register in which Huxley could feel at home—has been more prominent and accessible in India than it has been in the West. This may be changing. If it is, Huxley's religious writings have probably contributed to the change.

Huston Smith
Thomas J. Watson Professor of Religion and Distinguished Adjunct Professor of Philosophy, Emeritus, Syracuse University, and Adjunct Professor, Graduate Theological Union, Berkeley

THE DIVINE WITHIN

1

THE MINIMUM WORKING HYPOTHESIS

This essay subsequently appeared as part of Sebastian's notebook in *Time Must Have a Stop* (1945).

Research into sense-experience—motivated and guided by a working hypothesis; leading, through logical inference to the formulation of an explanatory theory; and resulting in appropriate technological action. That is natural science.

No working hypothesis means no motive for research, no reason for making one experiment rather than another, no way of bringing sense or order into the observed facts.

Contrariwise, too much working hypothesis means finding only what you already *know* to be there and ignoring the rest. Dogma turns a man into an intellectual Procrustes. He goes about forcing things to become the signs of his word-patterns, when he ought to be adapting his word-patterns to become the signs of things.

Among other things religion is also research. Research into, leading to theories about and action in the light of, nonsensuous, nonpsychic, purely spiritual experience.

To motivate and guide this research what sort and how much of a working hypothesis do we need?

None, say the sentimental humanists; just a little bit of Wordsworth, say the nature-worshipers. Result: they have no motive impelling them to make the more arduous experiments; they are unable to explain such non-sensuous facts as come their way; they make very little progress in charity.

At the other end of the scale are the Catholics, the Jews, the Moslems, all with historical, 100-percent revealed religions. These people have their working hypotheses about nonsensuous reality; which means that they have a motive for doing something about it. But because their working hypotheses are too elaborately dogmatic, most of them discover only what they were initially taught to believe. But what they believe is a hotch-potch of good, less good and even bad. Records of the infallible intuitions of great saints into the highest spiritual reality are mixed up with records of the less reliable and infinitely less valuable intuitions of psychics into the lower levels of nonsensuous reality; and to these are added mere fancies, discursive reasonings and sentimentalisms, projected into a kind of secondary objectivity and worshiped as divine facts. But at all times and in spite of these handicaps a persistent few have continued to research to the point where at last they find themselves looking through their dogmas, out into the Clear Light of the Void beyond.

For those of us who are not congenitally the members of an organized church, who have found that humanism and nature-worship are not enough, who are not content to remain in the darkness of ignorance, the squalor of vice, or the other squalor of respectability, the minimum working hypothesis would seem to run to about this:

That there is a Godhead, Ground, Brahman, Clear Light of the Void, which is the unmanifested principle of all manifestations.

That the Ground is at once transcendent and immanent.

That it is possible for human beings to love, know and, from virtually, to become actually identical with the divine Ground.

That to achieve this unitive knowledge of the Godhead is the final end and purpose of human existence.

That there is a Law or Dharma which must be obeyed, a Tao or Way which must be followed, if men are to achieve their final end.

That the more there is of self, the less there is of the Godhead; and that the Tao is therefore a way of humility and love, the Dharma a living Law of mortification and self-transcending awareness. This, of course, accounts for the facts of history. People like their egos and do not wish to mortify them, get a bigger kick out of bullying and self-adulation than out of humility and compassion, are determined not to see why they shouldn't "do what they like" and "have a good time." They get their good time; but also and inevitably they get wars and syphilis, tyranny and alcoholism, revolution, and in default of an adequate religious hypothesis the choice between some lunatic idolatry, such as nationalism, and a sense of complete futility and despair. Unutterable miseries! But throughout recorded history the great majority of men and women have preferred the risk—no, the positive certainty—of such disasters to the tiresome whole-time job of seeking first the kingdom of God. In the long run, we get exactly what we ask for.

2

SEVEN MEDITATIONS

BEING

God is. That is the primordial fact. It is in order that we may discover this fact for ourselves, by direct experience, that we exist. The final end and purpose of every human being is the unitive knowledge of God's being.

What is the nature of God's being? The invocation to the Lord's Prayer gives us the answer. "Our Father which *art* in heaven." God is, and is ours—immanent in each sentient being, the life of all lives, the spirit animating every soul. But this is not all. God is also the transcendent Creator and Law-Giver, the Father who loves and, because He loves, also educates His children. And finally, God is "in heaven." That is to say, He possesses a mode of existence which is incommensurable and incompatible with the mode of existence possessed by human beings in their natural, unspiritualized condition. Because He is ours and immanent, God is very close to us. But because He is also in heaven, most of us are very far from God. The saint is one who is as close to God as God is close to him.

It is through prayer that men come to the unitive

knowledge of God. But the life of prayer is also a life of mortification, of dying to self. It cannot be otherwise; for the more there is of self, the less there is of God. Our pride, our anxiety, our lusts for power and pleasure are God-eclipsing things. So too is that greedy attachment to certain creatures which passes too often for unselfishness and should be called, not altruism, but alter-egoism. And hardly less God-eclipsing is the seemingly self-sacrificing service which we give to any cause or ideal that falls short of the divine. Such service is always idolatry, and makes it impossible for us to worship God as we should, much less to know Him. God's kingdom cannot come unless we begin by making our human kingdoms go. Not only the mad and obviously evil kingdoms, but also the respectable ones—the kingdoms of the scribes and pharisees, the good citizens and pillars of society, no less than the kingdoms of the publicans and sinners. God's being cannot be known by us, if we choose to pay our attention and our allegiance to something else, however creditable that something else may seem in the eyes of the world.

BEAUTY

Beauty arises when the parts of a whole are related to one another and to the totality in a manner which we apprehend as orderly and significant. But the first principle of order is God, and God is the final, deepest meaning of all that exists. God, then, is manifest in the relationship which makes things beautiful. He resides in that lovely interval which harmonizes events on all the planes, where we discover beauty. We apprehend Him in the alternate voids and fullnesses of a cathedral; in the spaces that separate the salient features of a picture; in the living geometry of a flower, a sea shell, an animal; in the pauses and intervals between the notes of music, in their differences of tone and sonority; and finally, on the plane of conduct, in the love and gentleness, the confidence and humility, which give beauty to the relationships between human beings.

Such then, is God's beauty, as we apprehend it in the sphere of created things. But it is also possible for us to apprehend it, in some measure at least, as it is in itself. The beatific vision of divine beauty is the knowledge, so to say, of Pure Interval, of harmonious relationship apart from the things related. A material figure of beauty-in-itself is the cloudless evening sky, which we find inexpressibly lovely, although it possesses no orderliness of arrangement, since there are no distinguishable parts to be harmonized. We find it beautiful because it is an emblem of the infinite Clear Light of the Void. To the knowledge of this Pure Interval we shall come only when we have learned to mortify attachment to creatures, above all to ourselves.

Moral ugliness arises when self-assertion spoils the harmonious relationship which should exist between sentient beings. Analogously, aesthetic and intellectual ugliness arise when one part in a whole is excessive or deficient. Order is marred, meaning distorted and, for the right, the divine relation between things or thoughts, there is substituted a wrong relation—a relationship that manifests symbolically, not the immanent and transcendent source of all beauty, but that chaotic disorderliness which characterizes creatures when they try to live independently of God.

LOVE

God is love, and there are blessed moments when even to unregenerate human beings it is granted to know Him as love. But it is only in the saints that this knowledge becomes secure and continuous. By those in the earlier stages of the spiritual life God is apprehended predominantly as law. It is through obedience to God the Law-Giver that we come at last to know God the loving Father.

The law which we must obey, if we would know God as love, is itself a law of love. "Thou shalt love God with all thy soul, and with all thy heart, with all thy mind and with all thy strength. And thou shalt love thy neighbor as thyself." We cannot love God as we should, unless we love our neighbors as we should. We cannot love our neighbors as we should, unless we love God as we should. And, finally, we cannot realize God as the active, all-pervading principle of love, until we ourselves have learned to love Him and our fellow creatures.

Idolatry consists in loving a creature more than we love God. There are many kinds of idolatry, but all have one thing in common: namely, self-love. The presence of self-love is obvious in the grosser forms of sensual indulgence, or the pursuit of wealth and power and praise. Less manifestly, but none the less fatally, it is present in our inordinate affections for individuals, persons, places, things, and institutions. And even in men's most heroic sacrifices to high causes and noble ideals, self-love has its tragic place. For when we sacrifice ourselves to any cause or ideal that is lower than the highest, less than God Himself, we are merely sacrificing one part of our unregenerate being to another part which we and other people regard as more creditable. Self-love still persists, still prevents us from obeying perfectly the first of the two great commandments. God can be loved perfectly only by those who have killed out the subtlest, the most nobly sublimated forms of self-love. When this happens, when we love God as we should and therefore know God as love, the tormenting problem of evil ceases to be a problem, the world of time is seen to be an aspect of eternity, and in some inexpressible way, but no less really and certainly, the struggling, chaotic multiplicity of life is reconciled in the unity of the all-embracing divine charity.

PEACE

Along with love and joy, peace is one of the fruits of the spirit. But it is also one of the roots. In other words, peace is a necessary condition of spirituality, no less than an inevitable result of it. In the words of St. Paul, it is peace which keeps the heart and mind in the knowledge and love of God.

Between peace the root and peace the fruit of the spirit there is, however, a profound difference in quality. Peace the root is something we all know and understand, something which, if we choose to make the necessary effort, we can achieve. If we do not achieve it, we shall never make any serious advance in our knowledge and love of God, we shall never catch more than a fleeting glimpse of that other peace which is the fruit of spirituality. Peace the fruit is the peace which passes all understanding; and it passes understanding, because it is the peace of God. Only those who have in some measure become God-like can hope to know this peace in its enduring fullness. Inevitably so. For, in the world of spiritual realities, knowledge is always a function of being; the nature of what we experience is determined by what we ourselves are.

In the early stages of the spiritual life we are concerned almost exclusively with peace the root, and with the moral virtues from which it springs, the vices and weaknesses which check its growth. Interior peace has many enemies. On the moral plane we find, on the one hand, anger, impatience, and every kind of violence; and, on the other (for peace is essentially active and creative), every kind of inertia and slothfulness. On the plane of feeling, the great enemies of peace are grief, anxiety, fear, all the formidable host of the negative emotions. And on the plane of the intellect we encounter foolish distractions and the wantonness of idle curiosity. The overcoming of these enemies is a most laborious and often painful process, requiring incessant mortification of natural tendencies and all-too-human habits. That is why there is, in this world of ours, so little interior peace among individuals and so little exterior peace between societies. In the words of the *Imitation*: "All men desire peace but few indeed desire those things which make for peace."

HOLINESS

Whole, hale, holy—the three words derive from the same root. By etymology no less than in fact holiness is spiritual health, and health is wholeness, completeness, perfection. God's holiness is the same as His unity; and a man is holy to the extent to which he has become single-minded, one-pointed, perfect as our Father in heaven is perfect.

Because each of us possesses only one body, we tend to believe that we are one being. But in reality our name is Legion. In our unregenerate condition we are divided beings, half-hearted and double-minded, creatures of many moods and multiple personalities. And not only are we divided against our unregenerate selves; we are also incomplete. As well as our multitudinous soul, we possess a spirit that is one with the universal spirit. Potentially (for in his normal condition he does not know who he is) man is much more than the personality he takes himself to be. He cannot achieve his wholeness unless and until he realizes his true nature, discovers and liberates the spirit within his soul and so unites himself with God.

Unholiness arises when we give consent to any rebellion or self-assertion by any part of our being against that totality which it is possible for us to become through union with God. For example, there is the unholiness of indulged sensuality, of unchecked avarice, envy, and anger, of the wantonness of pride and worldly ambition. Even the negative sensuality of ill health may constitute unholiness, if the mind be permitted to dwell upon the sufferings of its body more than is absolutely necessary or unavoidable. And on the plane of the intellect there is the imbecile unholiness of distractions, and the busy, purposeful unholiness of curiosity about matters concerning which we are powerless to act in any constructive or remedial way.

From our natural state of incompleteness to spiritual health and perfection there is no magically easy short cut. The way to holiness is laborious and long. It lies through vigilance and prayer, through an unresting guard of the heart, the mind, the will and the tongue, and through the one-pointed loving attention to God, which that guard alone makes possible.

GRACE

Graces are the free gifts of help bestowed by God upon each one of us, in order that we may be assisted to achieve our final end and purpose; namely, unitive knowledge of divine reality. Such helps are very seldom so extraordinary that we are immediately aware of their true nature as God-sends. In the overwhelming majority of cases they are so inconspicuously woven into the texture of common life, that we do not know that they are graces, unless and until we respond to them as we ought, and so receive the material, moral or spiritual benefits, which they were meant to bring us. If we do not respond to these ordinary graces as we ought, we shall receive no benefit and remain unaware of their nature or even of their very existence. Grace is always sufficient, provided we are ready to cooperate with it. If we fail to do our share, but rather choose to rely on self-will and self-direction, we shall not only get no help from the graces bestowed upon us; we shall actually make it impossible for further graces to be given. When used with an obstinate consistency, self-will creates a private universe walled off impenetrably from the light of spiritual reality; and within these private universes the self-willed go their way, unhelped and unillumined, from accident to random accident, or from calculated evil to calculated evil. It is of such that St. Francis de Sales is speaking when he says, "God did not deprive thee of the operation of his love, but thou didst deprive His love of thy cooperation. God would never have rejected thee, if thou hadst not rejected Him."

To be clearly and constantly aware of the divine, guidance is given only to those who are already far advanced in the life of the spirit. In its earlier stages we have to work, not by the direct perception of God's successive graces, but by faith in their existence. We have to accept as a working hypothesis that the events of our lives are not merely fortuitous, but deliberate tests of intelligence and character, specially devised occasions (if properly used) for spiritual advance. Acting upon this working hypothesis, we shall treat no occurrence as intrinsically unimportant. We shall never make a response that is inconsiderate, or a mere automatic expression of our self-will, but always give ourselves time, before acting or speaking, to consider what course of behavior would seem to be most in accord with the will of God, most charitable, most conducive to the achievement of our final end. When such becomes our habitual response to events, we shall discover, from the nature of their effects, that some at least of those occurrences were divine graces in the disguise sometimes of trivialities, sometimes of inconveniences or even of pains and trials. But if we fail to act upon the working hypothesis that grace exists, grace will in effect be nonexistent so far as we are concerned. We shall prove by a life of accident at the best, or, at the worst, of downright evil, that God does not help human beings, unless they first permit themselves to be helped.

JOY

Peace, love, joy—these, according to St. Paul, are the three fruits of the spirit. They correspond very closely to the three essential attributes of God, as summarized in the Indian formula, *sat, chit, ananda*—being, knowledge, bliss. Peace is the manifestation of unified being. Love is the mode of divine knowledge. And bliss, the concomitant of perfection, is the same as joy.

Like peace, joy is not only a fruit of the spirit, but also a root. If we would know God, we must do everything to cultivate that lower equivalent of joy, which it is within our power to feel and to express.

"Sloth" is the ordinary translation of that *acedia,* which ranks among the seven deadly sins of our Western tradition. It is an inadequate translation, for *acedia* is more than sloth; it is also depression and self-pity; it is also that dull world-weariness which causes us, in Dante's words, to be "sad in the sweet air that rejoiceth in the sun." To grieve, to repine, to feel sorry for oneself, to despair—these are the manifestations of self-willing and of rebellion against the will of God. And that special and characteristic discouragement we experience on account of the slowness of our spiritual advance—what is it but a symptom of wounded vanity, a tribute paid to our high opinion of our own merits?

To be cheerful when circumstances are depressing, or when we are tempted to indulge in self-pity, is a real mortification—a mortification all the more valuable for being so inconspicuous, so hard to recognize for what it is. Physical austerities, even the mildest of them, can hardly be practiced without attracting other people's attention; and because they thus attract attention, those who practice them are often tempted to feel vain of their self-denial. But such mortifications as refraining from idle talk, from wanton curiosity about things which do not concern us, and above all from depression and self-pity, can be practiced without anybody knowing of them. Being consistently cheerful may cost us a far greater effort than, for example, being consistently temperate; and whereas other people will often admire us for refraining from physical indulgences, they will probably attribute our cheerfulness to good digestion or a native insensibility. From the roots of such secret and unadmired self-denials there springs the tree whose fruits are the peace that passes all understanding, the love of God and of all creatures for God's sake, and the joy of perfection, the bliss of an eternal and timeless consummation.

3

RELIGION AND TEMPERAMENT

Our holy fathers herebefore taught us that we should know the measure of our gift, and work upon that; not taking upon us by feigning more than we have in feeling. . . . Who hath grace, be it never so little, and leaveth willfully the working thereof, and maketh himself to travail in another which he hath not yet, but only because he seeth or heareth that other men did so, soothly he may run awhile until he be weary, and then shall he turn home again; and unless he beware, he may hurt his feet by some fantasies ere he come home. But he that worketh in such grace as he hath, and desireth by prayer meekly and lastingly after more, and after feeleth his heart stirred to follow the grace which he desired, he may safely run if he keep meekness. . . . And, therefore, it is speedful that we know the gifts that are given us of God, that we may work in them, for by these we shall be saved; as some by bodily works and deeds of mercy, some by great bodily penance, some by sorrow and weeping for their sins all their life-time, some by preaching and teaching, some by

divers graces and gifts of devotion shall be saved
and come to bliss.

These words from Walter Hilton's *The Scale of Perfection* were written by an English monk of the fourteenth century. But the message they convey is beyond any particular time or place. In one form or another it has been enunciated by all the masters of the spiritual life, Western and Oriental, present and past. Liberation, salvation, the Beatific Vision, unitive knowledge of God—the end is always and everywhere the same. But the means whereby it is sought to achieve that end are as various as the human beings who address themselves to the task.

Many attempts have been made to classify the varieties of human temperament. Thus, in the West, we have the four-fold classification of Hippocrates in terms of the "humours" (phlegmatic, choleric, melancholic, and sanguine), a classification which dominated the theory and practice of medicine for more than two thousand years and whose terminology is indelibly imprinted upon every European language. Another popular system of classification, which has also left its trace in modern speech, was the seven-fold system of the astrologers. We still describe people in planetary terms—as jovial, mercurial, saturnine, martial. Both these systems had their merits, and there was even something to be said for the physiognomic classification in terms of supposed resemblances to various animals. All were based to some extent on observation.

In our own day a number of new essays in classification have been attempted—those of Stockard, of Kretschmer, of Viola, and, more satisfactory and better-documented than all the rest, of Dr. William Sheldon, whose two volumes on *The Varieties of Human Physique* and *The Varieties of Temperament* are among the most important of recent contributions to the science of Man.

Sheldon's researches have led him to the conclusion that the most satisfactory system of classification is in terms of three types of temperament, which he calls the viscerotonic, the somatotonic and the cerebrotonic. All human beings are of mixed type. But in some the various elements are evenly mixed, while in some one element tends to predominate at the expense of the other two. In some again the mixture is well balanced, whereas in others there is a disequilibrium which results in acute internal conflict and extreme difficulty in making adaptation to life. No form of hormone treatment or other therapy can change the fundamental pattern of temperament, which is a datum to be accepted and made the best of. In a word, the psycho-physical pattern is one of the expressions of karma. There are good karmas and bad karmas: but it is within the choice of the individual to make a bad use of the best karma and a good use of the worst. There is a measure of free will within a system of predestination.

A religion cannot survive unless it makes an appeal to all sorts and conditions of men. This being so, we must expect to find in all the existing world religions elements

31

of belief, of precept, and of practice contributed by each of the principal categories of human beings. Dr. Sheldon's findings confirm these expectations and provide new instruments for the analysis of religious phenomena. Let us now briefly consider the three polar types in their relations to the organized religions of the world.

The viscerotonic temperament is associated with what Dr. Sheldon has called endomorphic physique—the type of physique in which the gut is the predominant feature, and which has a tendency, when external conditions are good, to run to breadth, fat and weight. Characteristic of extreme viscerotonia are the following: slow reaction time, love of comfort and luxury, love of eating, pleasure in digestion, love of the ritual of eating in company (the shared meal is for him a natural sacrament), love of polite ceremony, a certain untempered quality of flabbiness; indiscriminate amiability; easy communication of feeling; tolerance and complacency; dislike of solitude; need of people when in trouble; orientation toward childhood and family relations.

The somatotonic temperament is associated with mesomorphic physique, in which the predominant feature is the musculature. Mesomorphs are physically strong, active and athletic. Among the characteristics of extreme somatotonia we find the following: assertiveness of posture and movement; love of physical adventure; need of exercise; love of risk; indifference to pain; energy and rapid decision; lust for power and domination; courage for combat; competitiveness; psychological callousness;

claustrophobia; ruthlessness in gaining the desired end; extroversion toward activity rather than toward people (as with the viscerotonic); need of action when troubled; orientation toward the goals and activities of youth.

The cerebrotonic temperament is associated with the ectomorphic physique, in which the predominance of the nervous system results in a high degree of sensitiveness. Extreme cerebrotonia has the following characteristics: restraint of posture and movement; physiological over-response (one of the consequences of which is extreme sexuality); love of privacy; a certain over-intentness and apprehensiveness; secretiveness of feeling and emotional restraint; dislike of company; shyness and inhibited social address; agoraphobia; resistance to habit formation and incapacity to build up routines; awareness of inner mental processes and tendency to introversion; need of solitude when troubled; orientation toward maturity and old age.

These are summary descriptions; but they are sufficient to indicate the nature of the contributions to religion made by each of the three polar types. In his unregenerate state, the viscerotonic loves polite ceremony and luxury, and makes a fetish of ritual eating in public. It is because of him that churches and temples are so splendidly adorned, that rituals are so solemn and elaborate, and that sacramentalism, or the worship of the divine through material symbols, plays so important a part in organized religion.

The ideal of universal brotherly love represents the rationalization, refinement and sublimation of the viscerotonic's native amiability toward all and sundry. Similarly, it is from his native sociophilia that the idea of the Church or fellowship of believers takes its origin. The various cults of divine childhood and divine motherhood have their source in his nostalgic harking back to his own infancy and earlier relations to the family. (It is highly significant in this context to note the difference between the ordinary, viscerotonic cult of the child Christ and the cerebrotonic version of it produced by the French Oratorians of the seventeenth century. In the ordinary cult, the infant Christ is conceived of, and represented as, a beautiful child about two years old. In the Oratorian cult, the child is much younger, and the worshiper is encouraged to think of infancy, not as a time of charm and beauty, but as a condition of abjection and helplessness only slightly less complete than that of death. Christ is to be thanked for having voluntarily taken upon himself the appalling humiliation of being a baby. Between this point of view, and the point of view implicit in one of Raphael's Madonnas and Infant Christs, there is fixed an almost unbridgeable temperamental gulf.)

To the somatotonic, religions owe whatever they have in them of hardness and energy. Proselytizing zeal, the courting of martyrdom and the readiness to persecute are somatotonic characteristics. So are the extremer forms of asceticism, and the whole stoic and puritanic temper. So is the dogmatic insistence on hell fire and the sterner aspects of God. So is the preoccupation with active good works, as opposed to the viscerotonic's preoccupation with sacraments and ritual and the cerebrotonic's with private devotion and meditation. Another significant peculiarity of the somatotonic is mentioned by Dr. Sheldon, who points out that it is among persons of this type that the phenomenon of sudden conversion is most frequently observed. The reason for this must be sought, it would seem, in their active extroversion, which causes them to be profoundly ignorant of the inner workings of their own minds. When religion opens up to their view the interior life of the soul, the discovery comes to them, very often, with the force of a revelation. They are violently converted, and proceed to throw themselves into the business of acting upon their new knowledge with all the energy characteristic of their type. Religious conversion is no longer common in educated circles; but its place has been taken, as Dr. Sheldon points out, by psychological conversion. For it is upon unbalanced somatotonics that psychoanalysis produces its most striking effects, and it is they who are its most fervent believers and most energetic missionaries.

Very different is the case with the cerebrotonic, who habitually lives in contact with his inner being, and for whom the revelations of religion and psychiatry are not startlingly novel. For this reason, and because of his emotional restraint, he is little subject to violent conversion. For him, change of heart and life tends to come gradually. Along with the viscerotonic, who lacks the energy to get himself violently converted, the cerebrotonic has a peculiarly wretched time of it when he happens to be born into a sect which regards violent conversion as a necessary condition of salvation. His temperament is such that he simply cannot experience the convulsion which comes so easily to his somatotonic neighbors. Because of this inability, he is forced either to simulate conversion by an act of conscious or unconscious fraud, or else to regard himself, and be regarded by others, as irretrievably lost.

The great cerebrotonic contribution to religion is mysticism, the worship of God in contemplative solitude without the aid of ritual or sacraments. Because he feels no need of it, the cerebrotonic is sometimes moved, with the Buddha, to denounce ritualistic worship as one of the fetters holding back the soul from liberation.

The unregenerate viscerotonic likes luxury and "nice things" around him. When he becomes religious, he gives up "nice things" for himself, but wants them in his church or temple. Not so the cerebrotonic. To him the life of voluntary poverty seems not only tolerable, but often supremely desirable; and he likes to worship in a shrine as austerely naked as his cell. When the cerebrotonic love of bareness and poverty becomes associated with somatotonic proselytizing zeal, we have iconoclasm.

Among cerebrotonic inventions are hermitages and contemplative orders. Most systems of spiritual exercises are devised by cerebrotonics as an aid to private devotion and a preparation for mystical experience. And finally the great systems of spiritual philosophy, such as those of Shankara, of Plotinus, of Eckhart, are the work of cerebrotonic minds.

So much, then, for the elements contributed to religion by the three polar types of temperament. Two questions now present themselves for our consideration. First, which of the types has been most influential in the framing of the world's great religions? And, second, which of the types is best fitted to discover the truth about ultimate Reality?

The religions of India are predominantly viscerotonic and cerebrotonic religions of ritual and mysticism, having little proselytizing zeal and intolerance, and setting a higher value on the contemplative life than on the active. The same seems to be true of the Taoism of China, at any rate in its uncorrupted forms.

Confucianism would seem to be predominantly viscerotonic—a religion of forms and ceremonials, in which the cult of the family is centrally important.

Mohammedanism is decidedly more somatotonic than any of the religions native to India and China. In its primitive form it is hard, militant and puritanical; it encourages the spirit of martyrdom, is eager to make proselytes and has no qualms about levying "holy wars" and conducting persecutions. Some centuries after the prophet's death it developed the Sufi school of mysticism—a school whose strict Islamic orthodoxy its theologians have always had some difficulty in defending.

In Christianity we have a religion of which, until recent years, the central core has always been cerebrotonic and viscerotonic, contemplative and ritualistic. But, to a much greater extent than is the case with Buddhism and

Hinduism, these cerebrotonic and viscerotonic elements have always been associated with others of a strongly somatotonic nature. Christianity has been a militant, proselytizing and persecuting religion. At various periods of its history, stoicism and puritanism have flourished within the church, and at certain times active "good works" have been esteemed as highly as, or even more highly than, contemplation. This is especially the case at the present time. For, as Dr. Sheldon has pointed out, our age has witnessed a veritable somatotonic revolution. The expression of this revolution in the political field is too manifest to require comment. In the sphere of personal living the revolt against pure contemplation and the sacramental reverence for material things may best be suited in the advertising pages of our newspapers and magazines. Where religion is concerned, the revolt is not so much against the viscerotonic elements of Christianity as against the cerebrotonic or contemplative. The two key words of contemporary Western religion are respectively viscerotonic and somatotonic, namely "fellowship" and "social service." The things which these words stand for are good and precious; but their full value can be realized only when the contemplation of ultimate Reality gives meaning to the emotional warmth of fellowship and direction to the activity of service.

Risking a generalization, we may say that the main social function of the great religions has been to keep the congenitally energetic and often violent somatotonics from destroying themselves, their neighbors and society at large. Highly significant in this context is the *Bhagavad Gita,* which is addressed to a princely kshatriya, a hereditary and professional somatotonic. Its teaching of nonattached action was supplemented, in India, by the theory and practice of caste, with its all-important doctrine of the supremacy of spiritual authority over temporal power. Orthodox Christianity holds the same doctrine in regard to the supremacy of spiritual authority. During the last four hundred years, however, this doctrine has been assailed, not only in practice by ambitious rulers, but also in theory, by philosophers and sociologists. As far back as the sixteenth century, Henry VIII made himself, in Bishop Stubb's words, "the Pope, the whole Pope and something more than the Pope." Since that time his example has been followed in every part of Christendom, until now there is no organized temporal power which acknowledges even theoretically the supremacy of any kind of spiritual authority. The triumph of unrestrained somatotonia is now complete.

We now come to our second question: Which of the three polar types is best fitted to discover the truth about ultimate Reality? The question is one which can be referred only to the judgment of the experts—in this case, the great theocentric saints of the higher religions. The testimony of these men and women is unmistakable. It is in pure contemplation that human beings come nearest, in the present life, to the beatific vision of God. But the desire and the aptitude for contemplation are cerebrotonic characteristics. (But of course those who belong predominantly to the other polar types can always arrive at contemplation, if they fulfill the necessary conditions for receiving the grace of unitive knowledge. It may, however, be doubted whether persons of viscerotonic and somatotonic temperament would ever think of embarking upon the road which leads to contemplation, if the way had not first been explored by cerebrotonics whose soul is, in some sort, *naturaliter contemplativa*.)

To what extent is the viscerotonic justified in his claim that ritual, group worship, and sacramentalism enable him to establish contact with ultimate Reality? This is a very difficult question to answer. That such procedures permit those who practice them to get in touch with something greater than themselves seems to admit of no doubt. But what the nature of that something may be—whether some mediated aspect of spiritual Reality, or possibly some kind of psychically objective crystallization of the devotional feeling experienced by the long succession of worshipers who have used the same ceremonial in the past—I will not venture even to try to decide.

One practical conclusion remains to be recorded. Analysis seems to show that religion is a system of relativities within an absolute frame of reference. The end which religion proposes is knowledge of the unalterable fact of God. Its means are relative to the heredity and social upbringing of those who seek that end. This being so, it seems extremely unwise to promote any one of these purely relative means to the rank of a dogmatic absolute. For example, an organized fellowship for the furtherance of spiritual ends and the preservation of traditional knowledge is, obviously and as a matter of empirical experience, a most valuable thing. But we have no right to proceed to a quasi-deification of Church and a dogma of infallibility. *Mutatis mutandis,* the same thing may be said of rituals, sacraments, sudden conversions. All these are means to the ultimate end—means which for some people are enormously valuable, for others, of different temperament, of little or no value. For this reason they should not be treated as though they were absolutes. That way lies idolatry.

The case of ethical precepts is different. Experience shows that such states of mind as pride, anger, covetousness and lust are totally incompatible with the knowledge of ultimate Reality; and this incompatibility exists for persons of every variety of temperament and upbringing. Consequently these precepts may properly be inculcated in an absolute form. "If you want God, it is absolutely essential for you not to want to be Napoleon, or Jay Gould, or Casanova."

4

WHO ARE WE?

This essay is the text of a lecture given by Huxley at the Vedanta Temple in 1955.

My subject today is "Who Are We?" Now, in its totality, this is an enormous subject—a subject which no single person, least of all myself, is qualified to talk about. To answer it in its fullness, we would have to consider the relationships between man and nature, their natural environment animate and inanimate; between individual man and other individuals, and groups, and whole societies; between individuals living now and in past times; the cultural traditions of their own society and other societies. And this, of course, would be a theme for many lectures, given by many people over a long period of time.

But what I propose to speak about today is a limited field: what are we in relation to our own minds and bodies—or, seeing that there is not a single word, let us use it in a hyphenated form—our own mind-bodies? What are we in relation to this total organism in which we live?

Well, this seems pretty obvious. We go about, we live our life, and this seems to present no problem at all. But actually, this is simply because familiarity has bred a kind of contempt of the problem altogether. The moment we begin thinking about it in any detail, we find ourselves confronted by all kinds of extremely difficult, unanswered, and maybe unanswerable questions. Let us take a few examples: I say, I wish to raise my hand. Well, I raise it. But who raises it? Who is the "I" who raises my hand? Certainly it is not exclusively the "I" who is standing here talking, the "I" who signs the checks and has a history behind him, because I do not have the faintest idea how my hand was raised. All I know is that I expressed a wish for my hand to be raised, whereupon something within myself set to work, pulled the switches of a most elaborate nervous system, and made thirty or forty muscles—some of which contract and some of which relax at the same instant—function in perfect harmony so as to produce this extremely simple gesture. And of course, when we ask ourselves, how does my heart beat? how do we breathe? how do I digest my food?—we do not have the faintest idea.

The whole procedure is left to somebody else—somebody, incidentally, who is more or less infallible, provided we leave him alone. After all, this is the entire theory of psychosomatic medicine. Most of our diseases (as doctors are coming to see now) are caused by ourselves—this personal self-interfering with the functioning of the deeper physiological intelligence, which, when it is left in peace and not pushed or deranged by means of negative thought, is, as I have said, almost infallible.

And then there are still other more curious problems, because one can say, "Well, these are what used to be called 'the vegetative soul.'" The vegetative soul is built in. It is something we inherit, which just does things like digestion and regulating heartbeat automatically.

But we have to reflect that there is also another kind of indwelling self, which functions entirely differently from instinctive ways—which performs what I may call acts of *ad hoc* intelligence, acts which have never been done before in biological history, and yet which it performs with extraordinary skill, without the conscious self being in the least aware of how this is done. And this goes on on levels far below the human. Let me quote an example which most of you must have been familiar with at one time or another, the fact of a parrot imitating a human voice, or imitating the barking of a dog, or imitating laughter. What goes on when a parrot does this sort of thing? Presumably, the parrot has some sort of a conscious life. It hears the voice, it hears the barking or the laughter, and, probably in some sort of way corresponding to our wish to do something, it wishes to imitate this. But then, what happens after this? When you come to think of it, it is one of the most extraordinary things you can imagine. Something incomparably more intelligent than the parrot itself sets to work and proceeds to organize a series of sound organs, which are totally different from those of man. After all, man has teeth, a soft palate, a flat tongue. The parrot has a rough tongue, a beak, and no teeth; and it proceeds to organize this absolutely different apparatus to reproduce words and laughter so exactly that we are very often deceived by it, and think that what is in fact the parrot talking is the person himself making an utterance. The more you reflect on this, the stranger it is, because obviously in the course of evolutionary history parrots have not been imitating human beings from time immemorial. This is a purely *ad hoc* piece of intelligent action carried on by some form of intelligence within the parrot, which is quite different, as far as one can see, from the parrot itself.

And the same problem of imitation comes up in relation to very small children. You make a face at a child, and it will imitate the face. Again, who is doing the imitation? Somebody within the child is organizing for the first time in its history a whole mass of muscles connected with an elaborate nervous system to pull this muscle up, this muscle down, let one go, let another be tensed, in order to reproduce this grimace which the child has seen on the face of an adult.

This also is a most mysterious thing, so that what we find really is that we as personalities—as what we like to think of ourselves as being—are in fact only a very small part of an immense manifestation of activity, physical and mental, of which we are simply not aware. We have some control over this inasmuch as some actions being voluntary we can say, I want this to happen, and somebody else does the work for us. But meanwhile, many actions go on without our having the slightest consciousness of them, and (as I said before) these vegetative actions can be grossly interfered with by our undesirable thoughts, our fears, our greeds, our angers, and so on, which may lead to very serious psychophysical derangements.

The question then arises, How are we related to this? Why is it that we think of ourselves as only this minute part of a totality far larger than we are—a totality which according to many philosophers may actually be coextensive with the total activity of the universe? In the West you go back as far as Leibnitz with his conception that every monad was potentially omniscient. And in modern times you have the same conception in Bergson and in William James, both of whom were of the opinion that the consciousness that we have is simply a kind of filtering down of some form of universal or cosmic consciousness, narrowed down for the purpose of helping us to survive biologically on the surface of this particular planet.

And this leads us, of course, to the whole problem of what the relation is between mind and brain. It is quite obvious that there is a relationship. At one time it was believed that thought was just produced by brain. There was a charming phrase used at the end of the eighteenth century: "The brain secretes thought as the liver secretes bile"—a remark which, the more you think of it, the sillier it is. After all, bile at least is of the same nature as the cells of the liver, whereas thought is of a radically different kind from electro-chemical events in the brain. Again here both Bergson and James are of one opinion that the brain is not productive of thought but acts, so to speak, as a kind of reducing valve preventing us from being too omniscient. Obviously, if we have to get out of the way of the traffic on Hollywood Boulevard, it is no good being aware of everything that is going on in the universe; we have to be aware of the approaching bus. And this is what the brain does for us: It narrows the field down so that we can go through life without getting into serious trouble.

But, as many people have experienced and as all the teachers of the great religions have insisted should be the case, we can and ought to open ourselves up and become what in fact we have always been from the beginning, that is to say, omniscient, or anyhow much more widely knowing than we normally think we are. We should realize our identity with what James called the cosmic consciousness and what in the East is called the Atman-Brahman. The end of life in all great religious traditions is the realization that the finite manifests the Infinite in its totality. This is, of course, a complete paradox when it is stated in words; nevertheless, it is one of the facts of experience for many people—or for some people at least—and should be a fact of experience for all.

Now, let us consider a little more this problem of how we are related to this deeper self. The superficial self—the self which we call ourselves, which answers to our names and which goes about its business—has a terrible habit of imagining itself to be absolute in some sense. If we look at it from the metaphysical point of view, I think we may say this is a mistaken placement of the Absolute. We know in an obscure and profound way that in the depths of our being—in what Eckhart calls "the ground of our being"—we are identical with the divine Ground. And we wish to realize this identity. But unfortunately, owing to the ignorance in which we live—partly a cultural product, partly a biological and voluntary product—we tend to look at ourselves, at this wretched little self, as being absolute. We either worship ourselves as such, or we project some magnified image of the self in an ideal or goal which falls short of the highest ideal or goal, and proceed to worship that.

Hence, the appalling dangers of idolatry. I remember as a boy reading in the Ten Commandments the warning against idolatry, and wondering why such a fuss should be made about this, because, after all, who cares whether people take off their hats to a statue or not! But it is much profounder than this. Idolatry is in fact the worship of a part—especially the self or projection of the self—as though it were the absolute totality. And as soon as this happens, general disaster occurs. Nothing is clearer in this present mid-point of the twentieth century than that its religion is idolatrous nationalism. There are the nominal religions—Christianity, Mohammedanism, Hinduism, Buddhism, and so on; but if you inquire what the actions of people mean, it is perfectly clear that the real religion is nationalism; that we worship the national state; that actually we make use of the traditional religions to buttress the national state; and that the new religions like

Communism are also used in the service of great national idolatry. Karl Marx made a great mistake in underrating nationalism. He seems to have imagined that under the influence of socialist and communist doctrines the masses of the people would give up nationalism. Not at all! He never foresaw what has in fact happened, that communist and socialist doctrines have become the servants, the instruments, of a particular nationalism just as in the same way (I am afraid) it looks as though orthodox Christianity and orthodox Mohammedanism and orthodox Judaism are fast becoming the instruments of their respective Western, Middle-Eastern, or Jewish nationalisms. This is one of the great tragedies, and it confirms the profound wisdom which we find in the Old Testament, condemning idolatry as being a thing of unutterable danger.

To return to the individual: he of course worships himself; or if he thinks he is altruistic, he is what may be called an alter-egoist—he worships some projection of himself. And in this absolutization of himself he is, I think, assisted by the fact that he is a creature with a language.

Now, we can never overestimate the importance of language in the life of human beings. Actually, that which causes us to be human rather than simply another of the apes is our ability to speak. This has given us the power to create a social heredity so that we can accumulate the knowledge amassed in past times; and it has given us the power to analyze experience, which comes to us in a very chaotic way, and to make sense of it for our particular biological and social purposes. This is the greatest gift which man has ever received or given himself, the gift of language.

But we have to remember that although language is absolutely essential to us, it can also be absolutely fatal because we use it wrongly. If we analyze our processes of living, we find that, I imagine, at least 50 percent of our life is spent in the universe of language. We are like icebergs, floating in a sea of immediate experience but projecting into the air of language. Icebergs are about four-fifths under water and one-fifth above. But, I would say, we are considerably more than that above. I should say, we are the best part of 50 percent—and, I suspect, some people are about 80 percent above in the world of language. They virtually never have a direct experience; they live entirely in terms of concepts.

This is inevitable. When we see a rose, we immediately say, rose. We do not say, I see a roundish mass of delicately shaded reds and pinks. We immediately pass from the actual experience to the concept. In the history of art it has happened not infrequently that painters who have passed from conceptual representation of the world to direct representation have been thought completely insane. It is difficult for us to imagine now, but for about thirty years the Impressionists were regarded as mad and as being absolutely false to nature, when in point of fact they were the only painters at that period who were absolutely true to nature. They painted exactly what they saw and did not bother about the concepts in terms of which other painters did their seeing and their painting.

We cannot help living to a very large extent in terms of concepts. We have to do so, because immediate experience is so chaotic and so immensely rich that in mere self-preservation we have to use the machinery of language to sort out what is of utility for us, what in any given context is of importance, and at the same time to try to understand—because it is only in terms of language that we can understand what is happening. We make generalizations and we go into higher and higher degrees of abstraction, which permit us to comprehend what we are up to, which we certainly would not if we did not have language. And in this way language is an immense boon, which we could not possibly do without.

But language has its limitations and its traps. To start with, every language has been developed for specifically biological purposes in order to help man to cope with life on the surface of this planet. And most languages are remarkably poor, above all, in terms expressing the inner life of man, and also in terms which would describe the continuousness of experience. It is very significant that if we have to talk about the universe as the continuum which it is, we cannot do so in terms of any of the ordinarily existing languages, which deceive us all the time; it has to be done in terms of calculus, a special language invented for the express purpose of talking about the world as a continuum. We have this mania, so frequently stressed in all the Oriental texts, of thinking of ourselves and of every object in the world as being separate and self-subsistent, when, in fact, all are parts of a universal One. And unfortunately, the nature of language being what it is, we cannot get around this without making ourselves carefully aware of what we are doing and thinking when we use language. This is the only way of by-passing its intrinsic defects.

Added to the intrinsic defects, there are all kinds of traps which we lead ourselves into by taking language too seriously. We have been constantly warned against this. St. Paul is full of it. He speaks about "the newness of spirit," the "oldness of the letter," "the letter killeth," "the spirit giveth life"; and this is absolutely true. If we take the letter too seriously, we actually prevent ourselves from having certain types of direct experience which St. Paul was describing in terms of the word "spirit," so that what we have to do is to be profoundly aware of the language we are using—not to mistake the word for the thing. In the terms of Zen Buddhism, we have to be constantly aware that the finger which points at the moon is not the moon. In general, we think that the pointing finger—the word—is the thing we point at. And if you look at almost any literature of philosophy or religion, you will find this again and again, this obsession with words as though they were things, this mania. In reality, words are simply the signs of things. But many people treat things as though they were the signs and illustrations of words. When they see a thing, they immediately think of it as just being an illustration of a verbal category, which is absolutely fatal because this is not the case. And yet we cannot do without words. The whole of life is, after all, a process of walking on a tightrope. If you do not fall one way you fall the other, and each is equally bad. We cannot do without language, and yet if we take language too seriously we are in an extremely bad way. We somehow have to keep going on this knife-edge (every action of life is a knife-edge), being aware of the dangers and doing our best to keep out of them.

I think some progress has been made in recent years in the linguistic analysis, the semantics, which became extremely popular at one time, and then by the logical positivists, who have done very valuable work in the whole of the new development of logic since Boole, Peano, and Russell. (This is one of the great pieces of intellectual progress of the last fifty years, I would say.) All this is of immense importance, because it does permit anybody who wishes to do so to understand the pitfalls which lie within this necessary and vital medium of language. Of course, the logical positivists went a great deal too far. They got to a point of saying that if you could not in terms of language make a sentence which was logically foolproof, then the question asked was meaningless. But this is not true. This is actually a way very often of evading the question. There are plenty of questions which, it may be, one can never frame in terms of a sentence which shall be logically correct and make linguistic sense. Take a question like, Is the soul immortal? I am quite sure that a logical positivist would have no difficulty in saying that these words are perfectly meaningless. But at the same time the question still has a significance, even though we cannot frame it in any words available to us in such a way that it will make logical sense. And I do think that the logical positivists have evaded many difficulties simply by saying that questions which in fact have a meaning do not, just because they have no meaning merely in terms of words. They have a meaning on another level. And one of the problems of any kind of spiritual, intellectual, or moral development is to get beyond the merely verbal level to this level of immediate experience. We have to combine these things: to walk on this tightrope, to gather the data of perception, to be able to analyze it in terms of language, at the same time to be able to drop the language and to go on into the experience. It is very, very delicate and difficult.

We must briefly consider contemporary education—in fact, education as it has always been, as far as I can see— which is, of course, predominantly verbal. Children are taught an enormous number of things in terms of words. Practically all teaching is verbal. Look, for example, at what are called the liberal arts; they are little better than they were in the Middle Ages. In the Middle Ages the liberal arts were entirely verbal. The only two which were not verbal were astronomy and music. There was some faint attempt to look at the outside world in astronomy, and even music was not too nonverbal because it was regarded as a science and not as a pleasure. And it was entirely the theory of music that was taught. Fortunately, in the Middle Ages there were a number of mitigations to this. The life was so extremely, and so often very unpleasantly, close to nature that one could not be wholly verbal. The amount of cold, and dirt, and wild animals, and so on, kept people on their toes in a way which in a modern city they are not. We can live in a modern city as though we were living in a kind of paradise of words, or in those embodiments of words which are machines and gadgets. And this, I think, is a very unwholesome situation.

As I say, most education is predominantly verbal and suffers therefore from the defects which great religious teachers like St. Paul have pointed out: that the letter killeth, that this is a stultifying and dangerous thing. And one of the strangest facts about education is that although for hundreds of years we have been talking about *mens sana in corpore sano,* we really have not paid any serious attention to the problem of training the mind-body, the instrument which has to do with the learning, which has to do with the living. We give children compulsory games, a little drill, and so on, but this really does not amount in any sense to a training of the mind-body. We pour this verbal stuff into them without in any way preparing the organism for life or for understanding its position in the world— who it is, where it stands, how it is related to the universe. This is one of the oddest things.

Moreover, we do not even prepare the child to have any proper relation with its own mind-body. This is all the more remarkable because Professor Dewey, who after all is the prophet of modern education, was extremely preoccupied with this problem. I briefly touch on this because I do think it is very important. Dewey had a first-hand knowledge of the work of F. M. Alexander, who is an Australian—in his eighties now—who developed this remarkable technique by which he showed that the proper mental and physical functioning could not take place unless there was a certain normal and natural relationship between the trunk, and the neck, and head. And Dewey speaks of this in several passages. He says that Alexander's methods of training stand to education in general as education in general stands to ordinary life, which shows the enormous significance he attached to them. And yet, although literally millions of teachers now look up to Dewey as the great prophet, practically none that I know of have ever paid the smallest attention to this method, which Dewey regarded as of capital importance.

I think one of the reasons for the lack of attention to the training of the mind-body is that this particular kind of teaching does not fall into any academic pigeonhole. This is one of the great problems in education: Everything takes place in a pigeonhole. And when you get something like Alexander's work (or indeed like any system of general synthesis), who looks after it? It is neither biology, nor psychology, nor sociology, nor history, nor anything; therefore it does not exist! The pigeonholes must be there because we cannot avoid specialization; but what we do need in academic institutions now is a few people who run about on the woodwork between the pigeonholes, and peep into all of them and see what can be done, and who are not closed to disciplines which do not happen to fit into any of the categories considered as valid by the present educational system!

I do not think I can go into any other examples of the methods of training the mind-body, but I think I can risk a generalization. Many such methods, of course, have been empirically devised for particular purposes. And if you examine them all, you will find that they are all illustrations of one single principle, which is, that in some way we have to combine relaxation with activity. Take the piano teacher, for example. He always says, Relax, relax. But how can you relax while your fingers are rushing over the keys? Yet they have to relax. The singing teacher and the golf pro say exactly the same thing. And in the realm of spiritual exercises we find that the person who teaches mental prayer does too. We have somehow to combine relaxation with activity.

Let us take the analysis one stage further. Going back to what we said originally about the personal conscious self being a kind of small island in the midst of an enormous area of consciousness—what has to be relaxed is the personal self, the self that tries too hard, that thinks it knows what is what, that uses language. This has to be relaxed in order that the multiple powers at work within the deeper and wider self may come through and function as they should. In all psychophysical skills we have this curious fact of the law of reversed effort: the harder we try, the worse we do the thing. And we have therefore always to learn this paradoxical art of combining the maximum of relaxation of the surface self with the maximum activity of the lower selves or higher selves (whichever you like), the not-selves, which we carry about with us and which actually give us our being. And this is the principle which every one of these empirical discoveries in every field of psychophysical skill quite clearly illustrates. We have to learn, so to speak, to get out of our own light, because with our personal self—this idolatrously worshiped self—we are continually standing in the light of this wider self—this not-self, if you like—which is associated with us and which this standing in the light prevents. We eclipse the illumination from within. And in all the activities of life, from the simplest physical activities to the highest intellectual and spiritual activities, our whole effort must be to get out of our own light. Yet we must not abdicate our personal, conscious self.

Here again we are up against a paradox and a tightrope. We cannot let go, and just go to sleep, and hope this will happen. We have somehow to permit this to come up, and yet to organize it with the surface conscious mind in a way which shall be useful to ourselves and to others. This is what in theological terms is called "cooperating with grace."

And let us not forget, grace exists on every level. There is what may be called animal-grace, which is the grace of normal functioning of perfect health, which we are constantly interfering with—hence all the psychosomatic disorders. We must cooperate with this grace. Similarly, we must cooperate with what may be called intellectual grace. As everybody who has worked in any field knows quite well, there are the hunches and inspirations which come through. In the greatest works of art these are the inspirations of genius. But, as it has been remarked, genius is both inspiration and perspiration. You have to work at these things, otherwise they are no good. And to anybody who wants to read a most illuminating study of this problem, I recommend F. W. H. Myers's *Human Personality,* which has at last been reprinted. The chapter on genius there is of first-rate importance. The author illustrates very clearly by many examples this necessary collaboration with what may be called intellectual grace.

And then above that is what may be called spiritual grace: the awareness of the total universal consciousness, the awareness of God, the awareness of the finite as in some sort a manifestation of the total Infinite. And again we have to get out of the way and uneclipse ourselves to permit the light to come through.

These, as I say, seem to me the all extremely important facets of education, which have been wholly neglected. I do not think that in ordinary schools you could teach what are called spiritual exercises, but you could certainly teach children how to use themselves in this relaxedly active way, how to perform these psychophysical skills without the frightful burden of overcoming the law of reversed effort. You could probably teach them how to greatly increase their perceptive powers. This has been done, for example, in the most remarkable way by Professor Renshaw of the University of Ohio, who has immensely increased both the powers of perception and the powers of memory by applying Gestalt psychology in a perfectly sensible and simple way. Why children are not taught this one cannot imagine. It does not happen to have entered into any of the academic categories and so has never been brought into the general system.

Now we come to the final problem, the problem of becoming aware of what James called the cosmic consciousness, of the Atman-Brahman, of the unifying principle. In the Chinese conception the universe is perceived as the Yin and the Yang, the negative and the positive principles, which are equally valid in the world. You have the same conception in the Indian philosophy too: The goddess of creation is also the goddess of destruction; the negative is correlative to the positive; but the two are reconciled then in this fundamental principle, the Tao. And this, I think, is at the basis of all mystical religions. You see it very clearly in the writings of Eckhart just as you do in Oriental philosophy. And the practical problem arises: How do we get ourselves into a position where we can collaborate with grace? How can we open ourselves up to the grace of seeing God, to use Eckhart's words, "seeing God with the same eye that God sees us"?

How do we do this? It is an immense problem, and, I think, innumerable ways have been developed to help people to achieve this final end of man. Some are satisfactory; others, it seems to me, are not. On general principles, I would say that the means employed for this purpose should resemble the end envisaged. For example, the end envisaged is a form of consciousness entirely free from the partiality of individual ego-consciousness. We are partial, of course. We see the world in a partial way because we see ourselves as distinct, virtually divine, and absolute. And this is a perfectly partial and perfectly untrue way of looking at the universe. If I am desperately preoccupied with myself, it means that I am ignoring the immense majority of all the events in the universe. Naturally, we cannot know all the events in the universe, but we must be aware that this totality of things exists, and that our partial view is totally warped and self-stultifying. We try to help ourselves in this way, but "he that findeth his life shall lose it: and he that loseth his life . . . shall find it." All these paradoxical sayings, which keep cropping up in every religion, refer to this same thing—this necessity of getting rid of the essentially partial, limited, and ego-centered view of the world.

And, I think, in order to cultivate this point of view, we must, first of all, obviously have an intellectual preparation. It is no good saying you can work without any theology. You have to have some theology, and it is rather important it should be correct. And, I think, what may be called the basic theology of the identity of the finite with the Infinite, the total manifestation of the Infinite in the finite, the identity of Samsara and Nirvana, the one

Being expressed totally in every particular aspect of the many—this is the end; and this, it seems to me, we have to approach through a cultivation of a doctrine to many people not familiar. We have to remind ourselves—in the very beautiful words of Matthew Arnold—that to God

> *Every minute in its race,*
> *Crowd as we will its neutral space,*
> *Is but the quiet watershed*
> *Whence equally the seas of life and death are fed;*

that the minute in itself is essentially neutral; that both the positive and the negative—both life and death—go on in it; that God sends his rain upon the just and unjust; that there is an essentially equal view of the world. Although as biological creatures we cannot accept our own destruction, we have as intellectual creatures to admit that the negative powers have exactly the same right to exist as the positive powers; yet of course (another paradox), we have to do our best to preserve the positive powers, the positive aspects of the world, in every way we can. But intellectually we must be aware that every moment is a "quiet watershed whence equally the seas of life and death are fed." And this is a sort of reminder we have to go on making. It will not necessarily console us in moments of grief or crisis, but it is a preparation. It prepares the ground for what is the final end—this seeing of the world with the impartial eye of the divine intelligence.

We cannot, of course, press this thing. Nothing we can do will actually produce enlightenment. All we can do is to get out of our own light, use our will to will ourselves away. Eckhart has again another curious remark. He says, "God and God's will are one, I and my will are two." We have somehow to use our will to get rid of our will in order to collaborate with this totality of the universe, to accept events as they come in this impartial spirit, yet doing everything we can to promote the positive side of life.

One could go on talking even about the limited area of this subject I have chosen for a very long time— because it is immense. But I think I have said enough to make it clear that the principles, at any rate, are simple; that we as we think of ourselves are a very small part even of the physiological and subconscious life immediately available to us; that we do not control our bodies and we do not even control our thoughts. After all, the popular language is very clear on that subject. We say, "A thought came to me; this flashed upon me." We do not say, "I invented this thought." We accept what comes to us. And we have to learn how to take what is given by something which is not ourselves in any sense that we think of ourselves. And this, as I say, applies to every level of activity from the simplest physiological acts to acts of psychophysical skill, going up to the most complicated ones like playing the violin, playing the piano, and so on. And finally, it is exactly the same principle which holds good in the religious life, where the aim is somehow to get out of the light—what the Quakers call the Inner Light. We have to get out of the light and let it shine. (And most of our lives, of course, are spent in eclipsing this light with all possible means at our disposal.)

And the methods of doing this are fairly clear: We have to live a life where, with the minimum of negative emotions, the minimum of malice, the obvious moral commandments have to be fulfilled. And then there is this intellectual preparation of perceiving that the nature of the universe is such that our pretensions to be absolute and separate are ridiculous—not only ridiculous but fatal. We have to remember this all the time, as often as we can, and, I think, we have to prepare the mind in one way or another, to accept this uprush or downrush, whichever you like to call it, of the greater not-self, which we can also spell as Self with a large "S," the Atman-Brahman. This, I think, is as much as I can say at the present time.

5

THE PHILOSOPHY OF THE SAINTS

This essay later became the introduction to *The Perennial Philosophy* (1945).

Philosophia Perennis—the phrase was coined by Leibnitz; but the thing—the metaphysic that recognizes a divine Reality substantial to the world of things and lives and minds; the psychology that finds in the soul something similar to, or even identical with, divine Reality; the ethic that places man's final end in the knowledge of the immanent and transcendent Ground of all being—the thing is immemorial and universal. Rudiments of the Perennial Philosophy may be found among the traditionary lore of primitive peoples in every region of the world, and in its fully developed forms it has a place in every one of the higher religions. A version of this Highest Common Measure of all preceding and subsequent theologies was first committed to writing more than twenty-five centuries ago, and since that time the inexhaustible theme has been treated again and again, from the standpoint of every religious tradition and in all the principal languages of Asia and Europe.

Knowledge is a function of being. When there is a change in the being of the knower, there is a corresponding change in the nature and amount of knowing. For example, the being of a child is transformed by growth and education into that of a man; among the results of this transformation is a revolutionary change in the way of knowing and the amount and character of the things known. As the individual grows up, his knowledge becomes more conceptual and systematic in form, and its factual, utilitarian content is enormously increased. But these gains are offset by a certain deterioration in the quality of immediate apprehension, a blunting and loss of intuitive power. Or consider the change in his being which the scientist is able to induce mechanically by means of his instruments. Equipped with a spectroscope and a sixty-inch reflector, an astronomer becomes, so far as eyesight is concerned, a superhuman creature; and, as we should naturally expect, the knowledge possessed by this superhuman creature is very different, both in quantity and quality, from that which can be acquired by a star-gazer with unmodified, merely human eyes.

Nor are changes in the knower's physiological or intellectual being the only ones to affect his knowledge. What we know depends also on what, as moral beings, we choose to make ourselves. "Practice," in the words of William James, "may change our theoretical horizon, and this in a two-fold way: it may lead into new worlds and secure new powers. Knowledge we could never attain, remaining what we are, may be attainable in consequence of higher powers and a higher life, which we may morally achieve." To put the matter more succinctly, "Blessed are the pure in heart, for they shall see God." And the same idea has been expressed by the Sufi poet, Jalalud'din Rumi, in terms of a scientific metaphor: "The astrolabe of the mysteries of God is love."[1]

The Perennial Philosophy is primarily concerned with the one, divine Reality substantial to the manifold world of things and lives and minds. But the nature of this one Reality is such that it cannot be directly and immediately apprehended except by those who have chosen to fulfill certain conditions, making themselves loving, pure in heart, and poor in spirit. Why should this be so? We do not know. It is just one of those facts which we have to accept, whether we like them or not and however implausible and unlikely they may seem. Nothing in our everyday experience gives us any reason for supposing that water is made up of hydrogen and oxygen; and yet when we subject water to certain rather drastic treatments, the nature of its constituent elements becomes manifest. Similarly, nothing in our everyday experience gives us much reason for supposing that the mind of the average sensual man has, as one of its constituents, something resembling, or identical with, the Reality substantial to the manifold world; and yet, when that mind is

---

[1] In his book on the subject of contemplation and perfection, the eminent Roman Catholic theologian, Father Garrigou Lagrange, writes as follows: "All the canonized saints seem to have had the mystical union often, except those martyrs who may have had it only in the moment of their torture."

subjected to certain rather drastic treatments, the divine element, of which it is in part at least composed, becomes manifest, not only to the mind itself, but also, by its reflection in external behavior, to other minds. It is only by making physical experiments that we can discover the ultimate nature of matter and its potentialities. And it is only by making psychological and moral experiments that we can discover the intimate nature of mind and its potentialities. In the ordinary circumstances of average sensual life these potentialities of the mind remain latent and unmanifested. If we would realize them, we must fulfill certain conditions and obey certain rules, which experience has shown empirically to be valid.

In regard to few professional philosophers and men of letters is there any evidence that they did very much in the way of fulfilling the necessary conditions of direct spiritual knowledge? When poets or metaphysicians talk about the subject matter of the Perennial Philosophy, it is generally at secondhand. But in every age there have been some men and women who chose to fulfill the conditions upon which alone, as a matter of brute empirical fact, such immediate knowledge can be had; and of those a few have left accounts of the Reality they were thus enabled to apprehend and have tried to relate, in one comprehensive system of thought, the given facts of this experience with the given facts of their other experiences. To such firsthand exponents of the Perennial Philosophy those who knew them have generally given the name of "saint" or "prophet," "sage" or "enlightened one." And it is mainly to these, because there is good reason for supposing that they knew what they were talking about, and not to the professional philosophers and men of letters, that I have gone for my selections in my anthology *The Perennial Philosophy.*

In India two classes of scripture are recognized: the Shruti, or inspired writings which are their own authority, since they are the product of immediate insight into ultimate Reality; and the Smriti, which are based upon the Shruti and from them derive such authority as they have. "The Shruti," in Shankara's words, "depends upon direct perception. The Smriti plays a part analogous to induction, since, like induction, it derives its authority from an authority other than itself."

In recent years a number of attempts have been made to work out a system of empirical theology. But in spite of the subtlety and intellectual powers of such writers as Sorley, Oman, and Tennant, the effort has met with only a partial success. Even in the hands of its ablest exponents, empirical theology is not particularly convincing. The reason, it seems to me, must be sought in the fact that the empirical theologians have confined their attention more or less exclusively to the experience of those whom the theologians of an older school called "the unregenerate"—that is to say, the experience of people who have not gone very far in fulfilling the necessary conditions of spiritual knowledge. But it is a fact, confirmed and reconfirmed during two or three thousand years of religious history, that the ultimate Reality is not clearly and immediately apprehended, except by those who have made themselves loving, pure in heart and poor in spirit. This being so, it is hardly surprising that a theology based upon the experience of nice, ordinary, unregenerate people should carry so little conviction. This kind of an empirical theology is on precisely the same footing as an empirical astronomy, based upon the experience of naked-eye observers. With the unaided eye certain small faint smudges can be detected in various parts of the heavens; and doubtless an imposing cosmological theory could be based upon the observation of these smudges. But no amount of such theorizing, however ingenious, could ever tell us as much about the spiral nebulae as can direct acquaintance by means of a good telescope, camera, and spectroscope. Analogously, no amount of theorizing about such hints as may be darkly glimpsed within the ordinary unregenerate experience of the manifold world can tell us as much about divine Reality as can be directly apprehended by a mind in a state of detachment, charity, and humility. Natural science is empirical; but it does not confine itself to the experience of human beings in their merely human state, unmodified by instruments. Why empirical theologians should feel themselves obliged to submit to this handicap, goodness only knows. And of course, as long as they confine empirical experience within these all too human limits, they are doomed to the perpetual stultification of their best efforts. From the material they have chosen to consider, no mind, however brilliantly gifted, can infer more than a set of possibilities or, at the very best, specious probabilities. The self-validating certainty of direct awareness cannot in the very nature of things be achieved except by those equipped with the moral "astrolabe of God's mysteries." If one is not oneself a sage or saint, the best thing one can do, in the field of metaphysics, is to study the works of those who were, and who, because they had modified their merely human mode of being, were capable of a more than merely human kind and amount of knowledge.

6

RELIGION AND TIME

Religion is as various as humanity. Its reactions to life are sometimes intelligent and creative, sometimes stupid, stultifying, and destructive. Through its doctrines it presents sometimes an adequate picture of the nature and quality of ultimate Reality, sometimes a picture colored by the lowest of human cravings, and therefore wholly untrue. Its consequences are sometimes very good, sometimes monstrously and diabolically evil.

In considering a group of organized religions, or the religious beliefs and practices of a group of individuals, how can we distinguish between the truer and the less true, the better and the less good? One of the answers given by all the great religious teachers is that "by their fruits ye shall know them." But, unfortunately, fruits often take a long time to observe; the full consequences of adherence to a given religion will not be manifested in all circumstances, and the would-be critic must often wait, before passing judgment, until external events provide the opportunity for making a crucial observation. Nor is this all. The fruits of certain less good practices and less true beliefs do not take the form of positive wrong-doings or obviously recognizable disasters. They are of a subtler, more negative kind—not sins, but failures to achieve the highest development of which the individual or group is capable; not catastrophes, but the nonattainment of the fruits of the spirit, love, joy, and peace. But such failures and nonattainments can be measured only by observers of more than ordinary insight, or by those who are so placed that they can look back over a long span of the career of the individuals or groups under consideration.

It is clear, then, that, besides the criterion of fruits, we need another more readily applicable—a criterion by which to judge the roots and flowers from which the fruits spring. Thanks to the insight of specially gifted individuals and to the collective experience of generations of worshipers, such criterion for evaluating the doctrines and practices of religion have been discovered and only require to be intelligently applied.

The most elementary criterion is that which has reference to the unity or plurality of the object of worship. It has been found that the doctrines and practices of monotheism are, generally speaking, truer and better than those of polytheism, and lead to more satisfactory results, both for individuals and for societies. But the distinction between monotheism and polytheism is not enough. Two men may both be monotheists; but the nature of the God believed in by the first may be profoundly different from that of the God believed in by the second, and their religious practices may be as diverse as their theoretical conceptions. But the one God—and this is affirmed by all those who have fulfilled the conditions which alone make possible a clear insight into the nature and quality of Reality—is a God of love. In the light of these insights we may refine our criterion and assert that those beliefs will be truer, and those practices better, which have as their object a single God of love. But even a God of love can be conceived of, and therefore worshiped, in a variety of ways, and with diverse consequences for individuals and societies. To become fully adequate, our criterion requires to be further refined. Once again, the new qualification of the elementary criterion is provided by those theocentric mystics who alone have fulfilled the conditions upon which insight depends. The truer forms of religion are those in which God is conceived, not only as one and loving, but also as eternal (that is to say, outside time); and the better forms of religious practice are those which aim at creating in the mind a condition approximating to timelessness. (Reality cannot make itself known except to those who have fulfilled the necessary conditions of "mortification," and have rendered themselves commensurable with God by becoming, as far as they can, unified, loving and, in some measure, timeless.) Conversely, the less true forms of religious belief are those which emphasize God's everlastingness rather than his eternal presence in a nontemporal Now; and the less-good religious practices are those which stress the importance of petitionary prayer addressed to a temporal God for the sake of personal or social advantages in temporal affairs, and which, in general, substitute a preoccupation with future time for the mystic's concern with the time-less presence of eternal Reality.

In theory all the higher religions have insisted that the final end of man, the purpose of his existence upon earth, is the realization, partially in the present life, more completely in some other state, of timeless Reality. In practice, however, a majority of the adherents of these religions have always behaved as if man's primary concern were not with eternity, but with time. At any given moment several quite different religions go by the name of Christianity, say, or Buddhism, or Taoism—religions ranging all the way from the purest mysticism to the grossest fetishism.

In all the higher religions the doctrines about eternal Reality, and the practices designed to help worshipers to render themselves sufficiently timeless to apprehend an eternal God, bear a close family resemblance. Eckhart, as Professor Otto has shown in his "Mysticism East and West," formulates a philosophy which is substantially the same as that of Sankara; and the practical teaching of Indian and Christian mystics is identical in such matters as "holy indifference" to temporal affairs; mortification of memory for the past and anxiety about the future; renunciation of petitionary prayer in favor of simple abandonment to the will of God; purification not only of the will, but also of the imagination and intellect, so that the consciousness of the worshiper may partake in some measure of the intense undifferentiated timelessness of that which he desires to apprehend and be united with. For the theocentric mystics both of East and West, it is axiomatic that one must "seek first the kingdom of God" (the timeless kingdom of an eternal God) "and his righteousness" (the righteousness of eternity over and above the righteousness of life in time); and that, only if one does this, is there any prospect of "all the rest being added."

In the less true forms of the genuine religions and, still more, in the humanistic pseudo-religions of Nationalism, Fascism, Communism, and the like, the position is completely reversed. For here the fundamental commandment and its accompanying promise are, "Seek ye first all the rest, and the kingdom of God and his righteousness shall be added to you."

Among the religious, the seeking first of temporal values is always associated with the idea of a God who, being in time rather than eternity, is not spiritual but "psychical." Believers in a temporal God make use of passionately willed and intensely felt petitionary prayer for concrete benefits, such as health and prosperity before death and, afterward, a place in some everlasting heaven. These petitionary prayers are accompanied by rituals and sacraments which, by stimulating imagination and intensifying emotions, help to create that psychic "field," within which petitionary prayer takes on the power to get itself answered. The fact that "spiritual healing" (more accurately, "psychic healing") often works, and that prayers for one's own or other people's health, wealth, and happiness often get answered, is constantly put forward by the devotees of temporal religion as a proof that they are being directly helped by God. One might just as well argue that one is being directly helped by God because one's refrigerator works, or because somebody answers when one dials a number on the telephone. All one has a right to say of such things as "spiritual healing" and answers to prayer is that they are happenings permitted by God in exactly the same way as other natural psycho-physical phenomena are permitted. That the mind has extensive powers over and above those which are ordinarily used in everyday life has been known from time immemorial; and at all periods and in all countries these powers have been exploited, for good and for evil, by mediums, healers, prophets, medicine men, magicians, hatha yogis, and the other queer fish who exist and have always existed on the fringes of every society. During the last two or three generations some efforts have been made to investigate these powers and the conditions under which they are manifested. The phenomena of hypnotism and suggestion have been carefully explored. Under the auspices of the Society of Psychical Research a thoroughly respectable and critical literature of the abnormal has come into existence. Research into extrasensory perception is carried on in a number of university laboratories; and now, in at least one of those laboratories, there is piling up significant evidence for the existence of "Pk," or the ability of persons to interfere with the movements of material objects by means of a purely mental act. If people working under the most uninspiring laboratory conditions can perceive clairvoyantly, exercise foreknowledge, and affect the fall of dice by purely mental acts, then clearly we have no right whatever to invoke a direct intervention of God in the case of similar phenomena, just because they happen to take place in a church or to the accompaniment of religious rites.

In this context, it is highly significant that the great theocentric mystics have always drawn a sharp distinction between the "psychic" and the "spiritual." In their view, phenomena of the first class have their existence in an unfamiliar, but in no way intrinsically superior, extension of the space-time world. Spiritual phenomena, on the other hand, belong to the timeless and eternal order, within which the temporal order has its less real existence. The mystics' attitude to "miracles" is one of intellectual acceptance, and emotional and volitional detachment. Miracles happen, but they are of very little importance. Moreover, the temptation to perform "miracles" should always be resisted. For mystics, this temptation is particularly strong; for those who try to make themselves timelessly conscious of eternal Reality frequently develop unusual psychic powers in the process. When this happens, it is essential to refrain from using such powers; for the user thereby places an impediment between himself and the Reality with which he hopes to be united. This advice is given as clearly by the masters of Western spirituality as by the Buddhists and Vedantists. But, unfortunately for Christianity, the teaching of the gospels upon this subject is somewhat confused. Jesus denounces those who ask for "signs," but Himself performs many miracles of healing and the like. The explanation of this apparent inconsistency can probably be found in the passage, in which He asks His critics which is easier, to tell the sick man to rise and walk, or to tell him that his sins are forgiven him. The implication seems to be that physical "signs" are legitimate, if the person who performs them is so completely united with eternal Reality that he is able, by the very quality of his being, to modify the inner being of those, for whose sake the "signs" are performed. But this enormously important qualification has been generally neglected, and the adherents of the less true forms of the Christian religion attach enormous importance to such purely "psychic" phenomena as healing and the answer to petitionary prayer. By doing this they positively guarantee themselves against attaining that degree of union with timeless Reality which alone might render the performance of a "miracle" innocuous to the doer and permanently beneficial to the person on whom, or for whom, it is done.

Another form frequently taken by temporal religion is apocalypticism—belief in an extraordinary cosmic event to take place in the not-too-distant future, together with the practices deemed appropriate to this state of things. Here again intense preoccupation with future time positively guarantees the apocalypticist against the possibility of a timeless realization of eternal Reality.

In certain respects all the humanistic pseudo-religions, at present so popular, bear a close resemblance to the apocalyptic perversions of true religion. For in these also an intense preoccupation with hypothetical events in future time takes the place of the genuinely religious concern with Reality now, in the eternal present. But whereas believers in the approaching end of the world seldom find it necessary to coerce or slaughter those who do not agree with them, coercion and slaughter have formed an essential part of the program put forward by the crusaders for the humanistic pseudo-religions. For the revolutionary, whether of the right or the left, the supremely important fact is the golden age of peace, prosperity and brotherly love which, his faith assures him, is bound to dawn as soon as his particular brand of revolution has been carried through. Nothing stands between the people's miserable present and its glorious future, except a minority, perhaps a majority, of perverse or merely ignorant individuals. All that is necessary is to liquidate a few thousands, or it may be a few millions, of these living obstacles to progress, and then to coerce and propagandize the rest into acquiescence. When these unpleasant but necessary preliminaries are over, the golden age will begin. Such is the theory of that secular apocalypticism which is the religion of revolutionaries. But in practice, it is hardly necessary to say, the means employed positively guarantee that the end actually reached shall be profoundly different from that which the prophetic theorists envisaged.

Happiness is not achieved by the conscious pursuit of happiness; it is generally the by-product of other activities. This "hedonistic paradox" may be generalized to cover our whole life in time. Temporal conditions will be accepted as satisfactory only by those whose first concern is not with time, but with eternal Reality and with that state of virtually timeless consciousness, in which alone the awareness of Reality is possible. Furthermore, in any given society, temporal conditions will be generally felt to be tolerable, and will in fact be as free from the grosser evils as human conditions ever can be, only when the current philosophy of life lays more stress upon eternity than upon time, and only when a minority of individuals within the society are making a serious attempt to live out this philosophy in practice. It is highly significant, as Sorokin has pointed out, that a man born into the eternity-conscious thirteenth century had a much better prospect of dying in his bed than a man of our own time—the obsessed and therefore nationalistic, revolutionary, and violent twentieth century. *Si monumentum requiris, circumspice.* So runs the epitaph carved on Wren's tomb in St. Paul's cathedral. Similarly, if you require a monument to modern man's preoccupation with future time to the exclusion of present eternity, look round at the world's battlefields and back over the history covered by the lifetime of a man of seventy—the history of that late-Victorian "Generation of Materialism," so ably sketched in a recent volume by Professor Carlton Hayes, and the history of the generation which inevitably succeeded it, that of the wars and revolutions. Reality cannot be ignored except at a price; and the longer the ignorance is persisted in, the higher and the more terrible becomes the price that must be paid.

7

SOME REFLECTIONS
ON TIME

Time destroys all that it creates, and the end of every temporal sequence is, for the entity involved in it, some form of death. Death is wholly transcended only when time is transcended; immortality is for the consciousness that has broken through the temporal into the timeless. For all other consciousnesses there is at best a survival or a rebirth; and these entail further temporal sequences and the periodical recurrence of yet other deaths and dissolutions. In all the traditional philosophies and religions of the world, time is regarded as the enemy and the deceiver, the prison and the torture chamber. It is only as an instrument, as the means to something else, that it possesses a positive value; for time provides the embodied soul with opportunities for transcending time; every instant of every temporal sequence is potentially the door through which we can, if we so desire, break through into the eternal. All temporal goods are means to an end beyond themselves; they are not to be treated as ends in their own right. Material goods are to be prized because they support the body which, in our present existence, is necessary to the achievement of man's Final End. Moral goods have many and very obvious utilitarian values; but their highest and ultimate value consists in the fact that they are means to that selflessness, which is the precondition of the realization of the eternal. The goods of the intellect are truths and, in the last analysis, these are valuable insofar as they remove God-eclipsing delusions and prejudices. Aesthetic goods are precious because they are symbolic of, and analogous to, the unitive knowledge of timeless Reality. To regard any of these temporal goods as self-sufficient and final ends is to commit idolatry. And idolatry, which is fundamentally unrealistic and inappropriate to the facts of the universe, results at the best in self-stultification and at the worst in disaster.

Movement in time is irreversibly in one direction. "We live forwards," as Kierkegaard said, "but we can only understand backwards." Moreover the flux of duration is indefinite and inconclusive, a perpetual lapse possessing in itself no pattern, no possibility of balance of symmetry. Nature, it is true, imposes upon this perpetual perishing a certain appearance of pattern and symmetry. Thus, days alternate with nights, the seasons recur with regularity, plants and animals have their life cycles and are succeeded by offspring like themselves. But all these patternings and symmetries and recurrences are characteristic, not of time as it is in itself, but of space and matter as they are associated with time in our consciousness. Days and nights and seasons exist because certain heavenly bodies move in a certain way. If it took the earth not a year but a century to move round the sun, our sense of the intrinsic formlessness of time, of its irrevocable one-way lapse toward the death of all the entities involved in it, would be much more acute than it is at present; for most of us, in those hypothetical circumstances, would never live to see all the four seasons of the long year and would have no experience of that recurrence and renewal, those cosmic variations on known themes, which, under the present astronomical dispensation, disguise the essential nature of time by endowing it, or seeming to endow it, with some of the qualities of space. Now, space is a symbol of eternity; for in space there is freedom, there is reversibility of movement, and there is nothing in the nature of a space, as there is in that of time, which condemns those involved in it to inevitable death and dissolution. Moreover, when space contains material bodies, the possibility of orderliness, balance, symmetry, and pattern arises—the possibility, in a word, of that Beauty which, along with Goodness and Truth, takes its place in the trinity of manifested Godhead. In this context a highly significant point should be noted. In all the arts whose raw material is of a temporal nature, the primary aim of the artist is to spatialize time. The poet, the dramatist, the novelist, the musician—each takes a fragment of the perpetual perishing, in which we are doomed to undertake our one-way journey toward death, and tries to endow it with some of the qualities of space: namely, symmetry, balance, and orderliness (the Beauty-producing characteristics of a space containing material bodies), together with multidimensionality and the quality of permitting free movement in all directions. This spatialization of time is achieved in poetry and music by the employment of recurrent rhythms and cadences, by the confinement of the material within conventional forms, such as that of the sonnet or the sonata, and by the imposition upon the chosen fragment of temporal indefiniteness of a beginning, a middle, and an end. What is called *construction* in the drama and the narrative serves the same spatializing purpose. The aim in all cases is to give a form to the essentially formless, to impose symmetry and order upon what is actually an indefinite flux toward death. The fact that all the arts that deal with temporal sequences have always attempted to spatialize time indicates very clearly the nature of man's natural and spontaneous reaction to time, and throws a light on the significance of space as a symbol of that timeless state, toward which, through all the impediments of ignorance, the human spirit consciously or unconsciously aspires.

There has been an attempt on the part of certain Western philosophers of the last few generations to raise time from the position to which the traditional religions and the normal sentiments of humanity had assigned it. Thus, under the influence of evolutionary theories, time is regarded as the creator of the highest values, so that even God is emergent—the product of the one-way flux of perpetual perishing, not (as in the traditional religions) as the timeless witness of time, transcendent to it and, because of that transcendence, capable of immanence within it. Closely allied to the theory of emergence is the

Bergsonian view that "duration" is the primary and ultimate reality and that the "life-force" exists exclusively in the flux. On another line we have the Hegelian and Marxian philosophies of History, which is spelled with a capital H and hypostatized as a temporal providence working for the realization of the kingdom of heaven on earth—this kingdom of heaven on earth being, in Hegel's view, a glorified version of the Prussian State and in the view of Marx, who was exiled by the authorities of that State, of the dictatorship of the proletariat, leading "inevitably" by the process of the dialectic to the classless society. These views of history make the assumption that the Divine, or History, or the Cosmic Process, or *Geist,* or whatever the entity which uses time for its purposes may be called, is concerned with humanity in the mass, not with man and woman as individuals—and not with humanity at any given moment, but with humanity as a succession of generations. Now, there seems to be absolutely no reason for supposing that this is the case—absolutely no reason for supposing that there is a collective soul of succeeding generations capable of experiencing, comprehending, and acting upon the impulsions transmitted by *Geist,* History, Life-Force, and all the rest. On the contrary, all the evidence points to the fact that it is the individual soul, incarnated at a particular moment of time, which alone can establish contact with the Divine, to say nothing of other souls. The belief (which is based on obvious and self-evident facts) that Humanity is represented at any given moment by the persons who constitute the mass, and that all the values of Humanity reside in those persons, is regarded as absurdly shallow by these philosophers of history. But the tree is known by its fruits. Those who believe in the primacy of persons and who think that the Final End of all persons is to transcend time and realize that which is eternal and time-less, are always, like the Hindus, the Buddhists, the Tao-ists, the primitive Christians, advocates of nonviolence, gentleness, peace, and tolerance. Those, on the contrary, who like to be "deep" in the manner of Hegel and Marx, who think that "History" deals with Humanity-in-the-Mass and Humanity-as-successive-generations, not with individual men and women here and now, are indifferent to human life and personal values, worship the Molochs which they call the State and Society, and are cheerfully prepared to sacrifice successive generations of real, con-crete persons for the sake of the entirely hypothetical happiness which, on no grounds whatsoever, they think will be the lot of Humanity in the distant future. The politics of those who regard eternity as the ultimate re-ality are concerned with the present and with the ways and means of organizing the present world in such a way that it will impose the fewest possible obstacles in the way of individual liberation from time and ignorance; those, on the contrary, who regard time as the ultimate reality are concerned primarily with the future and re-gard the present world and its inhabitants as mere rubble, cannon-fodder are potential slave-labor to be exploited, terrorized, liquidated, or blown to smithereens, in order that persons who may never be born, in a future time about which nothing can be known with the smallest degree of certainty, may have the kind of a wonderful time which present-day revolutionaries and war-makers think they ought to have. If the lunacy were not criminal, one would be tempted to laugh.

8

ON A SENTENCE FROM SHAKESPEARE

This essay later appeared in *Time Must Have a Stop* (1945).

If you say absolutely everything, it all tends to cancel out into nothing. Which is why no explicit philosophy can be dug out of Shakespeare. But as a metaphysic-by-implication, as a system of beauty-truth, constituted by the poetical relationships of scenes and lines, and inhering, so to speak, in the blank spaces between even such words as "told by an idiot, signifying nothing," the plays are the equivalent of a great theological *Summa*. And of course, if you choose to ignore the negatives which cancel them out, what extraordinary isolated utterances of a perfectly explicit wisdom! I keep thinking, for example, of those two and a half lines in which Hotspur casually summarizes a whole epistemology, a whole ethic, a whole theology.

> But thought's the slave of life, and life's time's fool,
> And time that takes survey of all the world
> Must have a stop.

Three clauses, of which the twentieth century has

paid attention only to the first. Thought's enslavement to life is one of our favorite themes. Bergson and the Pragmatists, Adler and Freud, the Dialectical Materialists and the Behaviorists—all tootle their variations upon it. Mind, we are told, is nothing but a food-gathering mechanism; controlled by unconscious forces, either aggressive or sexual; the product of social and economic pressures; a bundle of conditioned reflexes.

All this is quite true so far as it goes; quite false if it goes no further. For obviously, if mind is only some kind of a nothing-but, none of its affirmations can make any claim to a general validity. But all nothing-but philosophies actually make such claims. Therefore they cannot be true; for if they were true, that would be the proof that they are false. Thought's the slave of life—yes, undoubtedly. But if it weren't also something else, we couldn't make even this partially valid generalization.

The significance of Hotspur's second clause is mainly practical. Life's time's fool. By merely elapsing, time makes nonsense of all that life consciously schemes for in the temporal order. No considerable action has ever had all, or nothing but, the results expected of it. Except under strictly controlled conditions, or in circumstances where we can abstract from reality, ignore individuals and concern ourselves only with vast numbers and the law of averages, any kind of accurate foresight is impossible. In all actual human situations more variables are involved than the human mind can take account of; and with the passage of time the variables tend to increase in number and change their character. All this is a matter of everyday experience. And yet the only faith of a majority of twentieth-century Americans and Europeans is faith in the Future—the bigger and better Future which they *know* that Progress is going to produce for them, like white rabbits out of a hat. For the sake of what their faith tells them about a Future, which their reason assures them to be almost completely unknowable, men are prepared to sacrifice their only tangible possession, the Present. During the last thirty years about 50 million of Europeans have been liquidated in wars and revolutions. Why? The nationalists and revolutionaries all give the same answer. "In order that the great-great-grandchildren of those who are now being liquidated may have an absolutely wonderful time in A.D. 2043." And (choosing, according to taste or political opinion, from among the Wellsian, Marxian, or Fascist blueprints) we solemnly proceed to visualize and describe the sort of wonderful time these lucky beggars are going to have. Just as our Victorian great-great-grandfathers solemnly visualized and described the sort of wonderful time *we* were going to have in the middle years of the twentieth century.

True religion concerns itself with the givenness of the timeless. And idolatrous religion is one which substitutes time for eternity—either past time, in the form of a rigid tradition, or else future time, in the form of Progress toward Utopia. And both are Molochs; both demand human sacrifice. Spanish Catholicism was a typical idolatry of past time. Nationalism, Communism, Fascism, all the twentieth-century pseudo-religions, are typical idolatries of future time.

What have been the consequences of Western man's recent shift of attention from past to future time? An intellectual progress from the Garden of Eden to Utopia and the Classless Society; a moral and political advance from compulsory orthodoxy and the divine right of kings to military and industrial conscription for everybody, the infallibility of the local political boss and the deification of the State. Before or behind, time can never be worshiped with impunity.

But Hotspur's summary has a final clause: time must have a stop. And not only *must,* as a prophecy or an ethical imperative, but also *does* have a stop, in the present indicative tense and as a matter of brute empirical experience, here and now, for all who so desire. It is only by taking the fact of eternity into account that we can deliver thought from its slavery to life. And it is only by deliberately paying our attention and our primary allegiance to eternity that we can prevent time from turning our lives into a pointless or diabolic foolery. Brahman, the Ground, the Clear Light of the Void, the Kingdom of God are all one timeless reality. Seek it first, and all the rest—from an adequate philosophy to a release from the compulsion to stultify and destroy ourselves—will be added. Or, to put the matter in Shakespearian language, if we cease to be "most ignorant" of what we are "most assured, our glassy essence"—the indwelling spirit,

the principle of our being, the *Atman*—then we shall be
other than that dreadful caricature of humanity who
    like an angry ape,
  Plays such fantastic tricks before high heaven
  As make the angels weep.

9

MAN AND REALITY

For those who live within its limits, the lights of the city are the only luminaries of the high sky. The street lamps eclipse the stars, and the glare of the whisky advertisements reduces even the moonlight to an almost invisible irrelevance.

The phenomenon is symbolical, a parable in action. Mentally and physically, man is the inhabitant, during the greatest part of his life, of a purely human and, so to say, homemade universe, scooped by himself out of the immense, nonhuman cosmos which surrounds it, and without which neither it nor he could exist. Within this private catacomb we build up for ourselves a little world of our own, constructed of a strange assortment of materials—interests and "ideals," words and technologies, cravings and day-dreams, artifacts and institutions, imaginary gods and demons. Here, among the magnified projections of our own personalities, we perform our curious antics and perpetrate our crimes and lunacies, we think the thoughts and feel the emotions appropriate to our man-made environment, we cherish the crazy ambitions that alone make sense in a madhouse. But all the time, in spite of the radio noises and the neon tubes, night and the stars are there—just beyond the last bus stop, just above the canopy of illuminated smoke. This is a fact which the inhabitants of the human catacomb find it all too easy to forget; but whether they forget or remember, a fact it always remains. Night and the stars are always there; the other, nonhuman world, of which the stars and night are but the symbols, persists and is the real world.

> *Man, proud man, drest in a little brief authority—*
> *Most ignorant of what he's most assured,*
> *His glassy essence—like an angry ape,*
> *Plays such fantastic tricks before high heaven*
> *As make the angels weep.*

So wrote Shakespeare in the only one of his plays which reveals any deep concern with the ultimate spiritual realities. It is the "glassy essence" of man that constitutes the reality of which he is most assured, the reality which sustains him and in virtue of which he lives. And this glassy essence is of the same kind as the Clear Light, which is the essence of the universe. Within us, this "spark," this "uncreated depth of the Soul," this *Atman*, remains unsullied and unflawed, however fantastic the tricks we may play—just as, in the outer world, night and the stars remain themselves in spite of all the Broadways and Piccadillies, all the searchlights and the incendiary bombs.

The great nonhuman world, which exists simultaneously within us and without, is governed by its own divine laws—laws which we are free to obey or disobey. Obedience leads to liberation; disobedience to a deeper enslavement to misery and evil, to a prolongation of our existence in the likeness of angry apes. Human history is a record of the conflict between two forces—on the one hand, the silly and criminal presumption that makes man ignorant of his glassy essence; on the other, the recognition that, unless he lives in conformity with the greater cosmos, he himself is utterly evil, and his world, a nightmare. In this interminable conflict, now one side gains the upper hand, and now the other. At the present time we are witnessing the temporary triumph of the specifically human side of man's nature. For some time now we have chosen to believe, and to act on the belief, that our private world of neon tubes and incendiaries was the only real world, that the glassy essence in us did not exist. Angry apes, we have imagined ourselves, because of our simian cleverness, to be angels—to be indeed, more than angels, to be gods, creators, framers of our destiny. What are the consequences of this triumph of the purely human side of man? The headlines in the morning papers furnish an unequivocal reply: the destruction of human values either by death or degradation or perversion to the ends of politics, revolution and war. When we think presumptuously that we are, or shall become in some future utopian state, "men like gods," then in fact we are in mortal danger of becoming devils, capable only (however exalted our "ideals" may be, however beautifully worked out our plans and blue-prints) of ruining our world and destroying ourselves. The triumph of humanism is the defeat of humanity.

Fortunately, as [Alfred Lord] Whitehead has pointed out, the moral order of the universe consists precisely in the fact that evil is self-stultifying. When evil is given free rein, either by individuals or by societies, it always ends by committing suicide. The nature of this suicide may be either physical or psychological. The evil individuals or societies may be literally killed off, or reduced to impotence through mere exhaustion; or else they may reach a condition, if the orgy of evil is too much prolonged, of such weariness and disgust that they find themselves forced, by a kind of sanguinary *reductio ad absurdum,* to surrender to the obvious truth that men are not gods, that they cannot control the destiny even of their own homemade world and that the only way to the peace, happiness, and freedom they so ardently desire is through the knowledge of and obedience to the laws of the greater, nonhuman cosmos.

"The further you go towards the East," Sri Ramakrishna was fond of saying, "the further you go away from the West." This is one of those apparently childish remarks, which we meet with so often among the writings and recorded sayings of religious teachers. But it is an apparent childishness that masks a real profundity. Within this absurd little tautology there lies, in a state of living, seminal latency, a whole metaphysic, a complete program of action. It is, of course, the same philosophy and the

same way of life as were referred to by Jesus in those sayings about the impossibility of serving two masters, and
the necessity of seeking first the kingdom of God and
waiting for all the rest to be added. Egoism and alter-
egoism (or the idolatrous service of individuals, groups,
and causes with which we identify ourselves so that their
success flatters our own ego) cut us off from the knowledge and experience of reality. Nor is this all; they cut us
off also from the satisfaction of our needs and the enjoyment of our legitimate pleasures. It is a matter of empirical experience and observation that we cannot for long
enjoy what we desire as human beings, unless we obey
the laws of that greater, nonhuman cosmos of which,
however much we may, in our proud folly, forget the
fact, we are integral parts. Egoism and alter-egoism advise us to remain firmly ensconced in the West, looking
after our own human affairs. But if we do this, our affairs
will end by going to pot; and if our alter-egoistic "ideals" have been very lofty, we shall, as likely as not, find
ourselves liquidating our neighbors on a gigantic scale—
and, incidentally, being liquidated by them. Whereas if
we ignore the counsels of egoism and alter-egoism, and
resolutely march toward the divine East, we shall create for ourselves the possibility of receiving the grace of
enlightenment and, at the same time, we shall find that
existence in our physical, Western home is a great deal
more satisfactory than it was when we devoted our attention primarily to the improvement of our human lot.
In a word, things in the West will go better because, as

we go toward the East, we are further from them—less attached to them, less passionately concerned about them, therefore less liable to start liquidating people on account of them. But, alas, as the author of the *Imitation* remarks: "All men desire peace, but few there are who desire the things that make for peace."

A measure of detachment from egoism and alter-egoism is essential even if we would make contact with the secondary aspects of cosmic reality. Thus, in order to be fruitful, science must be pure. That is to say, the man of science must put aside all thoughts of personal advantage, of "practical" results, and concentrate exclusively on the task of discovering the facts and coordinating them in an intelligible theory. In the long run, alter-egoism is as fatal to science as egoism. Typical of alter-egoistic science is that secretive, nationalistic research which accompanies and precedes modern war. Such science is dedicated to its own stultification and destruction, as well as to the destruction of every other kind of human good.

These are not the only detachments which the man of science must practice. He must liberate himself not only from the cruder egoistic and alter-egoistic passions, but also from his purely intellectual prejudices—from the trammels of traditional thought-patterns, and even of common sense. Things are not what they seem; or, to be more accurate, they are not only what they seem, but very much else besides. To act upon this truth, as the man of science must constantly do, is to practice a kind of intellectual mortification.

Analogous mortifications and detachments have to be practiced by the artist, when he is making his attempt to discover and express that divine relationship between the parts of the cosmos, which we call beauty. Similarly, on the plane of ethical conduct, the manifestations of goodness cannot be made by oneself or elicited from others unless there is an inhibition of personal and alter-egoistic cravings and aversions.

When we pass from the realm of the manifested and embodied aspects of reality to that of reality itself, we shall find that there must be an intensification of detachment, a widening and deepening of mortification. The symbol of death and rebirth recurs incessantly in the sayings and writings of the masters of the spiritual life. If God's kingdom is to come, man's must go; the old Adam has to perish in order that the new man may be born. In other words, ascetical self-mortification, at once physical, emotional, ethical, and intellectual, is one of the indispensable conditions of enlightenment, of the realization of divine immanence and transcendence. True, no amount of ascetic practices or of spiritual exercises can automatically guarantee enlightenment, which is always in the nature of a grace. The most we are justified in saying is that the egoism and alter-egoism, which ascetic practices are designed to root out, automatically perpetuate the state of nonenlightenment. We cannot see the moon and the stars so long as we choose to re-main within the aura of street lamps and whisky ad-vertisements. We cannot even hope to discover what is happening in the East, if we turn our feet and faces toward the West.

10

REFLECTIONS ON PROGRESS

This essay was eventually incorporated into the author's
The Devils of Loudun (1952).

Evolutionary change is regarded as progressive when it is
in the direction of increasing independence of, and control over, the environment. Judged by this criterion, the
history of life on our planet has not by any means been
uniformly progressive. Primitive forms have survived almost unmodified from the dawn of that history down
to the present. Man is the contemporary of unicellular
organisms which, despite their almost total dependence
on the environment, may very likely outlive their more
progressive rivals. Moreover, many organisms have undergone progressive changes over a long period of time,
only to regress toward a new and specialized kind of dependence upon the environment, as parasites upon more
advanced forms. And finally even those species which
have changed most progressively are all, at the present
time, at the end of evolutionary blind alleys, condemned
by their high degree of specialization either to remain
what they are, or, if they undergo a series of considerable
mutations, to die out through inability to adapt them-

selves, in their changed forms, to the environment. There is good reason to suppose that all the existing higher animals are living fossils, predestined to survival without much change, or, if change sets in, to extinction. Except for the human species, evolutionary progress would seem to be at an end.

Biological progress, like every other kind of evolutionary change, is brought about by means of mutations, whose consequences are inherited. Human progress might still conceivably be brought about in the same way; but at least within historical times it has not been so brought about. Moreover, since the great majority of mutations are harmful, it seems unlikely that future changes in the germ plasm will do anything to improve the constitution of a species, which is the product of so long an evolutionary development. (Hence the enormous dangers inherent in the use, even for peaceful purposes, of nuclear fission. Mutations can be artificially produced by the kind of radiations associated with nuclear fission—and most mutations, as we have seen, are harmful. It would be a very suitable punishment for man's overweening *hubris* if the final result of his efforts to dominate nature were the production of a race of harelipped, six-fingered imbeciles.) If there is to be hereditary progress in the human species, it will be brought about by the same kind of selective breeding as has improved the races of domesticated animals. It would be perfectly possible, within a few centuries, to raise the average level of human intelligence to a point far above the present. Whether such a vast eugenic experiment could be carried out except under the auspices of a world dictatorship, and whether, if carried out, its results would turn out to be socially desirable, are matters about which we can only speculate. Meanwhile it is worth remarking that the hereditary qualities of the more civilized peoples of the world are probably deteriorating. This is due to the fact that persons of poor physique and low intellectual endowments have a better chance of living under modern conditions than their counterparts ever had in the much severer conditions prevailing in the past. Human progress, within historical times, differs from biological progress in being a matter, not of heredity, but of tradition. This tradition, oral and written, has served as the vehicle by means of which the achievements of exceptional individuals have been made available for their contemporaries and successors, and the new discoveries of one generation have been handed on, to become the commonplace of the next.

Many and very various criteria have been used to measure this human progress-by-tradition. Sometimes it is envisaged as a continuation of biological progress—an advance in control and independence. Judged by this standard, the progress achieved in recent centuries by certain sections of the human race has been very great. True, it has not been quite so great as some people like to think. Earthquakes still kill their thousands, epidemics their millions, while famines due to drought, or floods, or insect pests, or the diseases of plants, slowly and painfully destroy their tens of millions. Moreover, many of the "conquests of nature" most loudly acclaimed at one moment have turned out, a few years later, to be a good deal less spectacular than was first imagined—have even taken on the aspect of defeats. Consider, for example, the progress achieved in the most important of all human activities—agriculture. New fields are brought under the plough, produce crops that permit an expansion of the population, and then, almost suddenly, turn into dust bowls and eroded hillsides. New chemicals for the control of insects, viruses, and fungi seem to work almost miraculously, but only until such time as mutation and natural selection produce new and resistant strains of the old enemies. Artificial fertilizers produce bumper harvests; but meanwhile they kill the indispensable earthworm and, in the opinion of a growing number of authorities, tend in the long run to reduce the fertility of the soil and to impair the nutritive qualities of the plants that grow on it. In the name of "efficiency," we disturb the delicate balance of nature; by eliminating one of the factors of the ecological mosaic, or artificially adding to another, we get our increased production, but after a few years outraged nature takes its revenge in the most unexpected and disconcerting way. And the list could be lengthened indefinitely. Human beings are never quite so clever as they think they are.

But the criteria by which biological progress is measured are not adequate when it comes to the measurement of human progress. For biological progress is thought of as applying exclusively to the species as a whole; whereas

it is impossible to think realistically about mankind without considering the individual as well as the race to which
he belongs. It is easy to imagine a state of things in which
the human species should have achieved their progress,
at the expense of the component individuals, considered
as personalities. Judged by specifically human standards,
such biological progress would be a regression toward a
lower, subhuman state.

In framing standards by which to measure human
progress we must take into account the values which,
in the opinion of individual men and women, make life
worth living. And this, in effect, has been done by all
the theorists of human progress from the later seventeenth century, when the idea first began to seem plau-
sible, down to the present day. During the eighteenth
and nineteenth centuries biological progress was reconciled with human progress by means of a doctrine of
pre-established harmony. It was assumed as practically
self-evident that advances in man's control over his environment would inevitably be accompanied by corresponding advances in individual happiness, in personal
and social morality, and in the quantity and quality of
creative activity in the spheres of art and science. Those
of us who are old enough to have been brought up in the
Victorian tradition can recall (with a mixture of amuse-
ment and melancholy) the basic and unquestioned as-
sumptions of that consoling *Weltanschauung.* Comte and
Spencer and Buckle expressed the matter in respectably
abstract language; but the gist of their creed was simply

this: that people who wore top hats and traveled in railway trains were incapable of doing the sort of things that the Turks were doing to the Armenians or that our European ancestors had done to one another in the bad old days before steam engines. Today, after two world wars and three major revolutions, we know that there is no necessary correlation between advanced technology and advanced morality. Many primitives, whose control over their environment is rudimentary, contrive nonetheless to be happy, virtuous, and, within limits, creative. Conversely, the members of civilized societies, possessed of the technological resources to exercise considerable control over their environment, are often conspicuously unhappy, maladjusted, and uncreative; and though private morals are tolerably good, collective behavior is savage to the point of fiendishness. In the field of international relations the most conspicuous difference between men of the twentieth century and the ancient Assyrians is that the former have more efficient methods of committing atrocities and are able to destroy, tyrannize, and enslave on a larger scale.

The truth is that all an increase in man's ability to control his environment can do for him is merely to modify the situation in which, by other than technological means, individuals and groups attempt to make specifically human progress in creativeness, morality, and happiness. Thus the city-dwelling factory worker may belong, biologically speaking, to a more progressive group than does the peasant; but it does not follow that he will find it any easier to be happy, good, and creative. The peasant is confronted by one set of obstacles and handicaps; the industrial worker, by another set. Technological progress does not abolish obstacles; it merely changes their nature. And this is true even in cases where technological progress directly affects the lives and persons of individuals. For example, sanitation has greatly reduced the incidence of contagious diseases, has lowered child mortality and lengthened the average expectation of life. At first sight this piece of technological progress would seem to be at the same time a piece of human progress. But when we look at the matter more closely, we discover that, even here, all that has happened is that the conditions for achieving human progress have been changed. Symptomatic of this change is the recent rise of geriatrics as an important branch of medicine, is the granting of pensions to the aged, is the shift of the balance of population, in countries with a low birth rate, toward the higher age groups. Thanks to sanitation, the aged are in process of becoming a socially important minority, and for this important minority the problems of human progress in happiness, goodness, and creativeness are peculiarly difficult. Even in the medical field, technological progress is never the same as human progress. For though we can say without qualification that it would be a good thing if, let us say, malaria could be abolished, yet the mere fact of improving the health of the victims of this disease would not in itself do more than change the conditions in which human progress is attempted. The healthy are not necessarily creative, good, or even happy; they merely have a better chance of being so than do the sick.

Advancing technology increases man's control over his environment, and the increasing control is hereditary in the sense that its methods are handed on by tradition from generation to generation. But, as we have seen, this equivalent of biological progress does not by itself constitute specifically human progress. Within the constantly changing situation created by advancing technology, men must try to achieve specifically human progress by means which are not of a technological nature—namely, politics and education. Politics is concerned with the organization of juridical and economical relationships within a given society, and between that society and other societies. Education, insofar as it is not merely vocational, aims at reconciling the individual with himself, with his fellows, with society as a whole, with the nature of which he and his society are but a part, and with the immanent and transcendent spirit within which nature has its being.

The difference between a good politico-economical arrangement and a bad one is simply this: that the good arrangement reduces the number of dangerous temptations to which the individuals and groups concerned are exposed, while the bad arrangement multiplies such temptations. Thus a dictatorship, however benevolent its intentions, is always bad, because it tempts a minority to indulge in the lust for power, while compelling the majority to act as the irresponsible and servile recipients of orders from above. If we wish to evaluate any existing or still ideal institution, whether political, economic, or ecclesiastical, we must begin by asking the same simple questions: what temptations does it, or is it likely to, create, and from what temptations does it, or is it likely to, deliver us? If it strongly and insistently tempts the individuals and groups concerned to indulge such notoriously deadly passions as pride, covetousness, cruelty, and the lust for power, if it forces hypocrisy and servility and unreasoning obedience upon whole sections of the population, then, on the face of it, the institution in question is undesirable. If, on the contrary, it offers little scope for the abuse of power, if it puts no premium on avarice, if its arrangements are such that cruelty and pride of place are not easily to be indulged, if it invites, not unreasoning obedience, but intelligent and responsible cooperation, then, on the face of it, the verdict should be favorable.

Hitherto most political and economic revolutions have failed to achieve the good results anticipated. They have swept away institutions which had become intolerable because they invited individuals and groups to succumb to dangerous temptations. But the new revolutionary institutions have led other individuals and groups into temptations which were either identical with the old, or, if not identical, no less dangerous. For example, power is as certain to be abused, whether it is exercised by rich men in virtue of their wealth, or by politicians and administrators in virtue of their position in a governmental or ecclesiastical hierarchy.

Large-scale political changes are made primarily in

the interest of an individual, party, or class; but a more-or-less sincere desire to achieve specifically human progress often enters in as a secondary motive. How far can such changes produce what is hoped of them? To what extent can a continuing advance in happiness, goodness, and creativeness be achieved by act of parliament? Of creativeness on the higher levels it would be unwise to speak. Why large numbers of men of genius should appear at one period, and why other periods should be without them is a profound mystery. It is different, however, with creativity on its lower levels, creativity as expressed in the arts and crafts of common life. It is obvious that in a society where all the necessary household goods are produced by machines in highly organized factories, the arts and crafts will not flourish. The conveniences of mass production have to be paid for by a diminution in creativeness on the lower, popular levels.

Goodness and happiness are notoriously hard to measure. All that can be said is that, given certain political and economic arrangements, certain temptations to evil and certain reasons for misery may be eliminated. Thus, an efficient police can diminish the temptations to crimes of violence, and equitable arrangements for the distribution of food can diminish the miseries attendant on hunger. Again, a paternal government can, by suitable legislation, diminish the miseries connected with periodical unemployment. Unfortunately economic security in an industrialized society has been achieved, up till now, at the expense of personal liberty. The miseries of anxiety have had to be paid for by the miseries of a dependence, which in some countries has degenerated into servitude. This is a world in which nobody ever gets anything for nothing. Advantages in one field have to be paid for by disadvantages in another field. Destiny only sells; it never gives. All we can do is to drive the best possible bargain. And if we choose to use our intelligence and good will, instead of our low cunning and our lust for power, we can make political arrangements that shall eliminate many dangerous temptations to evil and many causes of misery without, in the process, creating new troubles no less intolerable than those we have escaped.

Meanwhile we must remember that the removal, by political methods, of certain dangerous temptations and certain reasons for misery will not of itself guarantee a general advance in goodness and happiness. Even under the existing political and economic dispensations there is a minority of persons whose lives are prosperous, secure, and untroubled. And yet of these fortunate few how many are profoundly unhappy and how many are actively or passively evil! Within wide limits goodness and happiness are almost independent of external circumstances. True, a starving child cannot be happy; and a child brought up among criminals is unlikely to be good. But these are extreme cases. The great masses of the population live in a middle region, lying between the extremes of sanctity and depravity, wealth and destitution. Provided that they remain within this middle region of experience, individuals can undergo considerable changes of fortune without undergoing corresponding changes in the direction of vice or virtue, misery or happiness. Private life is very largely independent of public life and even, in some measure, of private circumstances. Certain classes of happiness and even a certain kind of goodness are the fruits of temperament and constitution. There are men and women, of whom it can be said, as it was said, for example, of St. Bonaventura, that they are "born without original sin." There are children who are congenitally unselfish, like that *Pippo buono,* who was to grow up into St. Philip Neri. And to match these inborn and gratuitous virtues, there is such a thing as an unearned joy, an almost causeless beatitude.

> *Four ducks on a pond,*
> *A grass-bank beyond,*
> *A blue sky in spring,*
> *White clouds on the wing;*
> *What a little thing*
> *To remember with tears—*
> *To remember for years!*

Such is the stuff of which a good part of our happiness is composed; and such stuff is the same at all periods, is available in every conjunction of public or private circumstances. Happiness from this kind of source cannot be increased or diminished by an act of parliament, or even by our own acts and the acts of those with whom we come in contact. It depends on our own innate ability to react to certain unchanging elements in the order of nature.

The ability so to react depends to a certain extent upon age as well as on the constitution of the individual. An adolescent newly discovering the world is happy with a kind of tremulous intensity never to be recaptured during the years of maturity. And this leads us to a very important point, which is that the life of a man is not in its nature progressive, but rises to a peak, continues for a while on a plateau of maturity, then declines through old age into decrepitude and death. The literatures of the world abound in lamentations over life's inevitable regression from youthful happiness. To an old man who has outlived his contemporaries and is declining into second childhood it is absurd to talk of the march either of biological or of human progress. In his own person he can experience only the opposite of an advance either toward greater control over the environment, or toward greater happiness, goodness, and creativeness. And at any given period, however progressive that period may seem to future historians, a third or thereabouts of all the individuals then living will be experiencing the biological and human regress associated with advancing years. Old age under Pericles or Lorenzo the Magnificent was just as sad, just as antiprogressive as old age under Abdul-Hamid or Chilperich. True, the old are in a position to maintain progress in goodness, if only because in later life many vices lose their attractiveness; but it is difficult for them to maintain progress in happiness and creativeness. If such specifically human progress is ever maintained through a considerable period, it must be through a succession of young and mature individuals, whose own lives are still in a progressive phase.

Historians, when they describe a certain age as progressive, never trouble to tell us who precisely it is that experiences the progress in question, nor how it is experienced. For example, all modern historians agree that the thirteenth century was a progressive period. And yet the moralists who actually lived during the thirteenth century were unanimous in bemoaning the decadence of their times. And when we read such a document as the Chronicle of Salimbene, we find ourselves wondering to what extent conclusions drawn from the sanctity of St. Francis, the architecture of the Gothic cathedrals, the philosophy of St. Thomas, and the poetry of Dante are relevant to the brutish and totally unregenerate lives of the great masses of the people. If the age was indeed progressive, who experienced the progress? And if most of the people living at the time failed to experience anything in the nature of biological or human progress, is it justifiable to speak of the age as progressive? Or is an age genuinely progressive simply because future historians, using standards of their own devising, judge it to be so?

In the long history of evolutionary change, biological progress has been confined to the upper levels of the vegetable and animal population. Analogously it may be that specifically human progress is a privilege of the exceptionally fortunate and the exceptionally gifted. Thus, while the Elizabethan drama was progressing from Kyd to Shakespeare, great numbers of dispossessed peasants were suffering from extreme malnutrition, and the incidence of rickets and scurvy was steadily on the increase. In other words, there was human progress for a few in certain fields, but in other fields and among the destitute many, there was biological and human regress. And yet today, we rank the Elizabethan age as an age of progress.

The experience of technological and even of human progress is seldom continuous and enduring. Human beings have an enormous capacity for taking things for granted. In a few months, even in a few days, the newly invented gadget, the new political or economic privileges, come to be regarded as parts of the existing order of things. When reached, every longed-for ceiling becomes a common floor. We do not spend our time comparing present happiness with past misery; rather we accept it as our right and become bitterly resentful if we are even temporarily deprived of it. Our minds being what they are, we do not experience progress continuously, but only in fits and starts, during the first phases of any new advance.

From politics as a means to human progress we now pass to education. The subject is almost boundless; but, fortunately, in this particular context only one aspect of it is relevant. For, in so far as they are not dependent upon temperament or fortunate accident, happiness, goodness, and creativeness are the products of the individual's philosophy of life. As we believe, so we are. And what we believe depends on what we have been taught—by our parents and schoolmasters, by the books and newspapers we read, by the traditions, clearly formulated or unspoken, of the economic, political, and ecclesiastical organizations to which we belong. If there is to be genuine human progress, happiness, goodness, and creativeness must be maintained by the individuals of successive generations throughout the whole span of lives that are by nature nonprogressive and in the teeth of circumstances that must often be unfavorable. Of the basic philosophies of life which can be imposed upon an individual, or which he can choose to make his own, some are favorable to the maintenance of happiness, goodness, and creativeness, others are manifestly inadequate.

Hedonism, for example, is an inadequate philosophy. Our nature and the world are such that, if we make happiness our goal, we shall not achieve happiness. The philosophy implicit in modern advertising (the source from which millions now derive their *Weltanschauung*) is a special form of hedonism. Happiness, the advertisers teach us, is to be pursued as an end in itself; and there is no happiness except that which comes to us from without, as the result of acquiring one of the products of advancing technology. Thus hedonism is linked with the nineteenth-century faith that technological progress is necessarily correlated with human progress. If rayon stockings make you happy, how much happier you must be with nylons, which are the product of a more advanced technology! Unfortunately the human mind does not happen to work this way. Consequently, those who consciously or unconsciously accept the philosophy expounded by the advertisers find it hard to maintain even happiness, let alone goodness or creativeness.

More adequate are those political philosophies, which for millions of our contemporaries have taken the place of the traditional religions. In these political philosophies intense nationalism is combined with a theory of the state and a system of economics. Those who accept these philosophies, either of their own free will or because they have from infancy been subjected to unremitting propaganda, are inspired in many cases to a life of devotion to the national and ideological cause. They thus achieve and maintain a kind of happiness and a kind of goodness. Unfortunately a high personal morality is often associated with the most atrocious public wickedness; for the nation and the party are deities in whose service the worshiper is justified in doing anything, however abominable, that seems to advance the sacred cause. And even the happiness that comes from the service of a cause greater than oneself is apt in these cases to be somewhat precarious. For where bad means are used to achieve a worthy end, the goal actually reached is never the good end originally proposed, but merely the inevitable consequence of using bad means. For this reason the happiness that comes from self-dedication to such political causes must always be tempered by the disappointment arising from the chronic failure to realize the longed-for ideal.

In devotional religions, such as certain forms of Christianity, Hinduism, and Buddhism, the cause to which the worshiper dedicates himself is supernatural and the full realization of his ideal is not "in this world." Consequently their adherents have a better chance of maintaining happiness and, except where rival sects are struggling for power, are less strongly tempted to public immorality than are the devotees of the political religions.

Stoicism antedated the stoics and has survived them. It is the name we give to men's attempt to achieve independence of, and control over, environment by psychological means rather than by mutation and selection or, on the human level, by an ever more efficient technology. Because it depends mainly on the surface will, and because, however powerful and well trained the surface will is, it is not a match for circumstances, the mere stoic has never wholly realized his ideal of happiness in independence and goodness in voluntary detachment.

The aims of stoicism are fully achieved not by stoics, but by those who, by contemplation or devotion, lay themselves open to "grace," to the "Logos," to "Tao," to the "Atman-Brahman," to the "inner light." Specifically human progress in happiness, goodness, and creativity, and the psychological equivalent of biological progress in independence and control, are best achieved by the pursuit of man's final end. It is by aiming at the realization of the eternal that we are able to make the best—and the best is a continuing progress—of our life in time.

11

FURTHER REFLECTIONS
ON PROGRESS

Continuing the discussion which was begun in the last issue of "Vedanta and the West," I shall try, in the present article, to throw some light on the idea of progress in its relation to man's Final End, the realization that "thou art That." Seen from the standpoint of the Perennial Philosophy, biological progress is a heritable advance in the quality and extent of consciousness. In the course of terrestrial evolution life has developed awareness, and in man, the highest product of that evolution, awareness has reached the point where any given individual can (if he so desires, knows how, and is prepared to fulfill certain conditions), open himself up to the unitive knowledge of spiritual reality. Biological evolution does not of itself lead automatically to this unitive knowledge. It leads merely to the possibility of such a knowledge. And it leads to this possibility through the development of free will and self-consciousness. But free will and self-consciousness are the root of specifically human ignorance and wrong-doing. The faculties that make the unitive knowledge of reality possible are the very faculties that tempt human beings to indulge in that literally insane and diabolic conduct of which man, alone of all the animals, is capable. This is a world in which nobody ever gets anything for nothing. The capacity to go higher is purchased at the expense of being able to fall lower. Only an angel of light can become the Prince of Darkness. On the lower levels of evolutionary development there is no voluntary ignorance or deliberate evil-doing; but, for this very reason, there is also no enlightenment. That is why, in spite of Buchenwald and Hiroshima, we have to give thanks for having achieved a human birth.

Any creature which lives according to instinct lives in a state of what may be called animal grace. It does, not its will, but the will of God-in-Nature. Man does not live by instinct; his patterns of behavior are not inborn, but acquired. He is at liberty, within the restraints imposed by society and his own habits of thought, to choose the better or the worse, the moral and intellectual means to the Final End or the moral and intellectual means to self-destruction. "Not my will, but Thine, be done." This is the essence of all religion. Free will is given that self-will may be annihilated in the spiritual equivalent of instinct. Biological progress is a straight line; but the spiritual progress which we are at liberty to superimpose on the human end-product of biological progress rises in a spiral toward a point corresponding to, but incommensurably far above, the position of the animal that lives according to instinct, or the will of God-in-Nature.

Specifically human progress in happiness, virtue, and creativeness is valuable in the last analysis, as a condition of spiritual advance toward man's Final End. Hunger, privation, and misery; covetousness, hatred, anger, and lust; hide-bound stupidity and insensitiveness—all these are obstacles in the way of spiritual advance. At the same time it should not be forgotten that if happiness, morals and creativeness are treated as ends in themselves instead of means to a further End, they can become obstacles to spiritual advance no less serious, in their way, than wretchedness, vice, and conventionality. Enlightenment is not to be achieved by the person whose aim in life is to "have a good time," to the puritan worshiper of repressive morality for its own sake, or to the aesthete who lives for the creation or appreciation of formal beauty. Idolatry is always fatal; and even the highest human goods cease to be goods if they are worshiped for their own sake and not used, as they are intended to be used, for the achievement of an ultimate good that transcends them.

We now come to progress in relation to the spiritual life—in relation, that is to say, to the conscious pursuit of man's Final End. Significant in this context is the Buddha's remark that he who says he is an *arhat* thereby proclaims that he is not an *arhat*. In other words, it is fatal to boast of achievement or to take satisfaction in an experience which, if it genuinely partakes of enlightenment, is a product of grace rather than of the personal effort. Progress in spirituality brings contrition as well as joy. The enlightenment is experienced as joy; but this bright bliss illuminates all that, within the self, remains unenlightened, dispelling our normal blind complacency in regard to faults and shortcomings and causing us to regret not merely what we are, but even the very fact of our separate individuality. In total and uninterrupted enlightenment there can be nothing but the love, joy, and peace which are the fruits of the spirit; but on the way to that consummation contrition must alternate with bliss, and progress can be measured by the nature of that which is repented—sins, imperfections, and finally our own individualized existence.

Side by side with genuine progress in spirituality is an illusory progress through experiences which are thought to be apprehensions of the ultimate Reality, but which are in fact nothing of the kind. These experiences belong to one or other of two main classes. In the first class we find those emotional intoxications induced by focusing devotion upon a figment of the imagination—for example, the mental image of some divine person. Certain classes of spiritual exercises, such as those devised by St. Ignatius Loyola, exist solely for the purpose of training the imaginative powers and of arousing intense emotions in relation to the fantasies thus deliberately conjured up. Genuine mystics, such as St. John of the Cross or the author of "The Cloud of Unknowing," insist that it is, in the very nature of things, impossible to come to a realization of ultimate Reality by the cultivation of the fancy and the feelings; for the fancy and the feelings belong to the separate ego, whereas the immanent and transcendent Godhead can only be realized when the separate ego has been stilled and put aside, when an empty space has been created in the mind so as to make room, as it were, for the Atman-Brahman. The ecstasy of fancy-begotten emotions is entirely different from unitive knowledge of the divine Ground.

The illusory experiences of the second class are those induced by a form of self-hypnosis. Great stress is laid in many of the Mahayana sutras on the necessity of avoiding the false *samadhi* of the *sravakas* and the *Pratyeka-Buddhas*. This is a negative condition, an absence of consciousness rather than its transfiguration. The world is escaped; it is not seen anew *sub specie aeternitatis*. "If the doors of perception were cleansed," wrote Blake, "the world would appear as it is, infinite and holy." But in this false *samadhi* there is no cleansing of perception; there is merely a turning away, a temporary abolition of perception. This is a reversion toward the condition of inanimate matter, not a progress toward the Final End of unitive knowledge of the divine reality within the soul and in and beyond the world.

12

SUBSTITUTES FOR LIBERATION

An urge to self-transcendence is almost as widespread and, at times, quite as powerful as the urge to self-assertion. Men desire to intensify their consciousness of being what they have come to regard as "themselves"; but they also desire—and desire very often with irresistible violence— the consciousness of being someone else. In a word, they long to get out of themselves, to pass beyond the limits of that island universe, within which every individual finds himself confined. This wish for self-transcendence is not identical with the wish to escape from physical or mental pain. In many cases, it is true, the wish to escape from pain reinforces the desire for self-transcendence. But the latter can exist without the former. If this were not so, healthy and successful persons, who have (in the jargon of psychiatry) "made an excellent adjustment to life," would never feel the urge to go beyond themselves. But in fact they do. Even among those whom nature and fortune have most richly endowed, we find, and find not infre- quently, a deep-rooted horror of their own selfhood, a passionate yearning to get free of the repulsive little iden- tity to which the very perfection of their "adjustment to life" has condemned them, unless they appeal to the Higher Court, without reprieve. "I am gall," writes [Gerard Manley] Hopkins,

> *I am gall, I am heartburn. God's most deep decree*
> *Bitter would have me taste: my taste was me;*
> *Bones built in me, flesh filled, blood brimmed the curse.*
> *Self-yeast of spirit a dull dough sours. I see*
> *The lost are like this, and their scourge to be*
> *As I am mine, their sweating selves; but worse.*

Complete damnation is being one's sweating self, but worse. Being one's sweating self, but not worse, merely no better, is partial damnation, and this partial damnation is everyday life.

If we experience an urge to self-transcendence, it is because, in some obscure way and in spite of our conscious ignorance, we know what we really are. We know (or to be more accurate, something within us knows) that the ground of our individual knowing is identical with the Ground of all knowing and all being; that the *Atman* (Mind in the act of choosing to take the temporal point of view) is the same as *Brahman* (Mind in its eternal essence). We know all this, even though we may never have heard of the doctrines in which the primordial fact has been described; even though, if we happen to be familiar with them, we may regard these doctrines as being so much moonshine. And we also know their practical corollary, which is that the final end, purpose, and point of our existence is to make room in the "thou" for the "That," is to step aside so that the Ground may come to the surface of our consciousness, is to "die" so completely that we can say, "I am crucified with Christ: nevertheless I live; yet not I, but Christ liveth in me." When the phenomenal ego transcends itself, the essential Self is free to realize, in terms of a finite consciousness, the fact of its own eternity, together with the correlative fact, that every particular in the world of experience partakes of the timeless and the infinite. This is liberation, this is enlightenment, this is the beatific vision, in which all things are perceived as they are "in themselves" and not as they are in relation to a craving and abhorring ego.

The obscure knowledge of what we really are accounts for our grief at having to seem to be what we are not, and for our often passionate desire to overstep the limits of the imprisoning ego. The only truly liberating self-transcendence is into the knowledge of the primordial fact. But this liberating self-transcendence is easier to describe than to achieve. For those who are deterred by the difficulties of the ascending road, there are other, less arduous alternatives. Self-transcendence is by no means invariably upward. Indeed, in most cases, it is an escape either downward into a state lower than that of personality, or else horizontally into something wider than the ego, but not higher, not essentially other. We are forever trying to mitigate the results of the Collective Fall into insulated selfhood by another, strictly private fall into animality or mental derangement, or by some more or less creditable self-dispersion into art or science, into politics, a hobby, or a job. Needless to say, these substitutes for self-transcendence, these escapes into subhuman or merely human surrogates for grace, are unsatisfactory at the best and, at the worst, disastrous.

Without an understanding of man's deep-seated urge to self-transcendence, of his very natural reluctance to take the hard, ascending way, and of his search for some bogus liberation either below or to one side of his personality, we cannot hope to make sense of the observed and recorded facts of history, of individual and social psychology. For this reason, I propose to describe a few of the more common grace-substitutes, into which and by means of which men and women have tried to escape from the tormenting consciousness of being themselves.

In France there is now one retailer of alcohol for every hundred inhabitants, more or less. In the United States there are probably at least a million desperate alcoholics, besides a much larger number of very heavy drinkers, whose disease has not yet become mortal. Regarding the consumption of intoxicants in the past we have no precise knowledge. In western Europe, among the Celts and Teutons, and throughout medieval and early modern times, the individual intake of alcohol was probably greater than it is today. On the many occasions when we drink tea or coffee or soda pop, our ancestors refreshed themselves with wine, beer, mead, and in later centuries, with gin, brandy, and other forms of "hard liquor."

The regular drinking of water was a penance imposed on wrong-doers, or accepted by the religious, along with occasional vegetarianism, as a very severe mortification.

Alcohol is but one of the many drugs employed by human beings as avenues of escape from the insulated self. Of the natural narcotics, stimulants, and hallucinators there is, I believe, not a single one, whose properties have not been known from time immemorial. Modern research has given us a host of brand-new synthetics; but in regard to the natural poisons it has merely developed better methods of extracting, concentrating, and recombining those already known. From poppy to curare, from Andean coca to Indian hemp and Siberian agaric, every plant or bush or fungus capable, when ingested, of stupefying, or exciting, or producing visions, has long since been discovered and systematically employed. The fact is profoundly significant; for it seems to prove that, always and everywhere, human beings have felt the radical inadequacy of their personal existence, the misery of being their insulated selves. Exploring the world around him, primitive man evidently "tried all things and held fast to that which was good." For the purposes of self-preservation, the good is every edible fruit and leaf, every wholesome root, seed, or nut. But in another context—the context of self-dissatisfaction and the desire for self-transcendence—the good is everything in nature by means of which the quality of individual consciousness can be changed. Such drug-induced changes may be manifestly for the worse, may be at the price of present

discomfort and future addiction, degeneration, and pre-
mature death. All this is of no account. What matters is
the awareness, if only for an hour or two, if only for a few
minutes, of being someone, or more often something,
other than the insulated self.

Ecstasy through intoxication is still an essential part
of the religion of many primitive peoples. It was once, as
the surviving documents clearly show, a no less essential
part of the religion of the Celts, the Teutons, the Greeks,
the peoples of the Middle East, and the Aryan conquerors of India. It is not merely that "beer does more than
Milton can to justify God's ways to man." Beer *is* the
god. Among the Celts, Sabazios was the divine name
given to the felt alienation of being dead drunk on ale.
Further to the south, Dionysus was, among other things,
the divine objectification of the psychophysical effects
of too much wine. In Vedic mythology, Indra was the
god of that now unidentifiable drug called *soma*. Hero,
slayer of dragons, he was the magnified projection upon
heaven of the strange and glorious otherness experienced
by the intoxicated.

In modern times beer and the other toxic shortcuts to
self-transcendence are no longer officially worshiped as
gods. Theory has undergone a change, but not practice;
for in practice millions upon millions of civilized men
and women continue to pay their devotions, not to the
liberating spirit, but to alcohol, to hashish, to opium and
its derivatives, to barbiturates and the other synthetic ad-
ditions to the age-old catalog of poisons capable of caus-

ing self-transcendence. In every case, of course, what seems a god is actually a devil, what seems a liberation is in fact enslavement.

Like intoxication, elementary sexuality, indulged in for its own sake and divorced from love, was once a god, worshiped not only as the principle of fertility, but also as a manifestation of the radical otherness immanent in every human person. In theory, elementary sexuality has long since ceased to be a god. But in practice it can still boast of a countless host of votaries.

There is an elementary sexuality which is innocent, and an elementary sexuality which is morally and aesthetically squalid. The sexuality of Eden and the sexuality of the sewer—both of them have power to carry the individual beyond the limits of his or her insulated ego. But the second and (one would sadly guess) the commoner variety takes those who indulge in it to a lower level of sub-humanity, evokes the consciousness, and leaves the memory, of a completer alienation than does the first. Hence the perennial attraction of debauchery.

In most civilized communities public opinion condemns debauchery and drug addiction as being ethically wrong. And to moral disapproval is added fiscal discouragement and legal repression. Alcohol is heavily taxed, the sale of narcotics is everywhere prohibited, and certain sexual practices are treated as crimes. But when we pass from drug-taking and elementary sexuality to the third main avenue of downward self-transcendence, we find, on the part of moralists and legislators, a very different and much more indulgent attitude. This seems all the more surprising since crowd-delirium, as we may call it, is more immediately dangerous to social order, more dramatically a menace to that thin crust of decency, reasonableness, and mutual tolerance, which constitutes a civilization, than either drink or debauchery. True, a generalized and longstanding habit of over-indulgence in sexuality may result, as J. D. Unwin has argued, in lowering the energy level of an entire society, thereby rendering it incapable of reaching or sustaining a high level of civilization. Similarly, drug-addiction, if sufficiently widespread, may lower the military, economic, and political efficiency of the society in which it prevails. In the seventeenth and eighteenth centuries alcohol was the secret weapon of the European slave traders; heroin, in the twentieth, of the Japanese militarists. Dead drunk, the negro was an easy prey. As for the Chinese heroin-addict, he could be relied upon to make no trouble for his conquerors. But these cases are exceptional. When left to itself, a society generally manages to come to terms with its favorite poison. The drug is a parasite on the body politic, but a parasite which its host has strength enough to keep under control. And the same applies to elementary sexuality. Against its excesses, societies contrive, in one way or another, to protect themselves.

Their defense against crowd-delirium is, in all too many cases, far less adequate. The professional moralists who inveigh against drunkenness are strangely silent about the equally disgusting vice of crowd-intoxication, of downward self-transcendence into subhumanity by the process of getting together in a mob.

"Where two or three are gathered together in my name, there is God in the midst of them." In the midst of two or three hundred the divine presence becomes more problematical. And when the numbers run into the two or three thousands, or tens of thousands, the likelihood of God being there, in the consciousness of each individual, declines almost to the vanishing point. For such is the nature of excited crowds (and every crowd is automatically self-exciting) and that where two or three thousand are gathered together, there is an absence not merely of deity but even of common humanity. The fact of being one of a multitude delivers a man from the consciousness of being an insulated self and carries him down into a less than personal realm, where there are no responsibilities, no right and wrong, no need for thought or judgment or discrimination—only a strong vague sense of together-ness, only a shared excitement, a collective alienation. And the alienation is at once more prolonged and less exhausting than that which follows self-poisoning by al-cohol or morphine. Moreover, crowd delirium can be indulged in, not merely without a bad conscience, but actually, in many cases, with a positive glow of conscious virtue. For, far from condemning the practice of down-ward self-transcendence through herd-intoxication, the leaders of church and state have actively encouraged this kind of debauchery, whenever it could be used for the furtherance of their own ends.

Individually and in the purposive groups which constitute a healthy society, men and women display a certain capacity for rational thought and free choice in the light of ethical principles. Herded into mobs, the same men and women behave as though they possessed neither reason nor free will. Crowd-intoxication reduces them to a condition of infra-personal and antisocial irresponsibility. Drugged by the mysterious poison which every excited crowd secretes, they fall into a state of heightened suggestibility. While they are in this state they will believe any nonsense and obey any command, however senseless or criminal. For men and women under the influence of herd-poison, "whatever I say three times is true"—and whatever I say three hundred times is divine revelation. That is why men in authority—priests and the leaders of peoples—have never unequivocally proclaimed the immorality of this form of downward self-transcendence. True, crowd-delirium evoked by members of the opposition and in the name of heretical principles has everywhere been condemned by those in power. But crowd-delirium aroused by government agents, crowd-delirium in the name of orthodoxy, is an entirely different matter. In all cases where it can be made to serve the interests of the men controlling church and state, downward self-transcendence by means of herd-intoxication is treated as something legitimate and even highly desirable. Pilgrimages and political rallies, corybantic revivals and patriotic parades—these things are ethically right so long as they are *our* pilgrimages, *our* rallies, *our* revivals, and *our* parades. The fact that most of those taking part in these affairs are temporarily dehumanized by herd-poison is of no account in comparison with the fact that their dehumanization can be used to consolidate the religious and political powers that be. Being in a crowd is the best-known antidote to independent thought. Hence the dictator's rooted objection to "mere psychology" and a private life. "Intellectuals of the world, unite! You have nothing to lose but your brains."

Drugs, elementary sexuality, and herd-intoxication— these are the three most popular avenues of downward self-transcendence. There are many others, not so well-trodden as these great descending highways, but leading no less surely to the same infra-personal goal. There is the way, for example, of rhythmic movement, so widely employed in all primitive religions. And closely associated with the ecstasy-producing rite of rhythmic movement is the ecstasy-producing rite of rhythmic sound. Music is as vast as human nature and has something to say to men and women on every level of their being, from the self-regardingly sentimental to the abstractly intellectual, from the spiritual to the merely visceral. In one of its forms, music is a powerful drug, partly stimulant, partly narcotic, but wholly alterative.

Another road to downward self-transcendence is the way of what Christ called "vain repetition." Yet another is self-inflicted pain, which is used in all religions to modify normal consciousness and as a means for the acquisition of psychic powers.

To what extent, and in what circumstances is it possible for a man to make use of the descending road as a way to genuine spiritual self-transcendence? At first sight it would seem obvious that the way down is not and can never be the way up. But in the realm of existence, things are not quite so simple as they are in our beautifully tidy world of words. In actual life a downward movement may be made the beginning of an ascent. When the shell of the ego has been cracked and there begins to be a consciousness of the subliminal and physiological otherness underlying personality, it sometimes happens that we catch a glimpse, fleeting but apocalyptic, of that other Otherness, which is the Ground of all being. So long as we are confined within our insulated selfhood, we remain unaware of the various not-selves with which we are associated—the organic not-self, the not-self of the personal subconscious, the collective not-self of the psychic medium, out of which our individualities have crystallized, and the not-self of the immanent and transcendent Spirit. Any escape, even by a descending road, out of insulated selfhood, makes possible at least a momentary awareness of the not-self at every level. There are recorded cases in which a single "anesthetic revelation" has served as the starting point of a new attitude toward life. In certain Tantric practices elementary sexuality is used as a road to spiritual awareness. At revival meetings it sometimes happens that persons intoxicated by herd-poisoning acquire a new knowledge which transforms them permanently. In a word, the downward road does not lead invariably to disaster. However, it leads there often enough to make the taking of it extremely inadvisable.

On the subject of horizontal self-transcendence very little need be said—not because the phenomenon is unimportant (far from it), but because it is too obvious to require analysis, and of occurrence too frequent to be readily classifiable.

In order to escape from the horrors of insulated selfhood most men and women choose, most of the time, to go neither up nor down, but sideways. They identify themselves with some cause wider than their own immediate interests, but not degradingly lower and, if higher, higher only within the range of current social values. This horizontal, or nearly horizontal, self-transcendence may be into something as trivial as a hobby, or as precious as married love. It can be brought about through self-identification with any human activity, from running a business to research in nuclear physics, from composing music to collecting stamps, from campaigning for political office to educating children or studying the mating habits of birds.

Horizontal self-transcendence is of the utmost importance. Without it, there would be no art, no science, no law, no philosophy, indeed, no civilization. And there would also be no war, no *odium theologicum* or *ideologicum,* no systematic intolerance, no persecution. These great goods and these enormous evils are the fruits of man's capacity for total and continuous self-identification with an idea, a feeling, a cause. How can we have the good without the evil, a high civilization without saturation bombing and the extermination of religious or political heretics? The answer is that we cannot have it, so long as our self-transcendence remains exclusively horizontal.

When we identify ourselves with an idea or a cause, we are in fact worshiping something homemade, something partial and parochial, something which, however noble, is all too human. "Patriotism," as a great patriot concluded, on the eve of her execution by her country's enemies, "patriotism is not enough." Neither is Socialism, nor Communism, nor Capitalism; neither is art, nor science, nor public order, or any particular religious organization or church. All these are indispensable, but none of them is enough. Civilization demands from the individual self-identification with the highest of human causes. But if this self-identification with what is human is not accompanied by a conscious and consistent effort to achieve upward self-transcendence into the universal life of the Spirit, the goods achieved will always be mingled with counterbalancing evils. "We make," wrote Pascal, "an idol of truth itself; for truth without charity is not God, but his image and idol, which we must neither love nor worship." And it is not merely wrong to worship an idol; it is also exceedingly inexpedient. For example, the worship of truth apart from charity—self-identification with the cause of science unaccompanied by self-identification with the Ground of all being—results in the kind of situation which confronts us today. Every idol, however exalted, turns out in the long run to be a Moloch, hungry for human sacrifices.

13

REFLECTIONS ON THE
LORD'S PRAYER—1

Familiarity does not necessarily breed comprehension; indeed, it often interferes with comprehension. We take the familiar thing for granted, and do not even try to find out what it is. To millions of men and women the sentences of the Lord's Prayer are the most familiar of all forms of words. They are far from being the most completely understood. That is why, in the past, it has been the subject of so many commentaries; and that is why it has seemed worthwhile to add these brief reflections to the list.

The invocation defines the nature of the God to whom the prayer is addressed. The full significance of the phrase can best be grasped by emphasizing in turn the individual words of which it is composed.

"*Our* Father which art in heaven."

God is ours in the sense that He is the universal source and principle, the being of all beings, the life of all that lives, the spirit of every soul. He is present in all creatures; but all creatures are not equally aware of His presence. The degree of this awareness varies with the quality of that which is aware, for knowledge is always a function of being. God's nature is fully comprehensible only to God Himself. Among creatures, knowledge of God's nature expands and becomes more adequate in proportion as the knower becomes more God-like. As St. Bernard puts it, "God who, in His simple substance is all everywhere equally, nevertheless, in efficacy, is in rational creatures in another way than in irrational, and in good rational creatures in another way than in the bad. He is in irrational creatures in such a way as not to be comprehended by them; by all rational creatures, however, He can be comprehended by knowledge; but only by the good is He also comprehended by love" and, we might add, by contemplation, which is the highest expression of man's love of God.

The final end of man's existence is this: to make himself fit to realize God's presence in himself and in other beings. The value of all that he thinks and does is to be measured in terms of his capacity for God. Thoughts and actions are good, when they make us, morally and spiritually, more capable of realizing the God who is *ours,* immanently in every soul and transcendently as that universal principle in which we live and move and have our being. They are bad when they tend to reinforce the barriers which stand between God and our souls, or the souls of other beings.

"Our *Father* which art in heaven."

A father begets, supports and educates, loves and yet punishes.

All sentient beings are capable of disobedience to the

Father's will, man preeminently so. Conversely, man is preeminently capable of obedience.

God as He is in Himself cannot be known except by those who are "perfect as their father in heaven is perfect." Consequently, the intrinsic nature of God's love for the world must remain, for the overwhelming majority of human beings, a mystery. But of God's love in relation to us, and from our point of view, we are able to form a sufficiently clear idea. And the same is true of what is called God's anger, or the stern and punishing aspect of the divine fatherhood. Any disobedience to God's will, any flouting of the nature of things, any departure from the norms governing the universes of matter, mind, and spirit, results in more or less serious consequences for those directly or even indirectly involved in the transgression. Certain of these undesirable consequences of disobedience are physical, as when some flouting of the laws of nature or of human nature leads, for example, to disease in the individual or war in the body politic. Others are moral and spiritual, as when bad habits of thought and conduct lead to degeneration of character and the erection of insurmountable barriers between the soul and God. These fruits of human disobedience are commonly regarded as the expression of God's anger.

In the same way, we commonly regard as the expression of God's love those desirable consequences, physical, moral, or spiritual, which flow from obedience to the divine will and conformity to the nature of things. This is the sense in which, for the "natural man," God is our father, at once loving and stern. God's fatherhood as it is in itself cannot be known to us until we have fitted ourselves for the beatific vision of divine reality.

"Our Father which *art* in heaven."

This is the keyword of the invocation; for the ultimate fact about God is the fact of His being. "Who is He?" (I quote St. Bernard once again.) "I can think of no better answer than, He who is. No name is more appropriate to the eternity which God is. If you call God good, or great, or blessed, or wise, or anything of this sort, it is included in these words, namely, He is."

Philosophers have written interminably of Being, Essence, Entities. Much of this speculation is meaningless and would never have been undertaken, if the philosophers in question had troubled to analyze their medium of expression. In the Indo-European languages, the verb *to be* is used in a number of different ways and with meanings which are by no means always identical. Owing to this fact, much which used to pass as metaphysics has now come to reveal itself, with the advance of linguistic studies, as no more than misunderstood grammar. Does this apply to such statements as that God is He who is? The answer is, no. For the statement that God is He who is, is one that can be, in some measure, empirically verified by anyone who cares to fulfill the conditions upon which mystical insight into reality depends. For in contemplation the mystic has a direct intuition of a mode of being incomparably more real and substantial than the existences—his own and that of other things and persons—of which, by a similar direct intuition, he is aware at ordinary times. That God *is,* is a fact that men can actually experience, and is the most important of all the facts that can be experienced.

Everything that can be said about God, "is included in these words, namely, He is." Because He is, we apprehend Him as ours and as father. And also, because He is, we apprehend Him as being "in heaven."

"Our Father which art in *heaven.*"

Throughout the prayer, heaven is contrasted with earth, as something different from it in kind. The terms have, of course, no spatial significance. The mind is its own place, and the Kingdom of Heaven is within. In other words, heaven is another and superior mode of consciousness. For the natural, unregenerate way of thinking, feeling, and willing, must be substituted another way. The life of earth must be lost that the life of heaven may be gained. At first, as every mystic has taught, the mode of consciousness which we call "heaven" will be ours only fitfully, during moments of contemplation. But in the highest stages of proficiency *samsara* and *nirvana* are one; the world is seen *sub specie aeternitatis;* the mystic is able to live uninterruptedly in the presence of God. He will continue to work among his fellow men, here on earth; but his spirit will be "in heaven," because it is assimilated to God.

So much for the invocation; we have now to consider the prayer proper. This is couched in the imperative tense; but the full extent of its significance is best understood if we translate the clauses into the indicative and regard them as a series of statements about the end of human life and the means whereby that end is to be achieved.

Another point to remember is that, though the phrases are uttered successively, each one is relevant, as a statement simultaneously of cause and effect, to all the others. If we were making a diagrammatic representation of the prayer, it would not be correct to symbolize it under the image of a straight line or an open curve. The appropriate symbol would be a closed figure, in which there is no beginning or end and in which every section is the forerunner and successor of every other—a circle or, better, a spiral, where the repetitions are progressive and take place, as the conditions of advance are fulfilled, at ever higher points of achievement.

"Hallowed be Thy name."

Applied to human being, the word "holiness" signifies the voluntary service of, and self-abandonment to, the highest, most real good. Hallowing, or making holy, is the affirmation, in words and actions, that the thing hallowed partakes of the highest, most real good. That which alone ought to be hallowed (and we must pray for strength to hallow it unceasingly) is the name of God— the God who *is,* and is therefore ours, the father and in heaven.

"The name of God" is a phrase which carries two principal meanings. Insofar as the Jews, like many other peoples of antiquity, regarded the name of a thing as identical with its inner principle or essence, the phrase means simply "God." "Hallowed be Thy name" is equivalent to "hallowed be Thou." The clause asserts that God is the highest, most real good, and that it is to the service of this good alone that we should dedicate our lives. What we pray for, when we repeat this clause, is living, experiential knowledge of this fact, and the strength unswervingly to act upon that knowledge.

So much for the first meaning of "Thy name." Its other meaning accords with that view of language which has prevailed in modern times. For us, the name of something is essentially different from that which is named. Words are not the things they stand for, but devices by means of which we are enabled to think about things. To one who considers the matter from the modern standpoint "the name of God" is not the equivalent of "God." Rather, it stands for those verbal concepts, in terms of which we think about God. These concepts are to be hallowed, not of course in and for themselves (for that would be mere magic), but inasmuch as they contribute to the effective and continuous hallowing of God in our lives. Knowledge is one of the conditions of love, and words are one of the conditions of any form of rational knowledge. Hence the importance, in the spiritual life, of a working hypothesis regarding the highest, most real good. Hallowing God's *name* is thinking verbalized thoughts about God, as a means to passing from mere intellectual knowledge to a living experience of reality. Discursive meditation precedes and is the preparation for contemplation; access to God Himself can be had through a proper use of the name of God. This is true, not only in the extended sense in which the word has hitherto been used, but also in the most limited and literal sense. Wherever spiritual religion has flourished, it has been found that a constant repetition of sacred names can serve a very useful purpose in keeping the mind one-pointed and preparing it for contemplation.

The relationship between this first clause of the prayer and the succeeding clauses may be summed up in a few sentences. The hallowing of God and of His name is an indispensable condition of achieving the other aims mentioned in the prayer—namely, the realization of God's kingdom and the doing of His will, and the fitting of the soul to receive from God grace, forgiveness, and liberation. Conversely, the better we succeed, through liberation, forgiveness, and grace, in doing God's will and realizing His kingdom, the more adequately shall we be enabled to hallow God's name and God Himself.

14

REFLECTIONS ON THE LORD'S PRAYER—II

"Thy kingdom come . . . in earth as it is in heaven."

The end of man's existence is to use his opportunities in space-time in such a way that he may come to the knowledge of God's kingdom of timeless reality—or, to put it the other way round, that he may be fit for reality to come to manifestation in and through Him. The "is," in "as it is in heaven," was introduced into the English translation as a mere linguistic convenience. But if we choose to underline it, so as to make it carry, like the "art" of the invocation, a suggestion of real and substantial being, the word will help us to realize more clearly what it is we are praying for—the strength to pass through time to a realization here, in time, of eternity, for the power to give eternity a chance of possessing us, not merely virtually, but in realized actuality. For the contemplative saints who are "perfect as their Father in heaven is perfect," *samsara* and *nirvana* are one, God's kingdom comes on earth as it is in heaven. Nor is the change merely personal and subjective. The influence of these people has power to change the world in which they live.

The end of human life cannot be achieved by the efforts of the unaided individual. What the individual can and must do is to make himself fit for contact with reality and the reception of that grace by whose aid he will be enabled to achieve his true end. That we may make ourselves fit for God, we must fulfill certain conditions, which are set forth in the prayer. We must hallow God's name, do God's will and forgive those who have trespassed against us. If we do this, we shall be delivered from the evil of selfhood, forgiven the sin of separateness and blessed with the bread of grace, without which our contemplation will be illusory and our attempts at amendment vain.

"Thy will be done, in earth as it is in heaven."

This phrase carries two meanings. So far as ultimate reality is concerned, the will of God is identical with God's being or kingdom. To pray that the will of God may be done in earth as in heaven is to pray, in other words, for the coming into time of the kingdom of eternity. But the words do not apply only to ultimate reality; they also apply to human beings. So far as we are concerned, "doing the will of God" is doing what is necessary to fit ourselves for the grace of enlightenment.

Earth is incommensurable with heaven, time with eternity, the ego with the spirit. The kingdom of God can come only to the extent to which the kingdom of the natural man has been made to go. If we would gain the life of union, we must lose the life of passion, idle curiosity, and distractions, which is the ordinary life of human selves. "Fight self," says St. Catherine of Siena, "and you need fear no other foe."

All this is very easy to read and write, but enormously difficult to put into practice. Purgation is laborious and painful; but purgation is the condition of illumination and union. Conversely, a certain measure of illumination is a condition of effective purgation. The stoic thinks to deny himself by making acts of the surface will. But the surface will is the will of the self, and his mortifications tend rather to strengthen the ego than eliminate it. He is apt to become, in the tremendous phrase coined by William Blake, "a fiend of righteousness." Having denied one aspect of his ego merely to strengthen another and more dangerous aspect, he ends up by being more impervious to God than he was before he started his process of self-discipline. To fight self exclusively with the self serves only to enhance our selfhood. In the psychological field there can be no displacing without replacing. For preoccupation with self must be gradually substituted by preoccupation with reality. There can be no effective mortification for enlightenment without meditation or devotion, which direct the attention away from self to a higher reality. As I have remarked before, all spiritual processes are circular, or rather spiral. In order to fulfill the conditions of enlightenment we must have the glimmerings, if not of enlightenment itself, at least of an idea of what enlightenment consists in. God's will must be done by us, if God's kingdom is to come in us; and God's kingdom must begin to come, if we are effectively to do God's will.

"Give us this day our daily bread."

It is possible that the word translated as "daily" may really carry another meaning and that the phrase should read: "Give us this day our bread of the (eternal) day." This would emphasize the fact, already sufficiently obvious to anyone familiar with the language of the gospels, that the bread referred to is a divine and spiritual nourishment—the grace of God. In the traditional translation the spiritual nature of the bread is taken for granted and an additional emphasis is laid on the thought already expressed in the words "this day."

A man cannot be nourished by the anticipation of tomorrow's dinner, or the recollection of what he ate a week ago. Bread serves its purpose only when consumed "this day"—here and now. It is the same with spiritual food. Remorseful thoughts about the past, pious hopes and aspirations for a better future contain no nourishment for the soul, whose life is always now, in the present, and not at any other un-actual moment of time. In its passage from the vegetative and animal level to the spiritual, life passes from what may be called the physiological eternity of mindless existence, through the human world of memory and anticipation, past and future, into another and higher timelessness, the eternal kingdom of God. In the ascending spiral of being, the contemplative saint stands at a point exactly corresponding, on his higher level, to the position of a flower or a bird. Both inhabit eternity; but whereas the flower's or the bird's eternity is the everlasting present of mindlessness, of natural processes working themselves out with little or no accompanying consciousness, the saint's eternity is experienced in union with that pure consciousness, which is the ultimate reality. Between these two worlds lies the human universe of foresight and retrospect, of fear and craving and memory and conditioning, of hopes and plans and daydreams and remorses. It is a rich world, full of beauty and goodness as well as of much evil and ugliness—but a world which is not the world of reality; for it is *our* world, man-made, the product of the thoughts and actions of beings who have forgotten their true end and have turned to things which are not their highest good. This is the truth proclaimed by all the great spiritual teachers of history—the truth that enlightenment, liberation, salvation, call it what you will, can come only for those who learn to live now in the contemplation of eternal reality, no longer in the past and future of human memories and habits, desires and anxieties.

Christ was especially emphatic on the urgent necessity of living in the spiritual present. He exhorted his disciples to model their life upon that of the flowers and the birds, and to take no thought for the morrow. They were to rely, not on their own anxious scheming, but upon the grace of God, which would be given in proportion as they gave up their own personal pretensions and self-will. The phrase of the Lord's Prayer, which we are now considering, sums up the whole gospel teaching on this head. We must ask God for grace *now,* for the good reason that the nature of grace is such that it can only come now, to those who are ready to live in the eternal present.

As usual, the practical problem for the individual is enormously difficult. Liberation cannot come unless we take no thought for tomorrow and live in the eternal present. But at the same time prudence is one of the cardinal virtues and it is wrong to tempt Providence by being rash and thoughtless.

> Oh wearisome condition of humanity!
>> Born under one law, to another bound;
> Vainly begot, and yet forbidden vanity;
>> Created sick, commanded to be sound.

For such a being (and Fulke Greville's description is eminently accurate) no problem can be anything but hard. This particular problem—the finding of a right relation between the world of eternal reality and the human world of time—is surely one of the hardest of all. We need grace in order to be able to live in such a way as to qualify ourselves to receive grace.

15

REFLECTIONS ON THE
LORD'S PRAYER—III

"Forgive us our trespasses, as we forgive them that trespass against us."

"As we forgive them that trespass against us" is a phrase which must be thought of as qualifying all the classes of the prayer. Forgiving is merely a special case of giving, and the word may be taken to stand for the whole scheme of nonegotistic life, which is at once the condition and the result of enlightenment. As we forgive, or, in other words, as we change our "natural," egotistic attitude toward our fellow beings, we shall become progressively more capable of hallowing the name of God, of doing God's will and cooperating with God to make His kingdom come. Moreover, the daily bread of grace, without which nothing can be achieved, is given to the extent to which we ourselves give and forgive. If one is adequately to love God, one must love one's neighbors—and one's neighbors include even those who have trespassed against us. Conversely, one must love God, if one is adequately to love one's neighbors. In the spiritual life, every cause is also an effect, and every effect is at the same time a cause.

We have now to consider in what sense God forgives

our trespasses or debts, as we forgive our debtors, or those who trespass against us.

On the human level, forgiveness is the waiving of an acknowledged right to payment or punishment. Some of these acknowledged rights are purely arbitrary and conventional. Others, on the contrary, seem to be more fundamental, more closely in accord with what we regard as just. But these fundamental notions of justice are the notions of the "natural," unregenerate man. All the great religious teachers of the world have insisted that these notions must be replaced by others—the thoughts and intuitions of the liberated and enlightened man. The Old Law is to be replaced by the New, which is the law of love, of *mahakarun,* of universal compassion. If men are not to enforce their "rights" for payment or punishment, then most certainly God does not enforce such rights. Indeed, it is absurd to say that such "rights" have any existence in relation to God. If they exist upon the human level, it is solely in virtue of the fact that we are either isolated selves or, at best, self-sacrificing members of groups which have the character of selves and whose selfish behavior vicariously satisfies the ego-feelings of those who have sacrificed themselves to these groups. The "natural" man is motivated either by selfishness or that social sublimation of selfishness which Philip Leon has aptly called "alter-egoism." But because God does not enforce any "rights" of the kind that unregenerate individuals and societies enforce, under the plea of justice, it does not follow that our acts are without their good or evil consequences. Here again the great religious teachers are unanimous. There is a law of *karma;* God is not mocked, and as a man sows, so shall he reap. Sometimes the reaping is extremely obvious, as when a habitual drunkard reaps bodily sickness and a failure of mental power. Very often, on the contrary, the reaping is of a nature which it is very difficult for any but enlightened eyes to detect. For example, Jesus was constantly inveighing against the Scribes and Pharisees. But the Scribes and Pharisees were models of austere respectability and good citizenship. The only trouble with them was that their virtues were only the virtues of unregenerate men—and such righteousness is as "filthy rags" in the sight of God; for even the virtues of the unregenerate are God-eclipsing and prevent those who have them from advancing toward that knowledge of ultimate Reality, which is the end and purpose of life. That which the Scribes and Pharisees reap is the more or less total inability to know the God they fondly imagine they are serving. God does not punish them, any more than he punishes the man who inadvertently steps over the edge of a cliff. The nature of the world is such that, if anyone fails to conform to its laws, whether of matter or mind or spirit, he will have to take the consequences, which may be immediate and spectacular, as in the case of the man who steps over the edge of the cliff, or remote, subtle and very far from obvious, as in the case of the virtuous man who is virtuous only in the manner of the Scribes and Pharisees.

Now, since God has no "rights" to enforce, he can

never be thought of as waiving such "rights." And since he is the principle of the world, he cannot suspend those laws or make exceptions to those uniformities, which are the manifestation of that principle. Does this mean, then, that God cannot forgive our debts and trespasses? In one sense it certainly does. But there is another sense in which the idea of divine forgiveness is valid and profoundly significant. Good actions and thoughts produce consequences which tend to neutralize, or put a stop to, the results of evil thoughts and actions. For as we give up the life of self (and note that, like forgiveness, repentance and humility are also special cases of giving), as we abandon what the German mystics called "the I, me, mine," we make ourselves progressively capable of receiving grace. By grace we are enabled to know reality more completely, and this knowledge of reality helps us to give up more of the life of selfhood—and so on, in a mounting spiral of illumination and regeneration. We become different from what we were and, being different, cease to be at the mercy of the destiny which, as "natural," unregenerate beings, we had forged for ourselves by our evil thoughts and actions. Thus the Pharisee who gives up his life of self-esteeming respectability and uncharitable righteousness, becomes capable thereby of receiving a measure of grace, ceases to be a Pharisee and, in virtue of that fact, ceases to be subject to the destiny forged by the man he once was and is no more. The making oneself fit to receive grace is effective repentance and atonement; and the bestowal of grace is the divine forgiveness of sins.

In a rather crude form, this truth is expressed in the doctrine which teaches that merits have the power to cancel out their opposites. Moreover, if divine forgiveness is the bestowal of grace, we can understand how vicarious sacrifices and the merits of others can benefit the soul. The enlightened person transforms not merely himself, but to some extent the world around him. The unregenerate individual is more or less completely without real freedom; only the enlightened are capable of genuinely free choices and creative acts. This being so, it is possible for them to modify for the better the destinies unfolding around them by inspiring the makers of these destinies with the wish and the power to give, so that they may become fit to receive the grace which will transform them and so deliver them from the fate they had been preparing for themselves.

"Lead us not into temptation, but deliver us from evil; for *thine* is the kingdom, and the power, and the glory."

The nature of the evil from which we pray to be delivered is defined by inference in the succeeding phrase. Evil consists in forgetting that kingdom, power, and glory are God's and acting upon the insane and criminal belief that they are ours. So long as we remain average, sensual, unregenerate individuals, we shall constantly be tempted to think God-excluding thoughts and perform God-eclipsing actions. Nor do such temptations cease as soon as the path of enlightenment is entered. All that happens is that, with every advance achieved, the temptations become more subtle, less gross and obvious, more profoundly dangerous. Belial and Mammon have no power over the advanced; nor will they succumb when Lucifer offers them his more material baits, such as worldly power and dominion. But for souls of quality Lucifer also prepares more rarefied temptations and many are those, even far advanced along the road to enlightenment, who have succumbed to spiritual pride. It is only to the perfectly enlightened and the completely liberated that temptations do not present themselves at all.

The final phrases of the prayer re-affirm its central, dominant theme, which is that God is everything and that man, as man, is nothing. Indeed, man, as man, is less than nothing; for he is a nothing capable of evil, that is to say capable of claiming as his own the things that are God's and, by that act, cutting himself off from God. But though man, as man, is nothing and can make himself less than nothing by becoming evil, man as the knower and lover of God, man as the possessor of a latent, inalienable spark of godhead, is potentially everything. In the words of Cardinal Bérulle, "man is a nothing surrounded by God, indigent of God, capable of God and filled with God if he so desires." This is the central truth of all spiritual religion, the truth that is, so to say, the major premise of the Lord's Prayer. It is a truth which the ordinary unregenerate man or woman finds it hard to accept in theory and harder still to act upon. The great religious teachers have all thought and acted theocentrically; the mass of ordinary human beings think and act anthropocentrically. The prayer which comes naturally to such people is the prayer of petition, the prayer for concrete advantages and immediate help in trouble. How profoundly different this is from the prayer of an enlightened being! Such a being prays not at all for himself, but only that God may be worshiped, loved, and known by him as God ought to be worshiped, loved, and known—that the latent and potential seed of reality within his own soul may become fully actualized. There is even a kind of irony to be found in the fact that this prayer of Christ's—the theocentric prayer of a supremely enlightened being— should have become the prayer most frequently repeated by millions upon millions of men and women, who have only a very imperfect notion of what it means and who, if they fully realized its revolutionary significance, so immensely remote from the more or less kindly humanism by which they govern their own lives, might even feel rather shocked and indignant. But in the affairs of the spirit, it is foolish to think in terms of large numbers and "public opinion." It may be true that the Lord's Prayer is generally misunderstood, or not understood at all. Nevertheless it is a good thing that it should remain the most familiar formulary used by a religion which, particularly in the more "liberal" of its contemporary manifestations, has wandered so far from the theocentrism of its founder, into an entirely heretical anthropocentrism or, as we now prefer to call it, "humanism." It remains with us, a brief and enigmatic document of the most uncompromising spirituality. Those who are dissatisfied with the prevailing anthropocentrism have only to look into its all too familiar, and therefore uncomprehended depths, to discover the philosophy of life and the plan of conduct for which they have been looking hitherto in vain.

16

DISTRACTIONS—I

Portions of these two essays later formed part of a chapter in the author's *Grey Eminence* (1941).

The petition, "Thy Kingdom come," has a necessary and unavoidable corollary, which is, "Our kingdom go." The condition of complete illumination is complete purgation. Only the purified soul can realize identity with Brahman; or, to change the religious vocabulary, union with God can never be achieved by the Old Adam, who must lose the life of self-will in order to gain the life of the divine will. These principles have been accepted as fundamental and axiomatic by all mystics, of whatever country, faith, and period.

When these principles are applied in practice, it is found that the personal kingdom which has to go, if the divine kingdom is to come, consists mainly of two great provinces, *passions* and *distractions*. Of the passions it is unnecessary to say much here, for the good reason that so much has been said elsewhere. Furthermore, it is, or should be, self-evident that "Thy kingdom" cannot possibly come for anyone who inhabits a homemade universe created for him by his own fear, greed, malice, and anxiety. To help men to overcome these passions is the aim of all ethical teaching; and that overcoming is an essential preliminary and accompaniment to the life of mystical spirituality. Those who imagine that they can achieve illumination without purgation are extremely mistaken. There is a letter addressed by St. Jeanne Chantal to one of the nuns of her order, a letter which should be placed in the hands of every beginner in the art of yoga or mental prayer.

> I can well believe it when you say that you do not know what to answer those novices who ask you what is the difference between union and contemplation. Lord God, how is it that my sister the Superior permits them such a thing, or that you permit it in her absence? Dear Jesus, where is humility? You must stop this at once, and give them books and lectures that treat of the practice of the virtues, and tell them that they must first set themselves to doing, and then they can talk about these exalted matters.

But enough of this first and all-too-familiar province of our personal kingdom. It is not of the passions, but of those less frequently publicized impediments to the unitive life, distractions, that I mean to write in this place.

Contemplatives have compared distractions to dust, to swarms of flies, to the movements of a monkey stung by a scorpion. Always their metaphors call up the image of a purposeless agitation. And this, precisely, is the interesting and important thing about distractions. The passions are essentially purposeful, and the thoughts, emotions and fancies connected with the passions always have more reference to the real or imaginary ends proposed, or to the means whereby such ends may be achieved. With distractions the case is quite different. It is of their essence to be irrelevant and pointless. To find out just how pointless and irrelevant they can be, one has only to sit down and try to recollect oneself. Preoccupations connected with the passions will most probably come to the surface of consciousness; but along with them will rise a bobbing scum of miscellaneous memories, notions, and imaginings—childhood recollections of one's grandmother's Yorkshire terrier, the French name for henbane, a White-Knightish scheme for catching incendiary bombs in midair—in a word, every kind of nonsense and silliness. The psychoanalytic contention that all the divagations of the subconscious have a deep passional meaning cannot be made to fit the facts. One has only to observe oneself and others to discover that we are no more exclusively the servants of our passions and biological urges than we are exclusively rational; we are also creatures possessed of a complicated psychophysiological machine that is incessantly grinding away and that, in the course of its grinding, throws up into consciousness selections from that indefinite number of mental permutations and combinations which its random functioning makes possible. Most of these permutations and combinations have nothing to do with our passions or our rational occupations; they are just imbecilities— mere casual waste products of psychophysiological activity. True, such imbecilities may be made use of by the passions for their own ends, as when the Old Adam in us throws up a barrage of intrinsically pointless abstractions in an attempt to nullify the creative efforts of the higher will. But even when not so used by the passions, even in themselves, distractions constitute a formidable obstacle to any kind of spiritual advance. The imbecile within us is as radically God's enemy as the passionately purposeful maniac, with his insane cravings and aversions. Moreover, the imbecile remains at large and busy long after the lunatic has been tamed or even destroyed. In other words, a man may have succeeded in overcoming his passions and replacing them by a fixed, one-pointed desire for enlightenment—he may have succeeded in this, and yet still be hindered in his advance by the uprush into consciousness of pointless and irrelevant distractions. This is the reason why all advanced spirituals have attached so much importance to such imbecilities and have ranked them as grave imperfections, even as sins. It is, I think, to distractions—or at least to one main class of distractions—that Christ refers in that strangely enigmatic and alarming saying, "that every idle word that men shall speak, they shall give account thereof in the day of judgment. For by thy words shalt thou be justified and by thy words shalt thou be condemned." Verbalized idiocies, spoken irrelevances, all utterances, indeed, that do not subserve the end of enlightenment must be classed as impediments, barriers between the soul and ultimate reality. They may seem harmless enough; but this harmlessness is only in relation to mundane things; in relation to spiritual and eternal ends, they are extremely harmful. In this context, I would like to quote a paragraph from the biography of that seventeenth-century French saint, Charles de Condren. A pious lady, named Mlle. de la Roche, was in great distress, because she found it impossible to make a satisfactory confession. "Her trouble was that her sins seemed to her greater than she could say. Her faults were not considerable; nevertheless she felt unable, so she said, ever to express them. If the confessor told her that he was content with her accusation of herself, she would answer that she was not satisfied and that, since she was not telling the truth, he could not give her absolution. If he pressed her to tell the whole truth, she found herself utterly incapable of doing so." Nobody knew what to say to this unfortunate woman, who came in time to be regarded as not quite right in the head. Finally she addressed herself to Condren, who relieved her of her misery by an explanation of her case which is of the highest interest. "It is true," he said, "that you have not adequately expressed your sins; but the fact is that, in this life, it is impossible to represent them in all their hideousness. We shall never know them as they really are, until we see them in the pure light of God. In your case, God has given you an impression of the deformity of sin, by which he makes you feel it to be incomparably graver than it appears to your understanding or can be expressed by your words. Hence your anguish and distress. You must therefore conceive of your sins as faith presents them to you, in other words, as they are in themselves; but you must content yourself with describing them in such words as your mouth can form." All that Condren says about poor Mlle. de la Roche's no doubt very trifling sins applies with equal force to our distractions. Judged by ordinary human standards, they may seem of no account. And yet, as they are in themselves, as they are in relation to the light of God (which they are able completely to eclipse, as the sun is darkened by a dust storm or a cloud of grasshoppers) these seemingly trifling imperfections are seen to have as great a power for evil in the soul as anger, or an ugly greed, or some obsessive apprehension.

It is because they mistrust the imbecile who, in the body of every human being, cohabits with the criminal lunatic, the easy-going animal, the good citizen and the potential, unawakened, deeply latent saint, it is because they recognize his truly diabolic power, that the contemplatives have always imposed upon themselves and their disciples such rigid self-denial in the matter of all distracting and irrelevant stimuli. The Old Adam's restless curiosity must be checked and his foolishness, his dissipation of spirit turned to wisdom and one-pointedness. That is why the would-be mystic is always told to refrain from busying himself with matters which do not refer to his ultimate goal, or in relation to which he cannot effectively do immediate and concrete good. This self-denying ordinance covers most of the things with which, outside business hours, the ordinary person is mainly preoccupied—news, the day's installment of the various radio epics, this year's car models and gadgets, the latest fashions. But it is upon fashions, cars, and gadgets, upon news and the advertising for which news exists, that our present industrial and economic system depends for its proper functioning. For, as ex-President Hoover pointed out not long ago, this system cannot work unless the demand for non-necessaries is not merely kept up, but continually expanded; and of course it cannot be kept up and expanded except by incessant appeals to greed, competitiveness, and love of aimless stimulation. Men have always been a prey to distractions, which are the original sin of the mind; but never before today has an attempt been made to organize and exploit distractions, to make of them, because of their economic importance, the core and vital center of human life, to idealize them as the highest manifestations of mental activity. Ours is an age of systematized irrelevances, and the imbecile within us has become one of the Titans, upon whose shoulders rests the weight of the social and economic system. Recollectedness, or the overcoming of distractions, has never been more necessary than now; it has also, we may guess, never been so difficult.

17

DISTRACTIONS — II

In an earlier article I gave some account of the psychological nature of distractions and of their significance as obstacles in the path of those who seek to attain enlightenment. In the paragraphs which follow, I shall describe some of the methods which have been found useful in overcoming these obstacles, in circumventing the tricks of the imbecile whom we carry about with us as a secondary personality.

Distractions afflict us not only when we are attempting formal meditation or contemplation, but also and even more dangerously in the course of our active, everyday life. Many of those who undertake spiritual exercises, whether yogic or Christian, tend all too frequently to confine their efforts at concentrating the mind strictly to business hours—that is to say, to the hours they actually spend in meditation. They forget that it is possible for a man or woman to achieve, during meditation, a high degree of mental concentration and even a kind of subjectively satisfying pseudo-ecstasy, while remaining at bottom an unregenerate ego. It is not an uncommon thing to meet with people who spend hours of each day doing spiritual exercises and who, in the intervals, display as much spite, prejudice, jealousy, greed, and silliness as the most "unspiritual" of their neighbors. The reason for this is that such people make no effort to adapt to the exigencies of ordinary life those practices which they make use of during their times of formal meditation. This is, of course, not at all surprising. It is much easier to catch a glimpse of reality under the perfect conditions of formal meditation than to "practice the presence of God" in the midst of the boredoms, annoyances, and constant temptations of family and professional life. What the English mystic, Benet Fitch, calls "active annihilation" or the sinking of the self in God at every moment of the day, is much harder to achieve than "passive annihilation" in mental prayer. The difference between the two forms of self-annihiliation is analogous to the difference between scientific work under laboratory conditions and scientific work in the field. As every scientist knows, a great gulf separates the achievement of results in the laboratory and the application of one's discoveries to the untidy and disconcerting world outside its walls. Laboratory work and work in the field are equally necessary in science. Analogously, in the practice of the unitive life, the laboratory work of formal meditation must be supplemented by what may be called "applied mysticism" during the hours of everyday activity. For this reason I propose to divide this article into two sections, the first dealing with distractions in times of recollection, the second with the obscuring and obstructive imbecilities of daily life.

All teachers of the art of mental prayer concur in advising their pupils never to struggle against the distractions which arise in the mind during recollection. The reason for this is simple. "The more a man operates, the more he is and exists. And the more he is and exists, the less God is and exists within him." Every enhancement of the separate personal self produces a corresponding diminution of the consciousness of divine reality. But the voluntary struggle against distractions automatically enhances the separate personal self and therefore reduces the individual's chance of coming to an awareness of reality. In the process of trying forcibly to abolish our God-eclipsing imbecilities, we merely deepen the darkness of our native ignorance. This being so, we must give up our attempt to fight distractions and find ways of circumventing and evading them. One method consists in simply "looking over the shoulder" of the imbecile who stands between us and the object of our meditation or our imageless contemplation. The distractions appear in the foreground of consciousness; we take notice of their presence, then lightly, without effort or tension of will, we shift the focus of attention to the reality in the background. In many cases the distractions will lose their obsessive "thereness" and gradually fade away.

Alternatively, when distractions come, the attempt to practice imageless contemplation or the "simple regard" may be temporarily given up, and attention directed to the distractions themselves, which are then used as objects of discursive meditation, preparatory to another return to the "simple regard" later on. Two methods of making profitable use of distractions are commonly recommended. The first consists in objectively examining the distractions, and observing which of them have their origins in the passions and which of them arise in the imbecile side of the mind. The process of following thoughts and images back to their source, of uncovering, here the purposive and passional, there the merely imbecile manifestations of egotism, is an admirable exercise in mental concentration, as well as a means for increasing that self-knowledge which is one of the indispensable pre-requisites to a knowledge of God. "A man," wrote Meister Eckhart, "has many skins in himself, covering the depths of his heart. Man knows so many other things; he does not know himself. Why, thirty or forty skins or hides, just like an ox's or a bear's, so thick and hard, cover the soul. Go into your own ground and learn to know yourself there." The dispassionate and scientific examination of distractions is one of the best ways of knowing the "thirty or forty skins" which constitute our personality, and discovering, beneath them, the Self, the immanent Godhead, the Kingdom of Heaven within us. Discursive meditation on the skins passes naturally into a simple regard directed to the ground of the soul.

The second method of making use of distractions for the purpose of defeating distractions is merely a variant on the first. The difference between the two methods is a difference in the quality of the emotional tone accompanying the examination of the disturbing thoughts and images. In the first method, the examination is dispassionate; in the second, it is accompanied by a sense of contrition and self-humiliation. In the words of the author of "The Cloud of Unknowing," "when thou feelest that thou mayest in no wise put them [distractions, imbecile and passional] down, cower then down under them as a caitiff and a coward overcome in battle, and think that it is but folly to strive any longer with them, and therefore thou yieldest thyself to God in the hands of thine enemies. And feel then thyself as though thou wert overcome forever. . . . And surely, I think, if this device be truly conceived, it is naught else but a true knowing and a feeling of thyself as thou art, a wretch and a filthy thing, far worse than naught: the which knowing and feeling is meekness. And this meekness meriteth to have God himself mightily descending, to venge thee on thine enemies, so as to take thee up and cherishingly dry thy ghostly eyes, as the father doth his child that is on the point to perish under the mouths of wild swine or mad biting bears."

We now come to the problem of dealing with distractions in common life—in the field rather than in the laboratory. Active annihilation or, to use the phrase made familiar by Brother Lawrence, the constant practice of the presence of God at all moments of the day, is a work of supreme difficulty. Most of those who attempt it make the mistake of treating field work as though it were laboratory work. Finding themselves in the midst of things, they turn away from things, either physically, by retreat, or psychologically, by an act of introversion.

But the shrinking from things and necessary external activities is an obstacle in the way of self-annihilation; for to shrink from things is to assert by implication that things still mean a great deal to one. Introversion from things for the sake of God may, by giving them undue importance, exalt things to the place that should be occupied by God. What is needed, therefore, is not physical flight or introversion from things, but the capacity to undertake necessary activity in a spirit of nonattachment, of self-annihilation in reality. This is, of course, the doctrine of the Gita. (It should be noted, however, that the Gita—if it is meant to be taken literally, which one hopes it isn't—suggests that it is possible to commit murder in a state of self-annihilation in God. In various forms, this doctrine of nonattachment has been used by aberrant sectaries of every religion to justify every kind of wickedness and folly, from sexual orgies to torture. But, as a matter of plain psychological fact, such activities are entirely unannihilable in God. Going to war, like the heroes of the Gita, indulging in unlimited sexual promiscuity, like some of the Illuminati of the West, are activities which cannot result in anything but an enhancement of the separate personal self and an eclipsing of divine reality. Nonattachment cannot be practiced except in relation to intrinsically good or ethically neutral actions; the idea that it can be practiced in relation to bad actions is a delusion, springing from the wish of the ego to go on behaving badly, while justifying such behavior by means of a high and apparently spiritual philosophy.)

To achieve the active annihilation, by which alone the distractions of common life may be overcome, the aspirant must begin by avoiding, not merely all bad actions, but also, if possible, all unnecessary and silly ones. Listening to the average radio program, seeing the average motion picture, reading the comic strips—these are merely silly and imbecile activities; but though not wicked, they are almost as unannihilable as the activities of lynching and fornication. For this reason it is obviously advisable to avoid them.

Meanwhile, what is to be done in the psychological field? First, it is necessary to cultivate a constant awareness of the reality that is everything and the personal self that is less than nothing. Only on this condition can the desired nonattachment be achieved. No less important than the avoidance of unnecessary and unannihilable activities and the cultivation of awareness is emptying of the memory and the suppression of foreboding. Anyone who pays attention to his mental processes soon discovers that a large proportion of his time is spent in chewing the cud of the past and foretasting the future. We return to the past, sometimes because random memories rise mechanically into consciousness; sometimes because we like flattering our egotism by the recalling of past triumphs and pleasures, the censoring and embellishing of past pains and defeats; sometimes, too, because we are sick of ourselves and, thinking to "repent of our sins" return with a gloomy satisfaction to old offenses. As for the future, our preoccupation with it is sometimes apprehensive, sometimes compensatory and wishful. In either case, the present is sacrificed to dreams of no longer existent or hypothetical situations. But it is a matter of empirical observation that the road to spiritual eternity is through the immediate animal eternity of the specious present. None can achieve eternal life who has not first learned to live, not in the past or in the future, but now—in the moment at the moment. Concerning the God-eclipsing folly of taking anxious thought for the future, the gospels have much to say. Sufficient unto the day is the evil thereof—and, we might add, sufficient unto the place. We make a habit of feeling disquietude about distant evils, in regard to which we can do no good, and we think that such disquietude is a sign of our sensibility and compassion. It would probably be more nearly true to say, with St. John of the Cross, that "disquietude is always vanity, because it serves no good. Yea, even if the whole world were thrown into confusion, and all things in it, disquietude on that account would still be vanity." What is true of things remote in space and in the future is also true of things remote in the past. We must teach ourselves not to waste our time and our opportunities to know reality by dwelling on our memories. Let the dead bury their dead. "The emptying of the memory," says St. John of the Cross, "though the advantages of it are not so great as those of the state of union, yet merely because it delivers souls from much sorrow, grief and sadness, besides imperfections and sin, is in itself a great good."

Such, then, in briefest summary, are some of the

methods by which distractions can be overcome, not merely in the laboratory of formal meditation, but also (which is much harder) in the world of common life. As always, it is enormously easier to write and read about such methods than to put them into practice.

18

IDOLATRY

Educated persons do not run much risk of succumbing to the more primitive forms of idolatry. They find it fairly easy to resist the temptation to believe that lumps of matter are charged with magical power, or that certain symbols and images are the very forms of spiritual entities and, as such, must be worshiped or propitiated. True, a great deal of fetishistic superstition survives even in these days of universal compulsory education. But though it survives, it is not regarded as respectable; it is not accorded any kind of official recognition or philosophical sanction. Like alcohol and prostitution, the primitive forms of idolatry are tolerated, but not approved. Their place in the accredited hierarchy of spiritual values is extremely low.

Very different is the case with the developed and civilized forms of idolatry. These have achieved, not merely survival, but the highest respectability. The pastors and masters of the contemporary world are never tired of recommending these forms of idolatry. And not content with recommending the higher idolatry, many philosophers and many even of the modern world's religious leaders go out of their way to identify it with true belief and the worship of God.

This is a deplorable state of affairs, but not at all a surprising one. For, while it diminishes the risk of succumbing to primitive idolatry, education (at any rate of the kind now generally current) has a tendency to make the higher idolatry seem more attractive. The higher idolatry may be defined as the belief in, and worship of, human creation as though it were God. On its moral no less than on its intellectual side, current education is strictly humanistic and anti-transcendental. It discourages fetishism and primitive idolatry; but equally it discourages any preoccupation with spiritual Reality. Consequently, it is only to be expected that those who have been most thoroughly subjected to the educational process should be the most ardent exponents of the theory and practice of the higher idolatry. In academic circles, mystics are almost as rare as fetishists; but the enthusiastic devotees of some form of political or social idealism are as common as blackberries. Significantly enough, I have observed, when making use of university libraries, that books on spiritual religion were taken out much less frequently than in public libraries, frequented by persons who had not had the advantages, and the disadvantages, of advanced education.

The many kinds of higher idolatry may be classified under three main headings, technological, political, and moral. Technological idolatry is the most ingenuous and primitive of the three; for its devotees, like those of the lower idolatry, believe that their redemption and liberation depend upon material objects, namely machines and

gadgets. Technological idolatry is the religion whose doctrines are explicitly or implicitly promulgated in the advertising pages of newspapers and magazines—the source
from which millions of men, women, and children in
the capitalist countries now derive their philosophy of
life. In Soviet Russia, during the years of its industrial-
ization, technological idolatry was promoted almost to
the rank of a state religion. More recently, the coming of
war has greatly stimulated the cult in all the belligerent
countries. Military success depends very largely on machines. Because this is so, machines tend to be credited
with the power of bringing success in every sphere of activity, of solving all problems, social and personal as well
as military and technical. So wholehearted is the faith
in technological idols that it is very hard to discover, in
the popular thought of our time, any trace of the ancient
and profoundly realistic doctrine of Hubris and Nemesis.
To the Greeks, Hubris meant any kind of overweening
and excess. When men or societies went too far, either
in dominating other men and societies, or in exploit-
ing the resources of nature to their own advantage, this
overweening exhibition of pride had to be paid for. In a
word, Hubris invited Nemesis. The idea is expressed very
clearly and beautifully in "The Persians" of Aeschylus.
Xerxes is represented as displaying inordinate Hubris, not
only by trying to conquer his neighbors by force of arms,
but also by trying to bend nature to his will more than
it is right for mortal man to do. For Aeschylus, Xerxes'
bridging of the Hellespont is an act as full of Hubris as the

invasion of Greece, and no less deserving of punishment at the hand of Nemesis. Today, our simple-hearted technological idolaters seem to imagine that they can have all the advantages of an immensely elaborate industrial civilization without having to pay for them.

Only a little less ingenuous are the political idolaters. For the worship of tangible material objects, these have substituted the worship of social and economic organizations. Impose the right kind of organizations on human beings, and all their problems, from sin and unhappiness to sewage disposal and war, will be automatically solved. Once more we look almost in vain for a trace of that ancient wisdom which finds so memorable an expression in the "Tao Te Ching"—the wisdom which recognizes (how realistically!) that organizations and laws are likely to do very little good where the organizers and law-makers on the one hand, the organized and law-obeyers on the other, are personally out of touch with Tao, the Way, the ultimate Reality behind phenomena.

It is the great merit of the moral idolaters that they clearly recognize the need of individual reformation as a necessary prerequisite and condition of social reformation. They know that machines and organizations are instruments which may be used well or badly according as the users are personally better or worse. For the technological and political idolaters, the question of personal morality is secondary. In some not too distant future—so runs their creed—machines and organizations will be so perfect that human beings will also be perfect, because it will be impossible for them to be otherwise. Meanwhile, it is not necessary to bother too much about personal morality. All that is required is enough industry, patience and ingenuity to go on producing more and better gadgets, and enough of these same virtues, along with a sufficiency of courage and ruthlessness, to work out suitable social and economic organizations and to impose them, by means of war or revolution, on the rest of the human race—entirely, of course, for the human race's benefit. The moral idolaters know very well that things are not quite so simple as this, and that, among the conditions of social reform, personal reform must take one of the first places. Their mistake is to worship their own ethical ideals instead of worshiping God, to treat the acquisition of virtue as an end in itself and not as a means—the necessary and indispensable condition of the unitive knowledge of God.

"Fanaticism is idolatry." (I am quoting from a most remarkable letter written by Thomas Arnold in 1836 to his old pupil and biographer-to-be, A. P. Stanley.) "Fanaticism is idolatry; and it has the moral evil of idolatry in it; that is, a fanatic worships something which is the creation of his own desires, and thus even his self-devotion in support of it is only an apparent self-devotion; for in fact it is making the parts of his nature or his mind, which he least values, offer sacrifice to that which he most values. The moral fault, as it appears to me, is the idolatry—the setting up of some idea which is most kindred to our own minds, and the putting it in the place of Christ, who alone cannot be made an idol and inspire idolatry, because He combines all ideas of perfection, and exhibits them in their just harmony and combination. Now, in my own mind, by its natural tendency—that is, taking my mind at its best—truth and justice would be the idols I should follow; and they would be idols, for they would not supply *all* the food which the mind wants, and whilst worshiping them, reverence and humility and tenderness might very likely be forgotten. But Christ Himself includes at once truth and justice and all these other qualities too. . . . Narrow-mindedness tends to wickedness, because it does not extend its watchfulness to every part of our moral nature and the neglect fosters the growth of wickedness in the parts so neglected."

As a piece of psychological analysis this is admirable, so far as it goes. But it does not go quite far enough; for it omits all consideration of what has been called grace. Grace is that which is given when, and to the extent to which, a human being gives up his own self-will and abandons himself, moment by moment, to the will of God. By grace our emptiness is fulfilled, our weakness reinforced, our depravity transformed. There are, of course, pseudographs as well as real graces—the accessions of strength, for example, that follow self-devotion to some form of political or moral idolatry. To distinguish between the true grace and the false is often difficult; but as time and circumstances reveal the full extent of their consequences on the personality as a whole, discrimination becomes possible even to observers having no special gifts of insight. Where the grace is genuinely "supernatu-ral," an amelioration in one aspect of personality is not paid for by atrophy or deterioration in another. Virtue is achieved without having to be paid for by the hardness, fanaticism, uncharitableness, and spiritual pride, which are the ordinary consequences of a course of stoical self-improvement by means of personal effort, either unas-sisted or reinforced by the pseudographics which are given when the individual devotes himself to a cause, which is not God, but only a projection of one of his own favor-ite ideas. The idolatrous worship of ethical values in and for themselves defeats its own object—and defeats it not only because, as Arnold rightly insists, there is a lack of all-round watchfulness, but also and above all because even the highest form of moral idolatry is God-eclipsing, a positive guarantee that the idolater shall fail to achieve unitive knowledge of Reality.

19

ACTION AND
CONTEMPLATION

The vocabulary of even intelligent and well-educated people is full of words and phrases which they glibly use without ever having troubled to analyze them or exactly determine their meaning. One could fill an entire volume with a discussion of such commonly used, but undefined and unanalyzed phrases. Here, however, I propose to deal with only one of them, the phrase *life of action,* so frequently used, in discussions of spiritual religion, in contradistinction to the *life of contemplation.* What exactly does this phrase mean? And, passing from the sphere of words to the spheres of facts and values, how is action related to contemplation, and how ought the two to be related?

In ordinary language, *life of action* connotes the sort of life led by film heroes, war correspondents, business executives, politicians, and so forth. Not so in the vocabulary of the religious life. To the religious psychologist the *active life* of common speech is merely worldly life, lived more or less unregenerately by people who have done little or nothing to rid themselves of the Old Adam and to establish contact with ultimate Reality. What the religious psychologist or theologian calls active life is the life of good works. To be active is to follow the way of Martha, who ministered to the needs of the master, while Mary (the personification, in the West, of the contemplative life) sat and listened to his words. So far as the contemplative is concerned, the *active life* is not the life of worldly affairs; it is the life of consistent and strenuous virtue.

Pragmatism regards action as the end and thought as the means to that end; and contemporary popular philosophy accepts the pragmatist position. In the philosophy underlying Eastern and Western spiritual religion this position is reversed. Here, contemplation is the end, action (in which is included discursive thought) is valuable only as a means to the beatific vision of reality. "Action," wrote St. Thomas Aquinas, "should be something added to the life of prayer, not something taken away from it." This is the fundamental principle of the life of spiritual religion. Starting from it, practical mystics have critically examined the whole idea of action, and have laid down rules for the guidance of those whose concern is with ultimate Reality rather than the world of selves. In the following paragraphs I shall summarize the Western mystical tradition in regard to the life of action.

In undertaking any action, those whose concern is with spiritual religion should model themselves upon God himself; for God created the world without in any way modifying His essential nature, and it is to this kind of action without attachment or involvement that the mystic should aspire. But to act in this way is impossible except for those who devote a certain amount of time to formal contemplation and who are able in the intervals constantly to "practice the presence of God." Both tasks are difficult, especially the latter, which is possible only to those far advanced along the road of spiritual perfection. So far as beginners are concerned, the doing even of good works may distract the soul from God. Action is safe only for proficients in the art of mental prayer. "If we have gone far in orison," says one Western authority, "we shall give much to action; if we are but middlingly advanced in the inward life, we shall give ourselves only moderately to outward life; if we have only a very little inwardness, we shall give nothing at all to what is external." To the reasons for this injunction already given, we may add others of a strictly utilitarian nature. It is a matter of experience and observation that well-intentioned actions performed by ordinary, unregenerate people, sunk in their selfhood and without spiritual insight, seldom do much good. St. John of the Cross put the whole matter in a single question and answer. Those who rush headlong into good works without having acquired through contemplation the power to act well—what do they accomplish? *"Poco mas que nada, y a veces nada, y aun a veces dano."* Little more than nothing, and sometimes nothing whatever, and sometimes even harm. One reason for hell being paved with good intentions is to be found in the intrinsically unsatisfactory nature of actions performed by ordinary unregenerate men and women. That is why spiritual directors advise beginners to give as little as possible to external action until such time as they are fit to act profitably. It is a noteworthy fact that, in the biographies of the great Christian mystics the period of activity has always been preceded by a preliminary stage of retirement from the world—a period during which these contemplatives learned to practice the presence of God so continuously and unwaveringly that the distractions of outward activity were powerless any longer to draw the mind away from reality. Indeed, for those who have reached a certain degree of proficiency in "active annihilation," action assumes a sacramental character and becomes a means for bringing them nearer to reality. Those for whom it is not such a means should refrain as far as possible from action—all the more so since, in all that concerns the saving of souls and the improving of the quality of people's thoughts and behavior, "a man of orison will accomplish more in one year than another man in all his life."

What is true of good works is true, *a fortiori*, of merely worldly activity, particularly when it is activity on a large scale, involving the cooperation of large numbers of individuals in every stage of unenlightenment. Good is a product of the ethical and spiritual artistry of individuals; it cannot be mass-produced. This brings us to the heart of that great paradox of politics—the fact that political action is necessary and at the same time incapable of satisfying the needs which called it into existence. Even when it is well intentioned (which it very often is not), political action is foredoomed to a partial, sometimes even a complete self-stultification. The intrinsic nature of the human instruments with which, and the human materials upon which political action must be carried out, is a positive guarantee against the possibility of such action yielding the good results expected of it.

For several thousands of years now men have been experimenting with different methods of improving the quality of human instruments and materials. It has been found that something can be done by strictly humanistic methods, such as the improvement of the social and economic environment and the various techniques of character training. With certain individuals, too, startling results are obtainable through conversion and catharsis. All these methods are good so far as they go; but they do not go far enough. For the radical and permanent transformation of personality, only one effective method has been discovered—that of the mystic. The great religious teachers of East and West have been unanimous in asserting that all human beings are called to achieve enlightenment. They have also unanimously asserted that the achievement of enlightenment is so difficult, and demands a degree of self-abnegation so horrifying to the average unregenerate human being, that, at any given moment of history, very few men and women will be ready even to attempt the labor. This being so, we must expect that large-scale political action will continue to yield the profoundly unsatisfactory results it has always yielded in the past.

The contemplative does not work exclusively for his own salvation. On the contrary, he has an important social function. At any given moment, as we have seen, only a few mystical, theocentric saints exist in the world. But few as they are, they can do an appreciable amount to mitigate the poisons which society generates within itself by its political and economic activities. They are the "salt of the earth," the antiseptic which prevents society from breaking down into irremediable decay.

This antiseptic and antidotal function of the theocentric saint is performed in a variety of ways. First of all, the mere fact that he exists is extremely salutary and important. The advanced contemplative is one who is no longer opaque to the immanent reality within, and as such he is profoundly impressive to the average unregenerate person, who is awed by his presence and even by the mere report of his existence into behaving appreciably better than he otherwise would do.

The theocentric saint is generally not content merely to be. He is almost always a teacher and often a man of action. Through teaching, he benefits surrounding society by multiplying the number of those who undertake the radical transformation of their character and thus increases the amount of antiseptics and antidotes in the chronically diseased body politic. As for the action into which so many advanced contemplatives have plunged, after achieving "active annihilation"—this is never political, but always concerned with small groups or individuals; never exercised at the center of society, but always on the margin; never makes use of the organized force of the state or church, but only of the noncoercive, spiritual authority which belongs to the contemplative in virtue of his contact with reality. It is a matter of plain historical fact that the greatest of the world's spiritual leaders have always refused to make use of political power. No less significant is the fact that, whenever well-intentioned contemplatives have turned from the marginal activities appropriate to spiritual leaders and have tried to use large-scale action to force an entire society, along some political short cut, into the Kingdom of Heaven, they have always failed. The business of a seer is to see; and if he involves himself in the kind of God-eclipsing activities which make seeing impossible, he betrays not only his better self, but also his fellow men, who have a right to his vision. Mystics and theocentric saints are not always loved or invariably listened to: far from it. Prejudice and the dislike of what is unusual may blind their contemporaries to the virtues of these men and women of the margin, may cause them to be persecuted as enemies of society. But should they leave their margin, should they take to competing for place and power within the main body of society, they are certain to be generally hated and despised as traitors to their seership. Only the greatest spirituals are fully consistent. The average, unregenerate person loves the thoughts, feelings, and actions that poison society, but also, and at the same time, loves the spiritual antidotes to the poison. It is as a poison-lover that he persecutes and kills the seers who tell him how to make himself whole; and it is as one who nostalgically yearns for vision that he despises the potential seer who forfeits his vision by wrong activity and the pursuit of power.

20

KNOWLEDGE AND UNDERSTANDING

Knowledge is acquired when we succeed in fitting a new experience into the system of concepts based upon our old experiences. Understanding comes when we liberate ourselves from the old and so make possible a direct, unmediated contact with the new, the mystery, moment by moment, of our existence.

The new is given on every level of experience—given perceptions, given emotions and thoughts, given states of unobstructed awareness, given relationships with things and persons. The old is our homemade system of ideas and word patterns. It is the stock of finished articles fabricated out of the given mystery by memory and analytical reasoning, by habit and the automatic associations of accepted notions. Knowledge is primarily a knowledge of these finished articles. Understanding is primarily direct awareness of the raw material.

Knowledge is always in terms of concepts and can be passed on by means of words or other symbols. Understanding is not conceptual, and therefore cannot be passed on. It is an immediate experience, and immediate experience can only be talked about (very inadequately), never shared. Nobody can actually feel another's pain or grief, another's love or joy or hunger. And similarly nobody can experience another's understanding of a given event or situation. There can, of course, be knowledge of such an understanding, and this knowledge may be passed on in speech or writing, or by means of other symbols. Such communicable knowledge is useful as a reminder that there have been specific understandings in the past, and that understanding is at all times possible. But we must always remember that knowledge of understanding is not the same thing as the understanding, which is the raw material of that knowledge. It is as different from understanding as the doctor's prescription for penicillin is different from penicillin.

Understanding is not inherited, nor can it be laboriously acquired. It is something which, when circumstances are favorable, comes to us, so to say, of its own accord. All of us are knowers, all the time; it is only occasionally and in spite of ourselves that we understand the mystery of given reality. Consequently we are very seldom tempted to equate understanding with knowledge. Of the exceptional men and women, who have understanding in every situation, most are intelligent enough to see that understanding is different from knowledge and that conceptual systems based upon past experience are as necessary to the conduct of life as are spontaneous insights into new experiences. For these reasons the mistake of identifying understanding with knowledge is rarely perpetuated and therefore poses no serious problem.

How different is the case with the opposite mistake, the mistake of supposing that knowledge is the same as understanding and interchangeable with it! All adults possess vast stocks of knowledge. Some of it is correct knowledge, some of it is incorrect knowledge, and some of it only looks like knowledge and is neither correct nor incorrect; it is merely meaningless. That which gives meaning to a proposition is not (to use the words of an eminent contemporary philosopher, Rudolf Carnap) "the attendant images or thoughts, but the possibility of deducing from it perceptive propositions, in other words the possibility of verification. To give sense to a proposition, the presence of images is not sufficient, it is not even necessary. We have no image of the electromagnetic field, nor even, I should say, of the gravitational field; nevertheless the propositions which physicists assert about these fields have a perfect sense because perceptive propositions are deducible from them." Metaphysical doctrines are propositions which cannot be operationally verified, at least on the level of ordinary experience. They may be expressive of a state of mind, in the way that lyrical poetry is expressive; but they have no assignable meaning. The information they convey is only pseudoknowledge. But the formulators of metaphysical doctrines and the believers in such doctrines have always mistaken this pseudoknowledge for knowledge and have proceeded to modify their behavior accordingly. Meaningless pseudoknowledge has at all times been one of the principal motivators of individual and collective action. And that is one of the reasons why the course of human history has been so tragic and at the same time so strangely grotesque. Action based upon meaningless pseudoknowledge is always inappropriate, always beside the point, and consequently always results in the kind of mess mankind has always lived in—the kind of mess that makes the angels weep and the satirists laugh aloud.

Correct or incorrect, relevant or meaningless, knowledge and pseudoknowledge are as common as dirt and are therefore taken for granted. Understanding, on the contrary, is as rare, very nearly, as emeralds, and so is highly prized. The knowers would dearly love to be understanders; but either their stock of knowledge does not include the knowledge of what to do in order to be understanders; or else they know theoretically what they ought to do, but go on doing the opposite all the same. In either case they cherish the comforting delusion that knowledge and, above all, pseudoknowledge *are* understanding. Along with the closely related errors of over-abstraction, over-generalization, and over-simplification, this is the commonest of all intellectual sins and the most dangerous.

Of the vast sum of human misery about one-third, I would guess, is unavoidable misery. This is the price we must pay for being embodied, and for inheriting genes which are subject to deleterious mutations. This is the rent extorted by Nature for the privilege of living on the surface of a planet, whose soil is mostly poor, whose climates are capricious and inclement, and whose inhabitants include a countless number of microorganisms capable of causing in man himself, in his domestic animals and cultivated plants, an immense variety of deadly or debilitating diseases. To these miseries of cosmic origin must be added the much larger group of those avoidable disasters we bring upon ourselves. For at least two thirds of our miseries spring from human stupidity, human malice, and those great motivators and justifiers of malice and stupidity, idealism, dogmatism, and proselytizing zeal on behalf of religious or political idols. But zeal, dogmatism, and idealism exist only because we are forever committing intellectual sins. We sin by attributing concrete significance to meaningless pseudoknowledge; we sin in being too lazy to think in terms of multiple causation and indulging instead in over-simplification, over-generalization, and over-abstraction; and we sin by cherishing the false but agreeable notion that conceptual knowledge and, above all, conceptual pseudoknowledge are the same as understanding.

Consider a few obvious examples. The atrocities of organized religion (and organized religion, let us never forget, has done about as much harm as it has done good) are all due, in the last analysis, to "mistaking the pointing finger for the moon"—in other words to mistaking the verbalized notion for the given mystery to which it refers or, more often, only seems to refer. This, as I have said, is one of the original sins of the intellect, and it is a sin in which, with a rationalistic bumptiousness as grotesque as it is distasteful, theologians have systematically wallowed. From indulgence in this kind of delinquency there has arisen, in most of the great religious traditions of the world, a fantastic over-valuation of words. Over-valuation of words leads all too frequently to the fabrication and idolatrous worship of dogmas, to the insistence on uniformity of belief, the demand for assent by all and sundry to a set of propositions which, though meaningless, are to be regarded as sacred. Those who do not consent to this idolatrous worship of words are to be "converted" and, if that should prove impossible, either persecuted or, if the dogmatizers lack political power, ostracized and denounced. Immediate experience of reality unites men. Conceptualized beliefs, including even the belief in a God of love and righteousness, divides them and, as the dismal record of religious history bears witness, sets them for centuries on end at each other's throats.

Over-simplification, over-generalization, and over-abstraction are three other sins closely related to the sin of imagining that knowledge and pseudoknowledge are the same as understanding. The over-generalizing over-simplifier is the man who asserts, without producing evidence, that "All X's are Y," or, "All A's have a single cause, which is B." The over-abstracter is the one who cannot be bothered to deal with Jones and Smith, with Jane and Mary, as individuals, but enjoys being eloquent on the subject of Humanity, of Progress, of God and History and the Future. This brand of intellectual delinquency is indulged in by every demagogue, every crusader. In the Middle Ages the favorite over-generalization was "All infidels are damned." (For the Moslems, "all infidels" meant "all Christians"; for the Christians, "all Moslems.") Almost as popular was the nonsensical proposition: "All heretics are inspired by the devil" and "All eccentric old women are witches." In the sixteenth and seventeenth centuries the wars and persecutions were justified by the luminously clear and simple belief that "All Roman Catholics (or if you happened to be on the Pope's side, all Lutherans, Calvinists, and Anglicans) are God's enemies." In our own day Hitler proclaimed that all the ills of the world had one cause, namely Jews, and that all Jews were subhuman enemies of mankind. For the communists, all the ills of the world have one cause, namely capitalists, and all capitalists and their middle-class supporters are subhuman enemies of mankind. It is perfectly obvious, on the face of it, that none of these over-generalized statements can possibly be true. But the urge to intellectual sin is fearfully strong. All are subject to temptation and few are able to resist.

There are in the lives of human beings very many situations in which only knowledge, conceptualized, accumulated, and passed on by means of words, is of any practical use. For example, if I want to manufacture sulphuric acid or to keep accounts for a banker, I do not start at the beginnings of chemistry or economics; I start at what is now the end of these sciences. In other words, I go to a school where the relevant knowledge is taught, I read books in which the accumulation of past experience in these particular fields are set forth. I can learn the functions of an accountant or a chemical engineer on the basis of knowledge alone. For this particular purpose it is not necessary for me to have much understanding of concrete situations as they arise, moment by moment from the depths of the given mystery of our existence. What is important for me as a professional man is that I should be familiar with all the conceptual knowledge in my field. Ours is an industrial civilization, in which no society can prosper unless it possesses an elite of highly trained scientists and a considerable army of engineers and technicians. The possession and wide dissemination of a great deal of correct, specialized knowledge has become a prime condition of national survival. In the United States, during the last twenty or thirty years, this fact seems to have been forgotten. Professional educationists have taken John Dewey's theories of "learning through doing" and of "education as life-adjustment," and have applied them in such a way that, in many American schools, there is now doing without learning, along with courses in adjustment to everything except the basic twentieth-century fact that we live in a world where ignorance of science and its methods is the surest, shortest road to national disaster. During the past half century every other nation has made great efforts to impart more knowledge to more young people. In the United States professional educationists have chosen the opposite course. At the turn of the century 56 percent of the pupils in American high schools studied algebra; today less than a quarter of them are so much as introduced to the subject. In 1955, 11 percent of American boys and girls were studying geometry; fifty years ago the figure was 27 percent. Four percent of them now take physics, as against 19 percent in 1900. Fifty percent of American high schools offer no courses in chemistry, 53 percent no courses in physics. This headlong decline in knowledge has not been accompanied by any increases in understanding; for it goes without saying that high school courses in life adjustment do not teach understanding. They teach only conformity to current conventions of personal and collective behavior. There is no substitute for correct knowledge, and in the process of acquiring correct knowledge there is no substitute for concentration and prolonged practice. Except for the unusually gifted, learning, by whatever method, must always be hard work. Unfortunately there are many professional educationists who seem to think that children should never be required to work hard. Wherever educational methods are based on this assumption, children will not in fact acquire much knowledge; and if the methods are followed for a generation or two, the society which tolerates them will find itself in full decline.

In theory, deficiencies in knowledge can be made good simply by changing the curriculum. In practice a change in the curriculum will do little good, unless there is a corresponding change in the point of view of professional educationists. For the trouble with American educationists, writes a distinguished member of their profession, Dr. H. L. Dodge, is that they "regard any subject from personal grooming to philosophy as equally important or interchangeable in furthering the process of self-realization. This anarchy of values has led to the displacement of the established disciplines of science and the humanities by these new subjects." Whether professional educationists can be induced to change their current attitudes is uncertain. Should it prove impossible, we must fall back on the comforting thought that time never stands still and that nobody is immortal. What persuasion and the threat of national decline fail to accomplish, retirement, high blood pressure, and death will bring to pass, more slowly, it is true, but much more surely.

The dissemination of correct knowledge is one of the essential functions of education, and we neglect it at our peril. But, obviously, education should be more than a device for passing on correct knowledge. It should also teach what Dewey called life adjustment and self-realization. But precisely how should self-realization and life adjustment be promoted? To this question modern educators have given many answers. Most of these answers belong to one or the other of two main educational families, the Progressive and the Classical. Answers of the Progressive type find expression in the provision of courses in such subjects as "family living, consumer economics, job information, physical and mental health, training for world citizenship and statesmanship, and last, and we are afraid least"

(I quote again the words of Dr. Dodge) "training in fundamentals." Where answers of the classical type are preferred, educators provide courses in Latin, Greek, modern European literature, in world history, and in philosophy—exclusively, for some odd reason, of the Western brand. Shakespeare and Chaucer, Virgil and Homer—how far away they seem, how irrevocably dead! Why, then, should we bother to teach the classics? The reasons have been stated a thousand times, but seldom with more force and lucidity than by Albert Jay Nock in his *Memoirs of a Superfluous Man*. "The literatures of Greece and Rome provide the longest, the most complete and most nearly continuous record we have of what the strange creature *Homo Sapiens* has been busy about in virtually every department of spiritual, intellectual and social activity. Hence the mind that has canvassed this record is much more than a disciplined mind; it is an experienced mind. It has come, as Emerson says, into a feeling of immense longevity, and it instinctively views contemporary man and his doings in the perspective set by this profound and weighty experience. Our studies were properly called formative, because, beyond all others, their effect was powerfully maturing. Cicero told the unvarnished truth in saying that those who have no knowledge of what has gone before them must for ever remain children. And if one wished to characterize the collective mind of this period, or indeed of any period, the use it makes of its powers of observation, reflection, logical inference, one would best do it by the word *immaturity*."

The Progressive and the Classical approaches to education are not incompatible. It is perfectly possible to combine a schooling in the local cultural tradition with a training, half vocational, half psychological, in adaptation to the current conventions of social life, and then to combine this combination with training in the sciences, in other words with the inculcation of correct knowledge. But is this enough? Can such an education result in the self-realization which is its aim? The question deserves our closest scrutiny. Nobody, of course, can doubt the importance of accumulated experience as a guide for individual and social conduct. We are human because, at a very early stage in the history of the species, our ancestors discovered a way of preserving and disseminating the results of experience. They learned to speak and were thus enabled to translate what they had perceived, what they had inferred from given fact and home-grown fantasy, into a set of concepts, which could be added to by each generation and bequeathed, a treasure of mingled sense and nonsense, to posterity. In Mr. Nock's words "the mind that has canvassed this record is an experienced mind." The only trouble, so far as *we* are concerned, is that the vicarious experience derived from a study of the classics is, in certain respects, completely irrelevant to twentieth-century facts. In many ways, of course, the modern world resembles the world inhabited by the men of antiquity. In many other ways, however, it is radically different. For example, in *their* world the rate of change was exceedingly slow; in *ours* advancing technology produces a state of chronic revolution. *They* took infanticide for granted (Thebes was the only Greek city which forbade the exposure of babies) and regarded slavery as not only necessary to the Greek way of life, but as intrinsically natural and right; *we* are the heirs of eighteenth- and nineteenth-century humanitarianism and must solve *our* economic and demographic problems by methods less dreadfully reminiscent of recent totalitarian practice. Because all the dirty work was done by slaves, *they* regarded every form of manual activity as essentially unworthy of a gentleman and in consequence never subjected their over-abstract, over-rational theories to the test of experiment; *we* have learned, or at least are learning, to think operationally. *They* despised "barbarians," never bothered to learn a foreign language, and could therefore naively regard the rules of Greek grammar and syntax as the Laws of Thought; *we* have begun to understand the nature of language, the danger of taking words too seriously, the ever present need for linguistic analysis. *They* knew nothing about the past and therefore, in Cicero's words, were like children. (Thucydides, the greatest historian of antiquity, prefaces his account of the Peloponnesian War by airily asserting that nothing of great importance had happened before his own time.) *We,* in the course of the last five generations, have acquired a knowledge of man's past extending back to more than half a million years and covering the activities of tribes and nations in every continent. *They* developed political institutions which, in the case of Greece, were hopelessly unstable and, in the case of Rome, were only too firmly fixed in a pattern of aggressiveness and brutality; but what *we* need is a few hints on the art of creating an entirely new kind of society, durable but adventurous, strong but humane, highly organized but liberty-loving, elastic, and adaptable. In this matter Greece and Rome can teach us only negatively—by demonstrating, in their divergent ways, what *not* to do.

From all this it is clear that a classical education in the humanities of two thousand years ago requires to be supplemented by some kind of training in the humanities of today and tomorrow. The Progressives profess to give such a training; but surely we need something a little more informative, a little more useful in this vertiginously changing world of ours, than courses in present-day consumer economics and current job information. But even if a completely adequate schooling in the humanities of the past, the present, and the foreseeable future could be devised and made available to all, would the aims of education, as distinct from factual and theoretical instruction, be thereby achieved? Would the recipients of such an education be any nearer to the goal of self-realization? The answer, I am afraid, is, No. For at this point we find ourselves confronted by one of those paradoxes, which are of the very essence of our strange existence as amphibians inhabiting, without being completely at home in, half a dozen almost incommensurable worlds—the world of concepts and the world of data, the objective world and the subjective, the world of personal consciousness and the world of the unconscious. Where education is concerned, the paradox may be expressed in the statement that the medium of education, which is language, is absolutely necessary, but also fatal; the subject matter of education, which is the conceptualized accumulation of past experience, is indispensable, but also an obstacle to be circumvented. "Existence is prior to essence." Unlike most metaphysical propositions, this slogan of the existentialists can actually be verified. "Wolf children," adopted by animal mothers and brought up in animal surroundings, have the form of human beings, but are not human. The essence of humanity, it is evident, is not something we are born with; it is something we make or grow into. We learn to speak, we accumulate conceptualized knowledge and pseudoknowledge, we imitate our elders, we build up fixed patterns of thought and feeling and behavior, and in the process we become human, we turn into persons. But the things which make us human are precisely the things which interfere with self-realization and prevent understanding. We are humanized by imitating others, by learning their speech, and by acquiring the accumulated knowledge which language makes available. But we understand only when, by liberating ourselves from the tyranny of words, conditioned reflexes, and social conventions, we establish direct, unmediated contact with experience. The greatest paradox of our existence consists in this: that, in order to understand, we must first encumber ourselves with all the intellectual and emotional baggage, which is an impediment to understanding. Except in a dim, preconscious way, animals do not understand a situation, even though, by inherited instinct or by an *ad hoc* act of intelligence, they may be reacting to it with complete appropriateness, *as though* they understood it. Conscious understanding is the privilege of men and women, and it is a privilege which they have earned, strangely enough, by acquiring the useful or delinquent habits, the stereotypes of perception, thought, and feeling, the rituals of behavior, the stock of second-hand knowledge and pseudoknowledge, whose possession is the greatest obstacle to understanding. "Learning," says Lao-tzu, "consists in adding to one's stock day by day. The practice of the Tao consists in subtracting." This does not mean, of course, that we can live by subtraction alone. Learning is as necessary as unlearning. Wherever technical proficiency is needed, learning is indispensable. From youth to old age, from generation to generation, we must go on adding to our stock of useful and relevant knowledge. Only in this way can we hope to deal effectively with the physical environment, and with the abstract ideas which make it possible for men to find their way through the complexities of civilization and technology. But this is not the right way to deal with our personal reactions to ourselves or to other human beings. In such situations there must be an unlearning of accumulated concepts; we must respond to each new challenge not with our old conditioning, not in the light of conceptual knowledge based on the memory of past and different events, not by consulting the law of averages, but with a consciousness stripped naked and as though new born. Once more we are confronted by the great paradox of human life. It is our conditioning which develops our consciousness; but in order to make full use of this developed consciousness, we must start by getting rid of the conditioning which developed it. By adding conceptual knowledge to conceptual knowledge, we make conscious understanding possible; but this potential understanding can be actualized only when we have subtracted all that we have added.

It is because we have memories that we are convinced of our self-identity as persons and as members of a given society.

> *The child is father of the Man;*
> *And I could wish my days to be*
> *Bound each to each by natural piety.*

What Wordsworth called "natural piety" a teacher of understanding would describe as indulgence in emotionally charged memories, associated with childhood and youth. Factual memory—the memory, for example, of the best way of making sulphuric acid or of casting up accounts—is an unmixed blessing. But psychological memory (to use Krishnamurti's term), memory carrying an emotional charge, whether positive or negative, is a source at the worst of neurosis and insanity (psychiatry is largely the art of ridding patients of the incubus of their negatively charged memories), at the best of distractions from the

task of understanding—distractions which, though socially useful, are nonetheless obstacles to be climbed over
or avoided. Emotionally charged memories cement the
ties of family life (or sometimes make family life impossible!) and serve, when conceptualized and taught as a
cultural tradition, to hold communities together. On the
level of understanding, on the level of charity, and on
the level, to some extent, of artistic expression, an individual has it in his power to transcend his social tradition,
to overstep the bounds of the culture in which he has
been brought up. On the level of knowledge, manners,
and custom, he can never get very far away from the
persona created for him by his family and his society. The
culture within which he lives is a prison—but a prison
which makes it possible for any prisoner who so desires
to achieve freedom, a prison to which, for this and a host
of other reasons, its inmates owe an enormous debt of
gratitude and loyalty. But though it is our duty to "honor
our father and our mother," it is also our duty "to hate
our father and our mother, our brethren and our sisters,
yea and our own life"—that socially conditioned life we
take for granted. Though it is necessary for us to add to
our cultural stock day by day, it is also necessary to subtract and subtract. There is, to quote the title of Simone
Weil's posthumous essay, a great "Need for Roots"; but
there is an equally urgent need, on occasion, for total
rootlessness.

In our present context this book by Simone Weil and
the preface which Mr. T. S. Eliot contributes to the En-

glish edition are particularly instructive. Simone Weil was a woman of great ability, heroic virtue, and boundless spiritual aspiration. But unfortunately for herself, as well as for her readers, she was weighed down by a burden of knowledge and pseudoknowledge, which her own almost maniacal over-valuation of words and notions rendered intolerably heavy. A clerical friend reports of her that he did not "ever remember Simone Weil, in spite of her virtuous desire for objectivity, give way in the course of a discussion." She was so deeply rooted in her culture that she came to believe that words were supremely important. Hence her love of argument and the obstinacy with which she clung to her opinions. Hence too her strange inability, on so many occasions, to distinguish the pointing finger from the indicated moon. "But why do you prate of God?" Meister Eckhart asked; and out of the depth of his understanding of given reality, he added, "Whatever you say of Him is untrue." Necessarily so; for "the saving truth was never preached by the Buddha," or by anyone else.

Truth can be defined in many ways. But if you define it as understanding (and this is how all the masters of the spiritual life have defined it), then it is clear that "Truth must be lived and there is nothing to argue about in this teaching; any arguing is sure to go against the intent of it." This was something which Emerson knew and consistently acted upon. To the almost frenzied exasperation of that pugnacious manipulator of religious notions, the elder Henry James, he refused to argue about anything. And the same was true of William Law. "Away, then, with the fictions and workings of discursive reason, either for or against Christianity! They are only the wanton spirit of the mind, whilst ignorant of God and insensible of its own nature and condition. . . . For neither God, nor heaven, nor hell, nor the devil, nor the flesh, can be any other way knowable in you or by you, but by their own existence and manifestation in you. And any pretended knowledge of any of those things, beyond and without this self-evident sensibility of their birth within you, is only such knowledge of them as the blind man hath of the light that has never entered into him." This does not mean, of course, that discursive reason and argument are without value. Where knowledge is concerned, they are not only valuable; they are indispensable. But knowledge is not the same thing as understanding. If we want to understand, we must uproot ourselves from our culture, bypass language, get rid of emotionally charged memories, hate our fathers and mothers, subtract and subtract from our stock of notions. "Needs must it be a virgin," writes Meister Eckhart, "by whom Jesus is received. Virgin, in other words, is a person, void of alien images, free as he was when he existed not."

Simone Weil must have known, theoretically, about this need for cultural virginity, of total rootlessness. But, alas, she was too deeply embedded in her own and other people's ideas, too superstitious a believer in the magic of the words she handled with so much skill, to be able to act upon this knowledge. "The food," she wrote, "that a collectivity supplies to those who form part of it has no equivalent in the universe." (Thank God! we may add, after sniffing the spiritual nourishment provided by many of the vanished collectivities of the past.) Furthermore, the food provided by a collectivity is food "not only for the souls of the living, but also for souls yet unborn." Finally, "the collectivity constitutes the sole agency for preserving the spiritual treasures accumulated by the dead, the sole transmitting agency by means of which the dead can speak to the living. And the sole earthly reality which is connected with the eternal destiny of man is the irradiating light of those who have managed to become fully conscious of this destiny, transmitted from generation to generation."

This last sentence could only have been penned by one who systematically mistook knowledge for understanding, homemade concepts for given reality. It is, of course, desirable that there should be knowledge of what men now dead have said about their understanding of reality. But to maintain that a knowledge of other people's understanding is the same, for us, as understanding, or can even directly lead us to understanding, is a mistake against which all the masters of the spiritual life have always warned us. The letter in St. Paul's phrase, is full of "oldness." It has therefore no relevance to the ever novel reality, which can be understood only in the "newness of the spirit." As for the dead, let them bury their dead. For even the most exalted past seers and avatars "never taught the saving truth." We should not, it goes without saying, neglect the records of dead men's understandings. On the contrary, we ought to know all about them. But we must know all about them without taking them too seriously. We must know all about them, while remaining acutely aware that such knowledge is not the same as understanding and that understanding will come to us only when we have subtracted what we know and made ourselves void and virgin, free as we were when we were not.

Turning from the body of the book to the preface, we find an even more striking example of that literally preposterous over-valuation of words and notions, to which the cultured and the learned are so fatally prone. "I do not know," Mr. Eliot writes, "whether she [Simone Weil] could read the Upanishads in Sanskrit—or, if so, how great was her mastery of what is not only a highly developed language, but a way of thought, the difficulties of which become more formidable to a European student the more diligently he applies himself to it." But like all the other great works of oriental philosophy, the Upanishads are not systems of pure speculation, in which the niceties of language are all important. They were written by Transcendental Pragmatists, as we may call them, whose concern was to teach a doctrine which could be made to "work," a metaphysical theory which could be operationally tested, not through perception only, but by a direct experience of the whole man on every level of his being. To understand the meaning of *Tat tvam asi,* "thou art That," it is not necessary to be a profound Sanskrit scholar. (Similarly, it is not necessary to be a proud Hebrew scholar in order to understand the meaning of "Thou shalt not kill.") Understanding of the doctrine (as opposed to conceptualized knowledge about the doctrine) will come only to those who choose to perform the operations that permit *Tat tvam asi* to become a given fact of direct, unmediated experience, or in Law's words "A self-evident sensibility of its birth within them." Did Simone Weil know Sanskrit, or didn't she? The question is entirely beside the point—is just a particularly smelly cultural red herring dragged across the trail that leads from selfhood to more-than-selfhood, from notionally conditioned ego or unconditioned spirit. In relation to the Upanishads or any other work of Hindu or Buddhist philosophy, only one question deserves to be taken with complete seriousness. It is this. How can a form of words, *Tat tvam asi,* a metaphysical proposition such as *Nirvana and samsara are one,* be converted into the direct, unmediated experience of a given fact? How can language and the learned foolery of scholars (for, in this vital context, that is all it is) be circumvented, so that the individual soul may finally understand the *That* which, in spite of all its efforts to deny the primordial fact, is identical with the *thou?* Specifically, should we follow the methods inculcated by Patanjali, or those of the Hinayana monks, those of the Tantrics of northern India and Tibet, those of the Far Eastern Taoists or the followers of Zen, those described by St. John of the Cross and the author of *The Cloud of Unknowing?* If the European student wishes to remain shut up in the prison of his private cravings and the thought-patterns inherited from his predecessors, then by all means let him plunge through Sanskrit, or Pali, or Chinese, or Tibetan, into the verbal study of "a way of thought, the difficulties of which become more formidable the more diligently he applies himself to it." If, on the other hand, he wishes to transcend himself by actually understanding the primordial fact described or hinted at in the Upanishads and the other scriptures of what, for lack of a better phrase, we will call "spiritual religion," then he must ignore the problems of language and speculative philosophy, or at least relegate them to a secondary position, and concentrate his attention on the practical means whereby the advance from knowledge to understanding may best be made.

From the positively charged collective memories, which are organized into a cultural or religious tradition, let us now return to the positively charged private memories, which individuals organize into a system of "natural piety." We have no more right to wallow in natural piety—that is to say, in emotionally charged memories of past happiness and vanished loves—than to bemoan earlier miseries and torment ourselves with remorse for old offenses. And we have no more right to waste the present instant in relishing future and entirely hypothetical pleasures than to waste it in the apprehension of possible disasters to come. "There is no greater pain," says Dante, "than, in misery, to remember happy times." "Then stop remembering happy times and accept the fact of your present misery," would be the seemingly unsympathetic answer of all those who have had understanding. The emptying of memory is classed by St. John of the Cross as a good second only to the state of union with God, and an indispensable condition of such union.

The word *Buddha* may be translated as "awakened." Those who merely know about things, or only think they know, live in a state of self-conditioned and culturally conditional somnambulism. Those who understand given reality as it presents itself, moment by moment, are wide awake. Memory charged with pleasant emotions is a soporific or, more accurately, an inducer of trance. This was discovered empirically by an American hypnotist, Dr. W. B. Fahnestock, whose book *Statuvolism, or Artificial Somnambulism,* was published in 1871. "When persons are desirous of entering into this state [of artificial somnambulism], I place them in a chair, where they may be at perfect ease. They are next instructed to throw their minds to some familiar place—it matters not where, so that they have been there before and seem desirous of going there again, even in thought. When they have thrown the mind to the place, or upon the desired object, I endeavor by speaking to them frequently to keep their mind upon it. . . . This must be persisted in for some time." In the end, "clairvoyancy will be induced." Anyone who has experimented with hypnosis, or who has watched an experienced operator inducing trance in a difficult subject, knows how effective Fahnestock's method can be.

Incidentally, the relaxing power of positively charged memory was rediscovered, in another medical context, by an oculist, Dr. W. H. Bates, who used to make his patients cover their eyes and revisit in memory the scenes of their happiest experiences. By this means muscular and mental tensions were reduced and it became possible for the patients to use their eyes and minds in a relaxed and therefore efficient way. From all this it is clear that, while positively charged memories can and should be used for specific therapeutic purposes, there must be no indiscriminate indulgence in "natural piety"; for such indulgence may result in a condition akin to trance—a condition at the opposite pole from the wakefulness that is understanding. Those who live with unpleasant memories become neurotic and those who live with pleasant ones become somnambulistic. Sufficient unto the day is the evil thereof—*and* the good thereof.

The Muses, in Greek mythology, were the daughters of Memory, and every writer is embarked, like Marcel Proust, on a hopeless search for time lost. But a good writer is one who knows how to *"donner un sens plus pur aux mots de la tribu."* Thanks to this purer sense, his readers will react to his words with a degree of understanding much greater than they would have had, if they had reacted, in their ordinary self-conditioned or culture-conditioned way, to the events to which the words refer. A great poet must do too much remembering to be more than a sporadic understander; but he knows how to express himself in words which cause other people to understand. Time lost can never be regained; but in his search for it, he may reveal to his readers glimpses of timeless reality.

Unlike the poet, the mystic is "a son of time present." "Past and present veil God from our sight," says Jalaluddin Rumi, who was a Sufi first and only secondarily a great poet. "Burn up both of them with fire. How long will you let yourself be partitioned by these segments like a reed? So long as it remains partitioned, a reed is not privy to secrets, neither is it vocal in response to lips or breathing." Along with its mirror image in anticipation, emotionally charged memory is a barrier that shuts us out from understanding.

Natural piety can very easily be transformed into artificial piety; for some emotionally charged memories are common to all the members of a given society and lend themselves to being organized into religious, political, or cultural traditions. These traditions are systematically drummed into the young of each successive generation and play an important part in the long drama of their conditioning for citizenship. Since the memories common to one group are different from the memories shared by other groups, the social solidarity created by tradition is always partial and exclusive. There is natural and artificial piety in relation to everything belonging to *us,* coupled with suspicion, dislike, and contempt in relation to everything belonging to *them.*

Artificial piety may be fabricated, organized, and fostered in two ways—by the repetition of verbal formulas of belief and worship, and by the performance of symbolic acts and rituals. As might be expected, the second is the more effective method. What is the easiest way for a skeptic to achieve faith? The question was answered three hundred years ago by Pascal. The unbeliever must act "as though he believed, take holy water, have masses said, etc. This will naturally cause you to believe and will besot you." (*Cela vous abêtira*—literally, will make you stupid.) We have to be made stupid, insists Professor Jacques Chevalier, defending his hero against the critics who have been shocked by Pascal's blunt language: we have to stultify our intelligence, because "intellectual pride deprives us of God and debases us to the level of animals." Which is, of course, perfectly true. But it does not follow from this truth that we ought to besot ourselves in the manner prescribed by Pascal and all the propagandists of all the religions. Intellectual pride can be cured only by devaluating pretentious words, only by getting rid of conceptualized pseudoknowledge and opening ourselves to reality. Artificial piety based on conditioned reflexes merely transfers intellectual pride from the bumptious individual to his even more bumptious church. At one remove, the pride remains intact. For the convinced believer, understanding or direct contact with reality is exceedingly difficult. Moreover the mere fact of having a strong reverential feeling about some hallowed thing, person, or proposition is no guarantee of the existence of the thing, the infallibility of the person, or the truth of the proposition. In this context, how instructive is the account of an experiment undertaken by that most imaginative and versatile of the Eminent Victorians, Sir Francis Galton! The aim of the experiment, he writes in his Autobiography, was to "gain an insight into the abject feelings of barbarians and others concerning the power of images which they know to be of human handiwork. I wanted if possible to enter into these feelings. . . . It was difficult to find a suitable object for trial, because it ought to be in itself quite unfitted to arouse devout feelings. I fixed on a comic picture, it was that of Punch, and made believe in its possession of divine attributes. I addressed it with much quasi-reverence as possessing a mighty power to reward or punish the behavior of men towards it, and found little difficulty in ignoring the impossibilities of what I professed. The experiment succeeded. I began to feel and long retained for the picture a large share of the feelings that a barbarian entertains towards his idols, and learned to appreciate the enormous potency they might have over him."

The nature of a conditioned reflex is such that, when the bell rings, the dog salivates, when the much worshiped image is seen, or the much repeated credo, litany, or mantram is pronounced, the heart of the believer is filled with reverence and his mind with faith. And this happens, regardless of the content of the phrase repeated, the nature of the image to which obeisance has been made. He is not responding spontaneously to given reality; he is responding to some thing, or word, or gesture, which automatically brings into play a previously installed post-hypnotic suggestion. Meister Eckhart, that acutest of religious psychologists, clearly recognized this fact. "He who fondly imagines to get more of God in thoughts, prayers, pious offices and so forth than by the fireside or in the stall, in sooth he does but take God, as it were, and swaddle His head in a cloak and hide Him under the table. For he who seeks God in settled forms lays hold of the form, while missing the God concealed in it. But he who seeks God in no special guise lays hold of Him as He is in Himself, and such as one lives with the Son and is the life itself."

"If you look for the Buddha, you will not see the Buddha." "If you deliberately try to become a Buddha, your Buddha is samsara." "If a person seeks the Tao, that person loses the Tao." "By intending to bring yourself into accord with Suchness, you instantly deviate." "Whosoever will save his life shall lose it." There is a Law of Reversed Effort. The harder we try with the conscious will to do something, the less we shall succeed. Proficiency and the results of proficiency come only to those who have learned the paradoxical art of simultaneously doing and not doing, of combining relaxation with activity, of letting go as a person in order that the immanent and transcendent Unknown Quantity may take hold. We cannot make ourselves understand; the most we can do is to foster a state of mind, in which understanding may come to us. What is this state? Clearly it is not any state of limited consciousness. Reality as it is given moment by moment cannot be understood by a mind acting in obedience to post-hypnotic suggestion, or so conditioned by its emotionally charged memories that it responds to the living *now* as though it were the dead *then*. Nor is the mind that has been trained in concentration any better equipped to understand reality. For concentration is merely systematic exclusion, the shutting away from consciousness of all but one thought, one ideal, one image, or one negation of all thoughts, ideals, and images. But however true, however lofty, however holy, no thought or ideal or image can contain reality or lead to the understanding of reality. Nor can the negation of awareness result in that completer awareness necessary to understanding. At the best these things can lead only to a state of ecstatic dissociation, in which one particular aspect of reality, the so-called *spiritual* aspect, may be apprehended. If reality is to be understood in its fullness, as it is given moment by moment, there must be an awareness which is not limited, either deliberately by piety or concentration, or involuntarily by mere thoughtlessness and the force of habit. Understanding comes when we are totally aware— aware to the limits of our mental and physical potentialities. This, of course, is a very ancient doctrine. "Know thyself" is a piece of advice which is as old as civilization, and probably a great deal older. To follow that advice, a man must do more than indulge in introspection. If I would know myself, I must know my environment: for as a body, I am part of the environment, a natural object among other natural objects; and, as a mind, I consist to a great extent of my immediate reactions to the environment and of my secondary reactions to those primary reactions. In practice "know thyself" is a call to total awareness. To those who practice it, what does total awareness reveal? It reveals, first of all, the limitations of the thing which each of us calls "I," and the enormity, the utter absurdity of its pretensions. "I am the master of my fate," poor Henley wrote at the end of a celebrated morsel of rhetoric, "I am the captain of my soul." Nothing could be further from the truth. My fate cannot be mastered; it can only be collaborated with and thereby, to some extent, directed. Nor am I the captain of my soul; I am only its noisiest passenger—a passenger who is not sufficiently important to sit at the captain's table and does not know, even by report, what the soul-ship looks like, how it works, or where it is going. Total awareness starts, in a word, with the realization of my ignorance and my impotence. How do electrochemical events in my brain turn into the perception of a quartet by Haydn or a thought, let us say, of Joan of Arc? I haven't the faintest idea—nor has anyone else. Or consider a seemingly much simpler problem. Can I lift my right hand? The answer is, No. I can't. I can only give the order; the actual lifting is done by somebody else. Who? I don't know. Why? I don't know. And when I have eaten, who digests the bread and cheese? When I have cut myself, who heals the wound? While I am sleeping, who restores the tired body to strength, the neurotic mind to sanity? All I can say is that "I" cannot do any of these things. The catalog of what I do not know and am incapable of achieving could be lengthened almost indefinitely. Even my claim to think is only partially justified by the observable facts. Descartes's primal certainty, "I think, therefore I am," turns out, on closer examination, to be a most dubious proposition. In actual fact, is it *I* who does the thinking? Would it not be truer to say, "Thoughts come into existence, and sometimes I am aware of them"? Language, that treasure house of fossil observations and latent philosophy, suggests that this is in fact what happens. Whenever I find myself thinking more than ordinarily well, I am apt to say, "An idea has occurred to me," or "It came into my head," or, "I see it clearly." In each case the phrase implies that thoughts have their origin "out there," in something analogous, on the mental level, to the external world. Total awareness confirms the hints of idiomatic speech. In relation to the subjective "I," most of the mind is out there. My thoughts are a set of mental, but still external facts. I do not invent my best thoughts; I find them.

Total awareness, then, reveals the following facts: that I am profoundly ignorant, that I am impotent to the point of helplessness, and that the most valuable elements in my personality are unknown quantities existing "out there," as mental objects more or less completely independent of my control. This discovery may seem at first rather humiliating and even depressing. But if I wholeheartedly accept them, the facts become a source of peace, a reason for serenity and cheerfulness. I am ignorant and impotent and yet, somehow or other, here I am—unhappy, no doubt, profoundly dissatisfied, but alive and kicking. In spite of everything, I survive, I get by, sometimes I even get on. From these two sets of facts—my survival on the one hand and my ignorance and impotence on the other—I can only infer that the not-I, which looks after my body and gives me my best ideas, must be amazingly intelligent, knowledgeable, and strong. As a self-centered ego, I do my best to interfere with the beneficent workings of this not-I. But in spite of my likes and dislikes, in spite of my malice, my infatuations, my gnawing anxieties, in spite of all my overvaluation of words, in spite of my self-stultifying insistence on living, not in present reality, but in memory and anticipation, this not-I, with whom I am associated, sustains me, preserves me, gives me a long succession of second chances. We know very little and can achieve very little; but we are at liberty, if we so choose, to cooperate with a greater power and a completer knowledge, an unknown quantity at once immanent and transcendent, at once physical and mental, at once subjective and objective. If we cooperate, we shall be all right, even if the worst should happen. If we refuse to cooperate, we shall be all wrong, even in the most propitious of circumstances.

These conclusions are only the first fruits of total awareness. Yet richer harvests are to follow. In my ignorance I am sure that I am eternally I. This conviction is rooted in emotionally charged memory. Only when, in the words of St. John of the Cross, the memory has been emptied, can I escape from the sense of my watertight separateness and so prepare myself for the understanding, moment by moment, of reality on all its levels. But the memory cannot be emptied by an act of will, or by systematic discipline or by concentration—even by concentration on the idea of emptiness. It can be emptied only by total awareness. Thus, if I am aware of my distractions—which are mostly emotionally charged memories or fantasies based upon such memories—the mental whirligig will automatically come to a stop and the memory will be emptied, at least for a moment or two. Again, if I become totally aware of my envy, my resentment, my uncharitableness, these feelings will be replaced, during the time of my awareness, by a more realistic reaction to the events taking place around me. My awareness, of course, must be uncontaminated by approval or condemnation. Value judgments are conditioned, verbalized reactions to primary reactions. Total awareness is a primary, choiceless, impartial response to the present situation as a whole. There are in it no limiting conditioned reactions to the primary reaction, to the pure cognitive apprehension of the situation. If memories of verbal formulas of praise or blame should make their appearance in consciousness, they are to be examined impartially as any other datum is examined. Professional moralists have confidence in the surface will, believe in punishments and rewards, and are adrenalin addicts who like nothing better than a good orgy of righteous indignation. The masters of the spiritual life have little faith in the surface will or the utility, for their particular purposes, of rewards or punishments, and do not indulge in righteous indignation. Experience has taught them that the highest good can never, in the very nature of things, be achieved by moralizing. "Judge not that ye be not judged" is their watchword and total awareness is their method.

Two or three thousand years behind the times, a few contemporary psychiatrists have now discovered this method. "Socrates," writes Professor Carl Rogers, "developed novel ideas, which have proven to be socially constructive." Why? Because he was "notably nondefensive and open to experience. The reasoning behind this is based primarily upon the discovery in psychotherapy that if we can add to the sensory and visceral experiencing, characteristic of the whole animal kingdom, the gist of a free undistorted awareness, of which only the human animal seems fully capable, we have an organism which is as aware of the demands of the culture as it is of its own physiological demands for food and sex, which is just as aware of its desire for friendly relationships as it is aware of its desire to aggrandize itself; which is just as aware of its delicate and sensitive tenderness toward others as it is of its hostilities toward others. When man is less than fully man, when he denies to awareness various aspects of his experience, then indeed we have all too often reason to fear him and his behavior, as the present world situation testifies. But when he is most fully man, when he is his complete organism, when awareness of experience, that peculiarly human attribute, is fully operating, then his behavior is to be trusted." Better late than never! It is comforting to find the immemorial commonplaces of mystical wisdom turning up as a brand new discovery in psychotherapy. *Gnosce teipsum*—know yourself. Know yourself in relation to your overt intentions and your hidden motives, in relation to your thinking, your physical functioning, and to those greater not-selves, who see to it that, despite all the ego's attempts at sabotage, the thinking shall be tolerably relevant and the functioning not too abnormal. Be totally aware of what you do and think and of persons, with whom you are in relationship, the events which prompt you at every moment of your existence. Be aware impartially, realistically, without judging, without reacting in terms of remembered words to your present cognitive reactions. If you do this, the memory will be emptied, knowledge and pseudoknowledge will be relegated to their proper place, and you will have understanding—in other words, you will be in direct contact with reality at every instant. Better still, you will discover what Carl Rogers calls your "delicate and sensitive tenderness towards others." And not only *your* tenderness, the cosmic tenderness, the fundamental all-rightness of the universe—in spite of death, in spite of suffering. "Though He slay me, yet will I trust Him." This is the utterance of someone who is totally aware. And another such utterance is, "God is love." From the standpoint of common sense, the first is the raving of a lunatic, the second flies in the face of all experience and is obviously untrue. But common sense is not based on total awareness; it is a product of convention, or organized memories of other people's words, of personal experiences limited by passion and value judgments, of hallowed notions and naked self-interest. Total awareness opens the way to understanding, and when any given situation is understood, the nature of all reality is made manifest, and the nonsensical utterances of the mystics are seen to be true, or at least as nearly true as it is possible for a verbal expression of the ineffable to be. One in all and all in One; samsara and nirvana are the same; multiplicity is unity, and unity is not so much one as not-two; all things are void, and yet all things are the Dharma-Body of the Buddha— and so on. So far as conceptual knowledge is concerned, such phrases are completely meaningless. It is only when there is understanding that they make sense. For when there is understanding, there is an experienced fusion of the End with the Means, of the Wisdom, which is the timeless realization of Suchness, with the Compassion which is Wisdom in action. Of all the worn, smudged, dog-eared words in our vocabulary, "love" is surely the grubbiest, smelliest, slimiest. Bawled from a million pulpits, lasciviously crooned through hundreds of millions of loudspeakers, it has become an outrage to good taste and decent feeling, an obscenity which one hesitates to pronounce. And yet it has to be pronounced; for, after all, Love is the last word.

21

THE SIXTH PATRIARCH

In Dwight Goddard's extremely valuable compilation, *A Buddhist Bible,* there is one document of which I am specially fond—"The Sutra Spoken by the Sixth Patriarch." That blending of Mahayana Buddhism with Taoism, which the Chinese called Ch'an and the Japanese of a later period called Zen, achieves its earliest formulation in this account of Hui-neng and his teaching. And whereas most of the other Mahayana sutras are written in a somewhat forbidding philosophical style, these recorded reminiscences and sayings of the Sixth Patriarch exhibit a freshness and liveliness which make them quite delightful.

Hui-neng's first "conversion" took place while he was still a youth. "One day, while I was selling firewood in the market, I heard a man reading a Sutra. No sooner had I heard the text of the Sutra than my mind became all of a sudden enlightened." Traveling to the Tung-tsen monastery, he was received by the Fifth Patriarch who asked "whence I came and what I expected to get from him. I replied that I was a commoner from Sun-chow, and then said, 'I ask for nothing but Buddhahood.'"

The boy was then sent to the granary of the monastery, where for many months he worked as a laborer, hulling rice.

One day the Patriarch assembled his monks and, after reminding them of the uselessness of merit in comparison with liberation, told them to go and "seek the transcendental wisdom within your minds and write me a stanza about it. He who gets the clearest idea of what Mind-Essence is, will receive the insignia and become the Sixth Patriarch."

Shin-shau, the most learned of the monks and the man who was by all expected to become the Sixth Patriarch, was the only one to do as the Abbot had commanded.

> *Our body may be compared to a Bodhi tree,*
> *While our mind is a mirror bright.*
> *Carefully we cleanse and watch them hour by hour,*
> *And suffer no dust to collect upon them.*

So he wrote; but the Fifth Patriarch told him to go back to his cell and try again. Two days later Hui-neng heard someone recite the stanza, knew immediately that its author had not achieved enlightenment and himself dictated, to someone who knew how to write, the following lines:

> *By no means is Bodhi a kind of tree,*
> *Nor is the bright reflecting mind a case of mirrors,*
> *Since mind is Emptiness,*
> *Where can the dust collect?*

That night the Fifth Patriarch summoned the youth to his cell and secretly invested him with the insignia.

Not unnaturally Hui-neng's fellow monks were jealous, and many years elapsed before he was generally recognized as the Sixth Patriarch. Here are a few examples of his utterances, as recorded by his disciples.

Since the object of your coming is for the Dharma, please refrain from having opinions about anything, but try to keep your mind perfectly pure and receptive. I will then teach you. When he had done this for a considerable time I said, "At the particular moment when you are thinking of neither good nor evil, what is your real self-nature?" As soon as he heard this, he became enlightened.

People living under illusion expect to expiate their sins by the accumulation of merit. They do not understand that the felicities to be gained thereby in future lives have nothing to do with the expiation of sin. If we get rid of the principle of sin within our own minds, then and only then is it a case of true repentance.

People under delusion are stubborn in holding to their own way of interpreting samadhi, which they define as "sitting quietly and continuously without letting any idea arise in the mind." Such an interpretation would class us with inanimate beings. It is not thinking which blocks the Path; it is attachment to any particular thought or opinion.

If we free our minds from attachment on the one hand and from the practice of repressing ideas on the other, the Path will be clear and open before us. Otherwise we shall be in bondage.

It has been the tradition of our school to take "non-objectivity" as our basis, "idea-lessness" as our object and "non-attachment" as our fundamental principle. "Non-objectivity" means not to be absorbed in objects when in contact with objects. "Idea-lessness" means not to be carried away by any idea which may arise in the process of exercising our mental faculties. "Non-attachment" means not to cherish craving or aversion in relation to any particular thing or word or idea. Non-attachment is the characteristic of Mind-essence or Suchness.

Where thinking is concerned, let the past be dead. If we allow our thoughts, past, present and future, to become linked up into a series, we put ourselves under bondage.

Our true Nature is intrinsically pure, and if we get rid of discriminative thinking, nothing but this intrinsic purity will remain. Nevertheless in our system of Dhyana, or spiritual exercises, we do not dwell upon purity. For if we concentrate our mind upon purity, we are merely creating another obstacle in the way of the realization of Suchness, namely the delusive imagination of purity.

The Sutra says, Our Essence of Mind is intrinsically pure. Let us each realize this for himself from one momentary sensation to another.

The account of the Patriarch's last days is unfortunately too long to quote in full. About a month before his death Hui-neng informed his disciples of his impending departure and gave them some final words of advice, among which the following are notable. "You are especially warned not to let the exercise for concentration of mind fall into mere quietism or into an effort to keep the mind in a blank state." And again, "Do your best, each of you. Go wherever circumstances lead you." Listen to this stanza:

"With those who are sympathetic
You may have discussion about Buddhism.
As to those whose point of view differs from ours,
Treat them courteously and try to make them happy.
Do not dispute with them, for disputes are alien to our
    school,
They are incompatible with its spirit.
To be bigoted, to argue with others in disregard of this
    rule
Is to subject one's Mind-essence to the bitterness of this
    mundane existence."

On his last day the Patriarch assembled his disciples and told them that they were not to weep or mourn for him after his death. "He who does so is not my disciple.

What you should do is to know your own mind and re-alize your own Buddha-nature, which neither rests nor moves, neither becomes nor ceases to be, neither comes nor goes, neither affirms nor denies, neither remains nor departs. If you carry out my instructions after my death, then my going away will make no difference to you. On the other hand, if you go against my teachings, even were I to remain with you, no benefit would be yours."

After this he sat reverently until the third watch of the night, then he said abruptly, "I am going now," and in a moment passed away. At that time a peculiar fragrance pervaded the room and a lunar rainbow appeared to link the earth and heaven; the trees in the grove turned pale and the birds and animals cried mournfully.

22

NOTES ON ZEN

This essay originally appeared as a review of the book *Cat's Yawn*, published by the First Zen Institute in 1947.

We are accustomed in religious literature to a certain large solemnity of utterance. God is sublime; therefore the words we use about God should also be sublime. So runs the unexpressed argument in favor of the grand style. In practice, however, it happens not infrequently that sublimity of utterance is carried to self-stultifying lengths. For example, at the time of the great Irish potato famine of a century ago, a special prayer was composed for recitation in all the churches of the Anglican communion. The purpose of this prayer was to entreat the Almighty to check the ravages of the blight which was destroying the Irish potato crop. But from the outset the word "potato" presented a difficulty. Quite obviously, in the eyes of Early Victorian divines, it was too low, common, and proletarian to be pronounced in a sacred place. The horribly vulgar fact of potatoes had to be concealed in the decent obscurities of periphrasis, and consequently God was requested to do something about an abstraction, sonorously called "the Succulent

Tuber." The sublime had soared up into the empyrean of the ludicrous.

In similar circumstances, we may guess, a Zen Master would also have avoided the word *potato,* not because it was too low for use in a religious context, but because it was too conventional and respectable. Not "Succulent Tuber," but plain, monosyllabic "spud" would have been his idea of a suitable alternative.

Sokei-an, the Zen Master who taught in New York from 1928 to the time of his death in 1945, conformed to the literary traditions of his school. When he issued a religious journal, the title he chose for it was *Cat's Yawn.* This studiedly absurd and anti-pompous name is a reminder to all who may be concerned that words are radically different from the things they stand for; that hunger can be stayed only by real potatoes and not by even the loftiest verbiage about the Succulent Tuber; that Mind, by whatever name we choose to call It, is always Itself and cannot be known except through a kind of direct action, for which words are only a preparation and an incitement.

In itself the world is a continuum; but when we think about it in terms of words, we are compelled, by the very nature of our vocabulary and syntax, to conceive of it as a something composed of separate things and distinct classes. Working upon the immediate data of reality, our consciousness fabricates the universe we actually live in. In the Hinayana scriptures craving and aversion are named as the factors making for the pluralization of

Suchness, the illusion of discreteness, egoity and the autonomy of the individual. To these world distorting vices of the will the Mahayana philosophers add the intellectual vice of verbalized thinking. The universe inhabited by ordinary, unregenerate people is largely homemade—a product of our desires, our hatreds and our language. By ascesis a man can learn to see the world, not through the refracting medium of craving and aversion, but as it is in itself. ("Blessed are the pure in heart, for they shall see God.") By meditation he can by-pass language—by-pass it at last so completely that his individual consciousness, deverbalized, becomes one with the unitary Consciousness of Suchness.

In meditation according to the methods of Zen, deverbalization of consciousness is achieved through the curious device of the *koan*. The *koan* is a paradoxical, even a nonsensical, proposition or question, upon which the mind is concentrated until, utterly thwarted by the impossibility of making sense out of a paralogism, it breaks through into a sudden realization that, beyond verbalized thinking, there exists another kind of awareness of another kind of reality. An example of the Zen method is supplied by Sokei-an in his brief essay, *Tathagata*. "A Chinese Zen master was giving a tea party one freezing night. . . ." Kaizenji said to his disciples: "There is a certain thing. It is as black as lacquer. It supports heaven and earth. It always appears in activity, but no one can grasp it in activity. My disciples, how can you grasp it?"

He was indicating the nature of *Tatha,* metaphorically

of course, just as Christian ministers explain the attributes of God. . . .

The disciples of Kaizenji did not know how to reply. Then finally one of them, Tai Shuso by name, answered: "You fail to grasp it because you try to grasp it in motion."

He was indicating that, when he meditated in silence, Tathagata appeared within himself.

Kaizenji dismissed the tea party before it had really begun. He was displeased with the answer. "If you had been his disciple, what answer would you have made so that the Master could have continued the tea party?"

My own guess is that the tea party might have been prolonged, at least for a few minutes, if Tai Shuso had answered in some such way as this: "If I cannot grasp *Tatha* in activity, then obviously I must cease to be *I,* so that *Tatha* may be able to grasp this ex-me and make it one with Itself, not merely in the immobility and silence of meditation (as happens to the Arhats), but also in activity (as happens to the Bodhisattvas, for whom Samsara and Nirvana are identical)." These, of course, are mere words; but the state described, or rather faintly hinted at, by these words would, if experienced, constitute enlightenment. And meditation upon the logically unanswerable question contained in the *koan* may suddenly take the mind beyond words to the condition of egolessness, in which *Tatha,* or Suchness, is realized in an act of unitive knowledge.

The wind of the spirit bloweth where it listeth, and

that which happens when free will collaborates with grace to achieve knowledge of Suchness cannot be theoretically foreknown, cannot be prejudged in terms of any system of theology or philosophy, cannot be expected to conform to any verbal formula. Experience is determined only by experience. In Zen literature this truth is expressed by calculatedly outrageous anecdotes about enlightened persons who make bonfire of the scriptures and even go so far as to deny that what Buddha taught deserves the name of Buddhism—for Buddhism is the unteachable, immediate experience of Suchness. A story illustrating another of the dangers of verbalization, namely its tendency to force the mind into grooves of habit, is cited in *Cat's Yawn,* together with commentary by Sokei-an.

One day when the monks were gathered in the Master's room, En Zenji asked Kaku this question: "Shaka and Miroku (i.e. Gotama Buddha and Maitreya, the future Buddha) are the slaves of another. Who is this other?"

Kaku answered: *"Ko Sho san, Koku Ri shi."* (Which means, "the third sons of the Ko and Sho families, and the fourth sons of the Koku and Ri families," a piece of nonsense signifying that the capacity to become identified with Suchness exists in every human being and that Gotama and Maitreya are what they are in virtue of being perfectly "the slaves" of that immanent and transcendent Buddha-Nature.)

The Master accepted his answer.

At that time Engo was the head of the monks of the temple. The Master related to him this incident. Engo said: "Pretty good, pretty good! But perhaps he hasn't yet grasped the real point. You shouldn't have given him your acknowledgment. Examine him again by a direct question."

When Kaku came into En Zenji's room the next day, the Zenji asked him the same question. Kaku replied: "I gave the answer yesterday."

The Master said: "What was your answer?"

"Ko Sho san, Koku Ri shi," said Kaku.

"No, no!" the Master cried.

"Yesterday you said 'Yes.' Why do you say 'No' today?"

"It was 'Yes' yesterday; but it is 'No' today," replied the Master.

On hearing these words Kaku was suddenly enlightened.

The moral of this story is that, in Sokei-an's words, "his answer fell into a pattern, a mould; he was caught by his own concept." And, having been caught, he was no longer free to become one with the freely blowing wind of Suchness. Any verbal formula—even a formula which correctly expresses the facts—can become, for the mind that takes it too seriously and idolatrously worships it as though it were the reality symbolized by the words, an obstacle in the way of immediate experience. To a Zen

Buddhist the idea that a man can be saved by giving assent to the propositions contained in a creed would seem
the wildest, the most unrealistic and dangerous of fancies.

Hardly less fantastic, in his eyes, would seem the idea
that high feelings can lead to enlightenment, that emotional experiences, however strong and vivid, are the
same as, or even remotely analogous to, the experience of
Suchness. Zen, says Sokei-an, "is a religion of tranquility. It is not a religion which arouses emotion, causing
tears to well from our eyes or stirring us to shout aloud
the name of God. When the soul and the mind meet in a
perpendicular line, so to speak, in that moment complete
unity between the universe and the self will be realized."
Strong emotions, however lofty, tend to emphasize and
strengthen the fatal illusion of the ego, which it is the
whole aim and purpose of religion to transcend. "Buddha
taught that there is no ego either in man or in dharma.
The term *dharma* in this case denotes Nature and all the
manifestations of nature. There is no ego in anything.
Thus what is known as 'the two kinds of non-ego' means
that there is 'no ego in man and no ego in things.'" From
metaphysics Sokei-an passes to ethics. "According to his
faith of non-ego," he asks, "how can we act in daily life!
This is one of the great questions. The flower has no ego.
In the spring it blooms, in the autumn it dies. The stream
has no ego within it. The wind blows and waves appear.
The river bed drops abruptly and there is a waterfall. We
ourselves must really feel these things within ourselves.
. . . We must realize by our own experience how this

non-ego functions within us. It functions without any hindrance, without any artificiality."

This cosmic non-ego is the same as what the Chinese call Tao, or what the Christians call the indwelling Spirit, with which we must collaborate and by which we must permit ourselves moment by moment to be inspired, making ourselves docile to Suchness in an unremitting act of self-abandonment to the Order of Things, to everything that happens except Sin, which is simply the manifestation of egoity and must therefore be resisted and rejected. Tao, or non-ego, or the divine immanence manifests itself on every level from the material to the spiritual. Deprived of that physiological intelligence which governs the vegetative functions of the body and through whose agency the conscious will is translated into action, lacking the aid of what may be termed "animal grace," we could not live at all. Moreover it is a matter of experience that the more the ego's superficial consciousness interferes with the workings of the animal grace, the sicker we become and the worse we perform all acts requiring a high degree of psycho-physical coordination. The emotions connected with craving and aversion impair the normal functioning of the organs and lead, in the long run, to disease. Similar emotions and the strain which arises from the desire for success prevent us from achieving the highest proficiency not only in such complex activities as dancing, making music, playing games, doing any kind of highly skilled work, but also in such natural psychophysical activities as seeing and hearing. Empirically it has been found that malfunctioning of the organs can be corrected, and proficiency in acts of skill increased, by inhibition of strain and negative emotions. If the conscious mind can be trained to inhibit its own self-regarding activities, if it can be persuaded to let go and give up its straining for success, the cosmic non-ego, the Tao that is immanent in all of us, can be relied upon to do what has to be done with something like infallibility. On the level of politics and economics the most satisfactory organizations are those which are achieved through "planning for unplanning." Analogously, on the psycho-physical levels, health and maximum proficiency are achieved by using the conscious mind to plan its collaboration and its subordination to that immanent Order of Things which is beyond the scope of our personal planning and with whose workings our busy little ego can only interfere.

Animal grace precedes self-consciousness and is something which man shares with all other living beings. Spiritual grace lies beyond self-consciousness, and only rational beings are capable of cooperating with it. Self-consciousness is the indispensable means to enlightenment; at the same time it is the greatest obstacle in the way, not only of the spiritual grace which brings enlightenment, but also of the animal grace, without which our bodies cannot function efficiently or even retain their life. The Order of Things is such that no one has ever got anything for nothing. All progress has to be paid for. Precisely because he has advanced beyond the animal level to the point where, through self-consciousness, he can achieve enlightenment, man is also capable, through that same self-consciousness, of achieving physical degeneration and spiritual perdition.

THE "INANIMATE" IS ALIVE

The experimenter's is a curious and special talent. Armed with a tea canister and some wire, with silk, a little sealing-wax, and two or three jam-pots, Faraday marched forth against the mysterious powers of electricity. He returned in triumph with their captured secrets. It was just a question of suitably juxtaposing the wax, the glass jars, the wires. The mysterious powers couldn't help surrendering. So simple—if you happened to be Faraday.

And if you happened to be Sir J. C. Bose, it would be simple, with a little clockwork, some needles, and filaments, to devise machines that would make visible the growth of plants, the pulse of their vegetable "hearts," the twitching of their nerves, the processes of their digestion. It would be so simple—though it cost even Bose long years of labor to perfect his instruments.

At the Bose Institute in Calcutta, the great experimenter himself was our guide. Through all an afternoon we followed him from marvel to marvel. Ardently and with an enthusiasm, with a copiousness of ideas that were almost too much for his powers of expression and left him impatiently stammering with the effort to elucidate methods, appraise results, unfold implications, he expounded them one by one. We watched the growth of a plant being traced out automatically by a needle on a sheet of smoked glass; we saw its sudden, shuddering reaction to an electric shock. We watched a plant feeding; in the process it was exhaling minute quantities of oxygen. Each time the accumulation of exhaled oxygen reached a certain amount, a little bell, like the bell that warns you when you are nearly at the end of your line of typewriting, automatically rang. When the sun shone on the plant, the bell rang often and regularly. Shaded, the plant stopped feeding; the bell rang only at long intervals, or not at all. A drop of stimulant added to the water in which the plant was standing set the bell wildly tinkling, as though some record-breaking typist were at the machine. Near it—for the plant was feeding out of doors—stood a large tree. Sir J. C. Bose told us that it had been brought to the garden from a distance. Transplanting is generally fatal to a full-grown tree; it dies of shock. So would most men if their arms and legs were amputated without an anesthetic. Bose administered chloroform. The operation was completely successful. Waking, the anesthetized tree immediately took root in its new place and flourished.

But an overdose of chloroform is as fatal to a plant as to a man. In one of the laboratories we were shown the instrument which records the beating of a plant's "heart." By a system of levers, similar in principle to that with which the self-recording barometer has made us familiar, but enormously more delicate and sensitive, the minute pulsations which occur in the layer of tissue immediately beneath the outer rind of the stem, are magnified—literally millions of times—and recorded automatically in a dotted graph on a moving sheet of smoked glass. Bose's instruments have made visible things that it has been hitherto impossible to see, even with the aid of the most powerful microscope. The normal vegetable "heart beat," as we saw it recording itself point by point on the moving plate, is very slow. It must take the best part of a minute for the pulsating tissue to pass from maximum contraction to maximum expansion. But a grain of caffeine or of camphor affects the plant's "heart" in exactly the same way as it affects the heart of an animal. The stimulant was added to the plant's water, and almost immediately the undulations of the graph lengthened out under our eyes and, at the same time, came closer together: the pulse of the plant's "heart" had become more violent and more rapid. After the pick-me-up we administered poison. A mortal dose of chloroform was dropped into the water. The graph became the record of a death agony. As the poison paralyzed the "heart," the ups and downs of the graph flattened out into a horizontal line halfway between the extremes of undulation. But so long as any life remained in the plant, this medial line did not run level, but was jagged with sharp irregular ups and downs that represented in a visible symbol the spasms of a murdered creature desperately struggling for life. After a little while, there were no more ups and downs. The line of dots was quite straight. The plant was dead.

The spectacle of a dying animal affects us painfully; we can see its struggles and, sympathetically, feel something of its pain. The unseen agony of a plant leaves us indifferent. To a being with eyes a million times more sensitive than ours, the struggles of a dying plant would be visible and therefore distressing. Bose's instrument endows us with this more than microscopical acuteness of vision. The poisoned flower manifestly writhes before us. The last moments are so distressingly like those of a man, that we are shocked by the newly revealed spectacle of them into a hitherto unfelt sympathy.

Sensitive souls, whom a visit to the slaughter-house has converted to vegetarianism, will be well advised, if they do not want to have their menu still further reduced, to keep clear of the Bose Institute. After watching the murder of a plant, they will probably want to confine themselves to a strictly mineral diet. But the new self-denial would be as vain as the old. The ostrich, the sword swallower, the glass-eating fakir are as cannibalistic as the frequenters of chop-houses, take life as fatally as do the vegetarians. Bose's earlier researches on metals—researches which show that metals respond to stimuli, are subject to fatigue and react to poisons very much as living vegetable and animal organisms do—have deprived the conscientious practitioners of *ahimsa* of their last hope. They must be cannibals, for the simple reason that everything, including the "inanimate," is alive.

This last assertion may seem—such is the strength of inveterate prejudice—absurd and impossible. But a little thought is enough to show that it is, on the contrary, an assertion of what is *a priori* probable. Life exists. Even the most strict and puritanical physicists are compelled, albeit grudgingly, to admit the horridly disquieting fact. Life exists, manifestly, in a small part of the world we know. How did it get there? There are two possible answers. Either it was, at a given moment, suddenly introduced into a hitherto completely inanimate world from outside and by a kind of miracle. Or else it was, with consciousness, inherent in the ultimate particles of matter and, from being latent, gradually extrinsicated itself in ever-increasingly complicated and perfect forms. In the present state of knowledge—or ignorance, put it how you will—the second answer seems the more likely to be correct. If it is correct, then one might expect that inanimate matter would behave in the same way as does matter which is admittedly animate. Bose has shown that it does. It reacts to stimuli, it suffers fatigue, it can be killed. There is nothing in this that should astonish us. If the conclusion shocks our sense of fitness, that is only due to that fact that we have, through generations, made a habit of regarding matter as something dead; a lump that can be moved, and whose only real attribute is extension. Motion and extension are easily measured and can be subjected to mathematical treatment. Life, especially in its higher, conscious forms, cannot. To deny life to matter and concentrate only on its measurable qualities was a sound policy that paid by results. No wonder we made a habit of it. Habits easily become a part of us. We take them for granted, as we take for granted our hands and feet, the sun, falling downstairs instead of up, colors, and sounds. To break a physical habit may be as painful as an amputation; to question the usefulness of an old-established habit of thought is felt to be an outrage, an indecency, a horrible sacrilege.

Crains dans le mur aveugle un regard qui t'épie.

It was all very well from a poet. One could smile indulgently at a pleasing and childish fancy. But when it came to laboratory experiments and graphs, things, it was felt, were getting more serious. It was time to make a protest.

Personally, I make no protest. Being only a literary man, and not one of those physicists whose professional interest it is to keep matter in its place, with only such attributes as render it amenable to mathematics, I am delighted. I love matter, I find it miraculous, and it pleases me when a serious man, like Bose, comes along and gives it a new certificate of merit.

READINGS IN MYSTICISM

I am often asked by friends or unknown correspondents to suggest a course of reading in the literature of mysticism. My own knowledge of that literature is very far from being exhaustive; but I have read enough to be able to give what I think may be useful advice to those who have had fewer opportunities for study than myself. In the paragraphs that follow I shall name and, where necessary, briefly describe certain books, from the reading of which one may derive a good working knowledge of the nature and historical development of mysticism. It should be noted that most of the books mentioned belong to the literature of Western spirituality. This is due, not to deliberate choice, but to the limitations imposed by ignorance and the inaccessibility of the relevant books. The compilation of even an elementary bibliography of Oriental mysticism is entirely beyond my powers, and I shall therefore mention only a few books which I personally have found illuminating and helpful.

Before embarking on my task, I feel impelled to utter a few words of warning in regard to mystical literature in general. There have been published, in recent years, vast numbers of books dealing with meditation and contemplation, yoga and mystical experience, higher consciousness and intuitive knowledge of Reality. Many of these books were written by people with excellent intentions, but lamentably ignorant of the history and science of mysticism, and lacking any genuine spiritual experience. In other cases the authors did not even have good intentions, but were concerned, not in the least with the knowledge of God, but with the exploitation of certain yogic and mystical practices for the purpose of getting wealth, success, and physical well-being. Such books, whether merely silly, ill-informed and "phony," or downright bad and pernicious, should be avoided at all cost. When choosing books on mysticism a good rule is to confine yourself to the writings either of acknowledged saints and persons whom you have good reason to believe are on the road to sanctity, or else of reputable scholars. Outside these two categories of writers, the reader whose concern is with enlightenment cannot hope to find the smallest profit.

The firsthand experiences of those who are not saints—not even better-than-average human beings—may be startling and exciting enough on their own psychic level; but they will certainly not be genuine experiences of ultimate Reality, or God. For such genuine spiritual experiences happen, as a general rule, only to those who have gone some way along the road of purgation, and themselves lead to an improvement in the quality of the experiencer's living—an improvement amounting in exceptional cases to that total transformation of character, manifesting itself in sanctity. Psychic experiences, which do not contribute to sanctification, are not experiences of God, but merely of certain unfamiliar aspects of our psychophysical universe. The validity of a supposed experience of God is in some sort guaranteed by the sanctification of the person who has the experience. Where there is no evidence of sanctification, there is no reason to suppose that the experience had anything to do with God. It is a significant fact that occultism and spiritualism have produced no saints.

In view of all this, the serious student should pay no attention to any descriptions of firsthand experiences, except those written by saints and by persons who show evidence of advancing toward saintliness, and to no secondhand documents except those written by sound scholars, who may be relied upon to give an accurate account of saints and their teachings.

Spirituality is the art of achieving union with God, and consists of two branches—asceticism and mysticism, the mortification of the self and that contemplation by means of which the soul makes contact with ultimate Reality. Mortification without contemplation, and contemplation without mortification are both useless, and may even be positively harmful. That is why all genuine mystical literature is also ascetical literature, while all good ascetical literature (such as "The Imitation of Christ") treats also, explicitly or by implication, of mystical prayer. The combination of asceticism and mysticism is very clearly seen in Buddhist and Hindu writings. Thus, in the Buddhist eightfold path, the first seven steps prescribe a complete course of mortification of the ego, while the eighth inculcates the duty of mystical contemplation. The ascetical teaching of the Buddha is found in the best known of the sermons attributed to him. Selections from these may be read in the recently published *Bible of the World* (a valuable anthology from the canonical books of the principal religions of the East and West) and in Warren's *Buddhism in Translation,* a more extended anthology. Edward Thompson's historical novel *The Youngest Disciple,* treats the later life and teachings of the Buddha in fictional form, but with strict fidelity to the original texts.

For detailed descriptions of the techniques employed by the Buddhists in contemplation, one may consult *The Path of Purity,* published by the Pali Text Society and, for what concerns the Northern school, the three volumes of translations from the Tibetan, edited by Evans Wentz and published by the Oxford University Press. The volume of Tibetan yoga contains a valuable collection of techniques of concentration, meditation, and contemplation. The biography of Milarepa graphically describes the life of a Buddhist saint. And the *Bardo Thodol,* or *Tibetan Book of the Dead* (one of the world's religious masterpieces), sets forth the significance of contemplation in relation to the after-life of man.

Those who wish to read brief, but scholarly, summaries of Buddhist thought and practices will find what they want in *What is Buddhism?* compiled and published by the Buddhist Lodge, London; *Mahayana Buddhism,* by Mi Suzuki, and *Buddhism,* by Professor Rhys Davids. Particular aspects of Buddhist spirituality are treated under numerous headings in Hastings's *Encyclopaedia of Religion and Ethic,* a valuable work of reference covering the entire field of religion.

The spiritual literature of Hinduism is so enormous that the unprofessional Western student must, in mere self-preservation, confine himself to a minute selection. Here are a few of the indispensable books. *The Bhagavad Gita,* with some good commentary, such as that by Aurobindo Ghose; the *Yoga Sutras of Patanjali,* with the commentaries of Vivekananda; the *Upanishads,* translated in the Sacred Books of the East series; *Sankara,* in Jacob's translation, or at second hand, in some brief history of Indian philosophy, such as Max Muller's or Deussen's; the life of Ramakrishna, and the writings of Vivekananda on the various kinds of yoga. From these books one may derive, not indeed a comprehensive view of Hindu spirituality, but at least a pretty accurate synthetic picture of its fundamental character. The knowledge so gained will be a fair and characteristic sample of the total knowledge which can only be acquired by years of intensive study.

Spirituality in the Far East is mainly Buddhist or Taoist. In the sphere of Buddhism, China was content to follow in the footsteps of the Mahayana teachers of northern India and Tibet. From sources derived from China, Japan developed that strange and not entirely satisfactory kind of spirituality, Zen mysticism. This is most conveniently studied in the writings of Professor Suzuki, who has published many volumes, dealing with Zen in all its aspects.

Taoist spirituality is best represented by the first and greatest of its canonical books, the *Tao Te Ching* of Lao-Tzu. To this most wonderful scripture one may return again and again, certain of finding, with every enrichment of one's own experience of life, ever deeper and subtler significances in its allusive, strangely abbreviated and enigmatical utterances.

In compiling my elementary bibliography of Western spirituality, I shall begin with a list of sound scholarly volumes dealing with its historical development, its philosophy, and its practical procedures, and go on to enumerate a few of the most valuable of its original, firsthand documents.

Perhaps the most comprehensive general history of Christian asceticism and mysticism is the *Christian Spirituality* of Father Pourrat. Three volumes of this work, covering the period from gospel times to the middle of the seventeenth century, have been translated into English.

Other sound and well-documented works are Evelyn Underhill's *Mysticism,* Dean Inge's *Christian Mysticism,* Saudreau's *Life of Union with God,* and Poulain's *The Graces of Interior Prayer.* This last book is probably the most elaborate, subtle, and exhaustive analysis of the psychology of mystical states ever attempted and, despite a certain rather forbidding dryness of style, deserves to be carefully read by any serious student of the subject.

Another great monument of French scholarship in this field is Henri Brémond's *Histoire Littéraire du Sentiment Re-*

ligieux en France, a work in eight volumes, of which, so far as I know, not all have yet been translated into English. Brémond's book treats exhaustively of the revival of mysticism in France during the seventeenth century, and is a treasure house of the most fascinating biographical material, copiously illustrated by citations, often of great literary beauty, from the works of the spiritual writers of the period.

Many Catholic writers have written volumes of detailed instruction on the art of mental prayer and contemplation. Among the best of these (and still, fortunately, accessible in a reprint) is the *Holy Wisdom* of Augustine Baker, an English Benedictine monk of the seventeenth century. Baker was himself an advanced mystic, and the book in which he embodies his teachings is wonderfully complete, lucid, and practical.

For those who wish to know something about other Catholic methods of meditation and contemplation, *The Art of Mental Prayer,* by Bede Frost, may be recommended. This is a brief, but thoroughly scholarly, modern work, summarizing the spiritual teachings of a number of mystical and ascetic writers from the sixteenth century onward. A good contemporary manual on the same subject is Father Leen's *Progress through Mental Prayer. Spiritual Exercises,* by A. Tillyard, includes in a single volume a number of the best-known Christian methods and of analogous methods employed by Hindu, Buddhist, and Sufi mystics.

Valuable modern studies of individual mystics include

Bede Frost's monumental volume on St. John of the Cross, Von Hügel's monograph on St. Catherine of Genoa and Wautier d'Aygalliers' *Ruysbroeck, the Admirable.* Slighter sketches of medieval and early-modern mystics may be found in Miss Underhill's *Mystics of the Church* and in *The Flowering of Mysticism,* by Rufus Jones.

We have now to consider the firsthand documents of mysticism—the autobiographies, the journals, the spiritual letters, the descriptive and speculative treatises left by the great masters of Western spirituality. Here are a few of the most significant. *The Confessions* of St. Augustine; *The Life of St. Teresa,* written by herself; *The Journal* of John Woolman; the spiritual letters of St. François de Sales, of St. Jeanne Chantal, of Fénelon; the *Mystical Theology* and *Divine Names* of Dionysius the Areopagite (interesting in themselves and historically significant as the bridge connecting Christian mysticism with neo-platonic and Oriental thought); the sermons and other writings of Meister Eckhart, the Western mystic who approaches most nearly to the Vedantic position; the short but incomparably profound and beautiful *Cloud of Unknowing,* by an anonymous English mystic of the fourteenth century; the *Theologia Germanica;* the various writings of Tauler; the "Imitation of Christ" and the "Following of Christ"—the latter once attributed to Tauler, but now given to another unknown author and regarded as somewhat heretical; the writings of St. John of the Cross; the *Introduction to the Devout Life* and *Treatise of the Love of God,* by St. François de Sales; the

Spiritual Doctrine of Lallemant and the little treatise by Surin, called "Abandonment." All these are not only admirable in themselves, but possess the further merit of being reasonably accessible. Anyone who reads even some of them, together with one or two of the scholarly volumes previously cited, will possess a very fair knowledge of Western mysticism, its character, its psychology, its practices, and its philosophy.

In conclusion, let me cite a paragraph on the reading of spiritual books from the pen of Augustine Baker.

But as for spiritual books, the intention of an internal liver ought not to be such as is that of those who live extroverted lives, who read them out of a vain curiosity, so as to be thereby enabled to discourse of such sublime matters without any particular choice or consideration whether they be suitable to their spirit for practice or not. A contemplative soul in reading such books must not say, this is a good book or passage, but, moreover, this is useful and proper for me, and by God's grace I will endeavor to put in execution, in due time and place, the good instructions contained in it, so far as they are good for me.

2 5

SYMBOL AND IMMEDIATE
EXPERIENCE

This essay is the text of a lecture given by Huxley at the
Vedanta Temple in 1960.

I would like to start this lecture by reading two or three
lines from the twenty-first chapter of the book of Revelation. This chapter contains a description of the New
Jerusalem, and it finishes like this: " . . . and the street
of the city was pure gold, as it were transparent glass.
And I saw no temple therein: for the Lord God Almighty
and the Lamb are the temple of it." In the same way, of
course, there was no temple and no religion, in the ordinary sense of the word, in Eden. Adam and Eve didn't
require a temple and didn't require the ordinary apparatus of religion, because they were in a position to hear
the voice of the Lord as they walked in the Garden in
the cool of the day. And when we look at the book of
Genesis, we find that religion, in the conventional sense
of the word, began only after the expulsion of Adam and
Eve from the Garden, and that the first record of it is
the building of the two altars by Cain and Abel; and,
unfortunately, this is also the record of the first religious

war. Cain, if you remember, was a husbandman, and a vegetarian like Hitler, and Abel was a herdsman and a meat eater; and they were divided passionately, evidently, on their different occupations. It gave them a kind of religious absolutism, with the sad result which we all know. Then, in the fourth chapter of Genesis, we find mention of a new phase in relation to religion. This is after the birth of Seth, who was Adam's third son. It says in the fourth chapter: "And to Seth, to him also there was born a son; and he called his name Enos. Then began men to call upon the name of the Lord." This, evidently, is the beginning of what may be called the conceptual kind of religion—the sort of liturgical side on the one hand and the verbalized side of religion on the other.

These two sets of references, at the beginning of the Bible and at the end, illustrate very clearly an important point: that there are two main kinds of religion. There is the religion of immediate experience (the religion, in the words of Genesis, of hearing the voice of God while walking in the Garden in the cool of the evening—the religion of direct acquaintance with the Divine in the world), and there is the religion of symbols (the religion of the imposition of order and meaning upon the world through verbal or nonverbal symbols and their manipulation—the religion of knowledge *about* the Divine rather than direct acquaintance *with* the Divine). And these two types of religion have, of course, always existed, and we have to discuss them both.

Let us begin with religion as the manipulation of

symbols, as imposing order and meaning upon the flux of experience. In practice we find that there are two types of symbol-manipulating religions. There is the religion of myth, and there is the religion of creed and theology. Myth is obviously a kind of nonlogical philosophy. It expresses (either in words, in the form of a story, very often in the form of some visible image, or even in the form of bodily movements—in the form of a dance or a complicated ritual) some generalized feeling about the nature of the world and of man's experience in regard to it. And the myth is an unpretentious thing, in this sense that it does not claim to be strictly true; it is merely expressive of our feelings about experience. And though it is a nonlogical philosophy, it is very often a very profound philosophy precisely because it is nonlogical and nondiscursive; because it permits in the story, or in the image, the picture, the statue, or in the dance, the bringing together into a single expressive whole of a number of the disparate and even apparently incommensurable and incompatible parts of our experience. It brings them together and shows them at one viewing as an indissoluble whole, exactly as we experience them. In this sense it is the most profound kind of symbolism. Let me take a single example of this: the myth of the Great Mother, which runs through all the earlier religions. (It is still very powerful in the religion of Hinduism.) This myth in almost all these religions shows the Mother as simultaneously the principle of life, of fecundity, of fertility, of kindness, of nourishing compassion; but at the same time as being the principle of death and destruction. In Hinduism, Kali is at once the infinitely kind and loving Mother and the terrifying Goddess of Destruction, who has a necklace of skulls and drinks the blood of human beings from a skull. And of course, this picture is profoundly realistic, because, obviously, if you give life you must necessarily give death—because life always ends in death and requires to be renewed through death. So we see here, I think, a very good example of this profound, nonlogical philosophy which can be expressed in mythological form. And when we ask whether myths are true or not, this is quite an irrelevant question; they just are not true. As I said before, they are simply expressive of our reactions to the mystery of the world in which we live.

I think it is worth mentioning here that in practice we find these earlier nonlogical, mythical religions very frequently associated with what have been called spiritual exercises, but which are in fact psychophysical exercises. We find very often that these religions make great use of the body in their religious approach to the world. We find them making use of chant and dance and gesture, and getting a genuine kind of revelation from this. It is as though the releasing of the physical tensions, which we build up by our anxious and ego-centered life, through these physical gestures constitute what the Quakers called an "opening" through which the profounder forces of life without and within us can flow more freely. And it is very interesting to see even within our own tradition how this occasional letting go and organizing the body for religious purposes has had profound and very salutary influences.

For example, why were the Quakers called "Quakers"? For the simple reason that they quaked. The early Quakers were renowned for this, that their meetings very frequently ended with the greater part of the assembly indulging in the strangest kind of violent bodily movements, which were profoundly releasing and which permitted, so to speak, the influx of the Spirit to pour into them. And, as a matter of history, the Quakers, as long as they quaked, had the greatest degree of inspiration and were at the height of their spiritual power. We have the same phenomenon in the Shakers; the Shakers shook just as the Quakers quaked. And we see in the contemporary religious movement called Subud precisely the same phenomenon, the coming upon the assembled people of these furiously violent and involuntary physical movements which produce this kind of a release and permit for many people (I don't know if they do it for all) the influx and the flowing through of deeply powerful spiritual forces. And here I would like to quote the remarks of an eminent French Islamic scholar who says: "Modern Europe (of course, modern Europe includes modern America) is almost alone in having renounced, out of bourgeois respectability and Gallican Puritanism, the participation of the body in the pursuits of the Spirit. In India, as in Islam, chants, rhythms, and dance are spiritual exercises." I think this is a profoundly true and important remark, and it is interesting to see how these rather isolated corners of our own tradition—the way in which this harnessing of the body to the needs of the Spirit, this permission to use the body that the Spirit may be left more free—have illustrated the fact which is so manifestly clear when we study the history of the Oriental religions.

We have to go on now to consider the problem of religion as the other kind of symbol system, not as the system of myths, but as the system of concepts, of creeds, of dogmas, of beliefs. This is a profoundly different kind of symbolism, and it is the one which in the West has been much the more important. The two types of religion— the religion of immediate experience, of direct acquaintance with the Divine, and this second kind of symbolic religion—have, of course, coexisted in the West. Mystics have always formed a minority in the midst of the official symbol-manipulating religions, and this has been a symbiosis, but a rather uneasy symbiosis. The members of the official religion tended to look upon the mystics as difficult, trouble-making people. They have even made puns about the name; they have called mysticism "misty schism," in the sense that this is not a clear doctrine. It is a cloudy doctrine, it is an antinomian doctrine, it is a doctrine which does not conform easily to authority; and they have disliked it in consequence. And on their side, of course, the mystics have spoken—not exactly with contempt, because they don't feel contempt, but with sadness and compassion about those who are devoted to the symbolic religion, because they feel that the pursuit and manipulation of symbols is simply incapable in the nature of things of achieving what they regard as the highest end: the union with God, the identification with the Divine. William Blake, who was essentially a mystic, and who was apt to express himself in rather violent terms about those he disagreed with, speaks in these terms of the relationship between the two types of religion. He has this little couplet where he says, "Come hither, my boy! Tell me what thou seest there." And the boy answers, "A fool, tangled in a religious snare."

Within the tradition of Western Christianity, the mystics have been assured of a tolerated position by the perpetration at an early stage in Christian development of what is called "a pious fraud." About the sixth century, there appeared a series of Christian neoplatonic volumes under the name of Dionysius the Areopagite, who was the first disciple of St. Paul in Athens. And these volumes were taken to be almost with apostolic rank. In point of fact, the books were written either at the end of the fifth or the beginning of the sixth century in Syria, and the unknown author merely signed the name of Dionysius the Areopagite to his books in order to give them a better hearing among his fellows. He was a neoplatonist who had adopted Christianity and who combined the doctrines of neoplatonic philosophy and the practice of ecstasy with the Christian doctrine.

The pious fraud was extremely successful. Of course Dionysius's books were translated into Latin in the ninth century by the early philosopher Scotus Erigena; they entered into the tradition of the Western church and acted as a kind of bulwark and guarantee for the mystical minority within the church thereafter. It was not until quite recent times that the pious fraud was recognized for what it was. But meanwhile it is interesting to notice that this curious bit of forgery played a very important, a very beneficent part in the Western Christian tradition.

We have to consider now the relationship between the two types of religion, the religion of immediate experience and the religion primarily concerned with symbols. In this context there are some very illuminating remarks by Abbot John Chapman, who was a Benedictine and one of the great spiritual directors of the twentieth century. He died, I suppose, about twenty-five or thirty years ago. His spiritual letters are works of very great interest, and he was obviously a man with profound mystical experience himself. He was able to help others along the same path. But in one of these letters he remarks on the great difficulty of reconciling, not merely uniting, mysticism and Christianity: "St. John of the Cross is like a sponge full of Christianity. If you squeeze it all out, the full mystical theory remains. Consequently, for fifteen years or so, I hated St. John of the Cross, and called him a Buddhist. I loved St. Teresa and read her over and over again. She is first a Christian, only secondly a mystic. Then I found I had wasted fifteen years, so far as prayer was concerned." And now, quickly, let us say what he meant by the word prayer in this context. He did not mean, of course, petitionary prayer. He was speaking about what is called the Prayer of Quiet, the prayer of waiting upon the Lord in a state of alert passivity and permitting the deepest elements within the mind to come to the surface.

Dionysius, in his *Mystical Theology* and in his other books, had constantly insisted upon the fact that in order to know God, to become directly acquainted with God rather than knowing about God, one must go beyond symbols and concepts. These are actual obstacles, according to him, to the immediate experience of the Divine. And empirically, this is found to be true by all the spiritual masters, both of the West and of the Oriental world.

The religion of direct experience of the Divine is usually regarded as the privilege of a very few people. I personally don't think this is necessarily true at all. I think that practically everybody is capable of this immediate experience, provided he sets about it in the right way and is prepared to do what is necessary about it. But, in fact, this has been taken for granted, that the mystics represent a very small minority among a huge majority who must be content with the religion of creeds and symbols and sacred books and liturgies and organizations and, of course, with beliefs. This is faith in the form of belief. Now, belief is a matter of very great importance. There has been published, in recent years, one of these great best sellers which is called *The Power of Belief;* and this is a very good title because belief is a very great source of power. It has power over the believer himself and permits the believing person to exercise power over others. It does, in a sense, move mountains. But this belief, like any other source of power, is in itself ethically neutral; it can be used just as well for evil as for good. We have in our own times this very fine spectacle of Hitler very nearly conquering the entire world through the power of belief in something which was not only manifestly untrue but also profoundly evil. We see then that this tremendous fact of belief, which is so constantly cultivated within the symbol-manipulating religions, is essentially ambivalent: it can be both good and bad. And the consequence is that religion as a system of beliefs has always, in point of history, been an ambivalent force which has given birth simultaneously to the Sister of Charity and to what the medieval poets called the Proud Prelate, the ecclesiastical tyrant. It gives birth to the highest form of art and also to the lowest form of superstition. It lights the fires of charity and it also lights the fires of the Inquisition—lights the fire that burns Servetus in the era of Calvin. It gives birth to a St. Francis or an Elizabeth Fry, but it also gives birth to a Torquemada. It gives birth to a George Fox and also gives birth to an Archbishop Laud. So we see that this tremendous force has always been ambivalent precisely because of the strange nature of belief and the strange capacity of man, when he embarks on his philosophical speculations, for coming up with extremely strange and fantastic answers.

Myths, on the whole, have been much less dangerous than theological systems, precisely because they are less precise and have less pretensions of being the absolute truth. Where you have a theological system, there is a claim that these propositions about events in the past and events in the future and the structure of the universe are absolutely true. Consequently, a reluctance to accept these propositions is regarded as a rebellion against God, worthy of the most undying punishment. And we see that these systems have, as a matter of historical record, been used as justifications for almost every act of aggression and imperialism and imperialistic expansion in the past. There is hardly a single large-scale crime in history which has not been committed in the name of God. And it is a terribly painful and troubling thing, I think, when one is studying the history of religions, to see how easily this tremendous force can be used for the most undesirable purposes. This of course was summed up many centuries ago in the hexameter of Lucretius, where he says, *"Tantum religio potuit suadere malorum"* ("Such great evils this religion is able to persuade men to commit"). But he should also have added, *"Tantum religio potuit suadere bonorum"* ("Such great good this religion is able to persuade men to commit"). Nevertheless, the good has clearly had to be paid for by a great deal of evil.

This sort of strife-producing, controversy-producing quality of religion as a system of theological symbols has brought about not only the jihads and crusades of one religion against another, it has produced an enormous amount of internal friction within the same religion. The *odium theologicum,* the theological hatred, is notorious for its virulence. The religious wars of the sixteenth and seventeenth centuries had a degree of ferocity which really surpasses all belief. They were unbelievably horrible—the Thirty Years' War, for example. And in this context, I think, we should remember what Professor Hofstadter said in his lecture, that "We are accustomed now to say, 'Oh what great evils naturalism as a philosophy has brought upon the world.' But in point of historical fact, supernaturalism has brought about just as great evils, and perhaps even greater ones in the past." So we must not allow ourselves to be carried away by this kind of rhetoric.

I mentioned before this extraordinary capacity of philosophers and theologians to produce fantastic ideas which they then dignify with the name of dogma or revelation. And as an example of this I would like to cite a few facts about the history of one of the fundamental ideas of Christianity, the idea of the atonement. Such information as I have here is based upon the excellent essay in Hastings's *Encyclopedia of Religion and Ethics*. The essay is by Dr. W. Adams Brown, who at one time was Professor of Theology at the Union Seminary in New York. He has set forth the history of this doctrine very lucidly, and summed it up very cogently at the end. Now let me quickly go through this because it illustrates, I think, very clearly, the dangers of this kind of symbol-manipulating religion.

In the earliest period of Christianity, Christ's death was regarded either as a covenant-sacrifice, comparable to the sacrifice of the paschal lamb in the Jewish religion (there is some gospel authority for this), or was regarded as a ransom, comparable to a price paid by a slave for his freedom or the price paid by a war prisoner to be released. Both these ideas are hinted at in the gospels. Later on, there came the notion that Christ's death was the bloody expiation for original sin. This was based on a very ancient idea that any wrong-doing required expiation by suffering on the part of the sinner himself, or on the part of a substitute for the sinner. For example, in the Old Testament we read that David sinned in making a census of his people, and was punished by a plague which killed seventy thousand of his subjects, but did not kill David. The expiation was by a substitute, and this idea was taken over in the later, post-gospel theology.

In patristic times we find a profound difference between the Greek theologians and the Latin theologians. The Greek theologians were not primarily concerned with the death of Christ; they were concerned with the life. The death was thought to be a mere incident in the life. Their view of the atonement was that it existed, not to save man from guilt, but to save him from the corruption into which he had fallen after the fall of Adam and Eve. And the consequence was that the life was therefore more important than the death. Irenaeus says that Christ came and lived the life of man in order that man might live a life comparable to Christ's, and that this was the saving quality of the atonement. Among the Latin fathers the stress was entirely different. There the idea was that man was being redeemed, not from corruption primarily, but from guilt. He was redeemed from the punishment which had to be inflicted upon him for the sin of Adam. And whereas the Greek theologians regarded God as, primarily, absolute Reality, absolute Spirit, the Latin theologians regarded God with the mind of the Roman warrior, as a governor and lawgiver, and consequently their theology tends to be in legalistic terms.

Now the doctrine is developed slowly. We get in St. Augustine a continual stress upon the guilt of original sin and the fact that the guilt is fully inherited by all members of the human race, so that an unbaptized child must necessarily go directly to hell. He has a very fine passage where he says that the floor of hell is paved with infants less than a span long. This view went on and was developed over the centuries. And then there was a long period of discussion about the question of the ransom: to whom was the ransom of Christ's death being paid? There were many theologians who insisted that the ransom was being paid to Satan, that God had handed the world over to Satan with a wish to take it back again, and therefore had to pay this enormous price to Satan for the privilege of taking it back—taking man back from the grip of Satan. On the other hand, there were theologians who insisted that the ransom was being paid to God, to satisfy the honor of God—that God had been infinitely offended, and that the only reparation for an infinite offense was an infinite satisfaction; consequently, that the only possible satisfaction was therefore the death of the God-man, of Christ. It was the latter view which prevailed in the more or less official doctrine which was formulated by St. Anselm in the twelfth century—that the reparation was paid for the satisfaction of God's honor. And we may remark, incidentally, that Anselm spoke about the "over-plus" of the satisfaction. This infinite Person being killed constituted a kind of fund of merit which could be used for the absolution of sins, and it was on the basis of this doctrine that the medieval church enlarged its practice of selling indulgences, which led in due course to the Reformation. So that again one sees the curious consequences of these different doctrines.

Then we come to the Reformation, and we find that Calvin felt that retributive justice was an essential part of the character of God, and that Christ was actually bearing punishment which was due to man—that every sin had to be punished, and that Christ (and these were the words he used) "bore the weight of the Divine anger, was smitten and afflicted, and experienced all the signs of an angry and avenging God." These views were modified by the Arminians and Socinians and Hugo Grotius in the sixteenth and seventeenth centuries, and have given place gradually to more ethical and spiritual views within modern Protestantism.

Now I would like to read this passage in which Professor Adams Brown sums up the whole of this very strange history. He says: "The atoning character of Christ's death is now found in its penal quality as suffering, now in its ethical character as obedience. It is represented now as a ransom to redeem men from Satan, now as a satisfaction due to the honor of God, now as a penalty demanded by his justice. Its necessity is grounded now in the nature of things, and, again, is explained as the result of an arrangement due to God's mere good pleasure or answering his sense of fitness. The means by which its benefits are mediated to men are sometimes mystically conceived, as in the Greek theology of the Sacrament; sometimes legally, as in the Protestant formula of imputation; and, still again, morally and spiritually, as in the more personal theories of recent Protestantism. Surveying differences so extreme, one might well be tempted to ask, with some recent critics, whether, indeed, we have here to do with an essential element in Christian doctrine, or simply with a survival of primitive ideas whose presence in the Christian system constitutes a perplexity rather than an aid to faith. . . . Yet," adds Professor Brown, "the differences which we have discussed are not greater than may be parallel in the case of every other Christian doctrine." And the reasons for these differences in particular doctrines are to be sought in fundamental differences in man's conception of God and of his relations to the world. Where God is thought of as absolute Spirit, the atonement is conceived as the Greek theologians conceived it. Where, in the theology of Roman Catholicism and earlier Protestantism, God is conceived primarily as governor and judge, legal phraseology seems the natural expression of religious faith. Where ethical doctrines come to the fore, as in modern views of the atonement, a kind of ethical and spiritual language is used.

This, I think, indicates very clearly the extraordinary difficulties we are up against when we embark upon a systematic theologization of experience, a transference of experience into conceptual and symbolic terms. It obviously leads to difficulties of the most extraordinary nature, and the advantages which certainly accrue from actual theological expressions seem to me certainly offset by very grave disadvantages which the history of organized religion clearly indicates.

Now what has been, as a matter of history, too, the attitude of the proponents of religion as immediate experience toward the religion expressed in terms of symbols? In an extreme form, Meister Eckhart expresses this attitude. He says, "Why do you pray to God? Everything you say about God is untrue." Here we have to make a short digression on the use of the word *truth* in religious literature. The word *truth* is used in at least three common senses. It is used as synonymous with Reality; we say, "God is Truth," which means that God is the primordial fact. It is used in the sense of immediate experience where in the Fourth Gospel it is said that God must be worshiped in Spirit and in truth, meaning an immediate apprehension of the divine Reality; and finally it is used in the common sense of the word as correspondence between symbolic propositions and the facts to which they refer. Eckhart, of course, was a theologian as well as a mystic, and he would not have denied that truth in the third sense was in some degree possible in theology; he would have said that some theological propositions were certainly truer than others. But he would have denied that there was any possibility of the final end of man, the union with God, being achieved by means of manipulating these symbols. And this insistence on the inefficacy of symbolic religion for this ultimate purpose of union with God has been stressed by all the Oriental religions too. We find it in the literature of Hinduism, the literature of Mahayana Buddhism, of Zen, of Taoism, and so on; and I would like to read one or two of the statements made by the Oriental mystics. Here is one from the Sutralamkara: "The truth, indeed, has never been preached by the Buddha, seeing that one has to realize it within oneself." And again, "What is known as the teaching of the Buddha is not the teaching of the Buddha." Again it has to be an interior experience. There were even Zen masters who prescribed that anybody who used the word "Buddha" had to have his mouth washed out with soap, because it was so remote from the goal of immediate experience which was proposed in this branch of Buddhism. There is yet another paradoxical phrase: "What is the ultimate teaching of Buddhism? You won't understand it until you have it." Meanwhile, Yoka Daishi says, don't be so ignorant and puerile to mistake the pointing finger for the moon at which you are pointing. The habit of imagining that the pointing finger is the moon condemns all efforts to realize oneness with Reality to total failure.

This has been the regular attitude of mystics at all times, and above all in the Orient. Oriental philosophy has always been what I may call a kind of "transcendental operationalism." It starts with somebody doing something about the Self, and then from the experience obtained going on to speculate and theorize about the significance of this experience; whereas all too frequently—above all in modern Western thought—you get a philosophy which is pure speculation, which is based on theoretical knowledge and ends only in theoretical confusion.

However, there have been many exceptions to this rule in the West, above all among the mystics, who have insisted just as strongly as their Oriental counterparts on the necessity for direct experience, and on the inefficacy of symbols and of the ordinary discursive processes of the mind. St. John of the Cross says categorically: "All that the imagination can imagine and the reason conceive and understand in this life is not and cannot be, a proximate means of union with God." And the same idea is expressed by the great Anglican mystic of the eighteenth century, William Law, who says, "To find or know God in reality by any outward proofs, or by anything but by God himself made manifest and self-evident in you, will never be your case, either here or hereafter. For neither God, nor heaven, nor hell, nor the devil, nor the flesh, can be any otherwise knowable in you or by you but by their own existence and manifestation in you. And all pretended knowledge of any of these things, beyond and without this self-evident sensibility of their birth within you, is only such knowledge of them as the blind man hath of the light that hath never entered into him." This, as I say, is the Western equivalent of this constant repetition which we find in all Oriental literature.

Very briefly, let us discuss what is the mystical experience. I take it that the mystical experience is essentially the being aware of and, while the experience lasts, being identified with a form of pure consciousness—of unstructured, transpersonal consciousness, lying, so to speak, upstream from the ordinary discursive consciousness of every day. It is a non-egotistic consciousness, a kind of formless and timeless consciousness, which seems to underlie the consciousness of the separate ego in time.

Now, why should this sort of consciousness be regarded as valuable? I think for two reasons: First of all, it is regarded as valuable because of the self-evident sensibility of value, as William Law would say. It is regarded as intrinsically valuable just as aesthetically the experience of beauty is regarded as valuable. It is like the experience of beauty, but much more so, so to speak. And it is valuable, secondarily, because as a matter of empirical experience it does bring about changes in thought and character and feeling which the experiencer and those about him regard as manifestly desirable. It makes possible a sense of unity, of solidarity, with the world. It brings about the possibility of a kind of universal love and compassion, that kind of ungrudging love and compassion which is stressed so much in the gospel, where Christ says, "Judge not, that ye be not judged." And there is a phrase which was used by St. Catherine of Siena on her deathbed, which again stresses this point with extreme significance, where with great force she said: "For no reason whatever should one judge the actions of creatures or their motives. Even when we see that it is an actual sin, we ought not to pass judgment on it, but have holy and sincere compassion and offer it up to God with humble and devout prayer." The mystic, I think, is made capable of this kind of love, and is able to understand organically such portentous phrases which for the ordinary person seem extremely difficult to understand—I mean phrases like "God is Love," or "Though He slay me, yet will I trust in Him." These phrases become comprehensible to one who has passed through this kind of experience. There is certainly an overcoming of the fear of death, a conviction that the soul has become identical with a kind of absolute principle which expresses itself every moment in its totality. There is an acceptance of suffering in the self, and a passionate desire to alleviate suffering in others. There is, in a word, a combination of what the Buddhists call *prajna paramita,* which is the wisdom of the other shore, with *maha karuna,* which is universal compassion. As Eckhart says, "What is taken in by contemplation is given out in love." And this is, as I say, the value of the experience.

As for the theology of the experience—when it is felt necessary to make a theology of it—this is profoundly simple, and is summed up in the three words which are at the base of virtually all Indian religion and philosophy: *"Tat tvam asi"* ("thou art That"), in the sense that the deepest part of the soul is identical with the divine nature—that the Atman, the deeper Self, is the same as Brahman, the universal principle. Or in Eckhart's words, that the Ground of the soul is the same as the Ground of the Godhead. And this idea of course has been expressed in many forms, particularly the idea of the Inner Light, the Spark of the Soul.

Now, very briefly, I must just touch on the means for reaching this state. Here, again, it has been constantly stressed that the means do not consist in mental activity and discursive reasoning. They consist in what Roger Fry, speaking about art, used to call "alert passivity," or in what a modern American mystic, Frank C. Laubach, has called "determined sensitiveness." This is a very remarkable phrase. You don't do anything, but you are determined to be sensitive to letting something be done within you. And one has this expressed by some of the great masters of the spiritual life in the West.

St. François de Sales, for example, writing to his pupil, St. Jeanne de Chantal, says:

> You tell me you do nothing in prayer. But what do you want to do in prayer except what you are doing, which is, presenting and representing your nothingness and misery to God? When beggars expose their ulcers and their necessities to our sight, that is the best appeal they can make. But from what you tell me, you sometimes do nothing of this, but lie there like a shadow or a statue. They put statues in palaces simply to please the prince's

eyes. Be content to be that in the presence of God: he will bring the statue to life when he pleases.

The words of St. Jeanne confirm her understanding of De Sales' counsel.

I have come to see that I do not limit my mind enough simply to prayer, that I always want to do something myself in it, wherein I do very wrong. . . . I wish most definitely to cut off and separate my mind from all that, and to hold it with all my strength, as much as I can, to the sole regard and simple unity. By allowing the fear of being ineffectual to enter into the state of prayer, and by wishing to accomplish something myself, I spoilt it all.

This attitude of the masters of prayer is in its final analysis exactly the same as that adopted by the teacher of any psychophysical skill. The man who teaches you how to play golf or tennis, or a singing teacher, a piano teacher, will always tell you the same thing: You must somehow combine activity with relaxation. You must let go of this clutching personal self in order to let this deeper Self within you come through and perform—one may say—its miracles, which you interfere with. And, in a certain sense, one can say that what we are doing all the time is to get into our own light. We eclipse our deeper Self by our superficial selves, and so don't permit this life-force, this light (whatever you like to call it), which is—as we discover as we let go—an empirical fact within us, to come through. In effect the whole of the technique of proficiency in every field, including this highest form of spiritual proficiency, is a diseclipsing process—a process of getting out of our own light and permitting this thing to come through.

And of course if anyone does not want to formulate this process in theological terms he does not have to; it is possible to think of it strictly in psychological terms. I myself happen to believe that this deeper Self within us is in some way continuous with the Mind of the universe, or whatever you like to call it; but you don't necessarily have to accept this. You can practice this entirely in psychological terms and on the basis of a complete agnosticism in regard to the conceptual ideas of orthodox religion. An agnostic can practice these things and yet come to gnosis, to knowledge; and the fruits of knowledge will be the fruits of the Spirit: love, joy, and peace, and the capacity to help other people. So that we see then, there is really no conflict between the mystical approach to religion and the scientific approach, simply because one is not committed by it to any cut and dried statement about the structure of the universe. One can remain completely an agnostic in regard to the orthodox conceptualizations of religion and yet, as I say, come to the gnosis and, finally, exhibit the fruits of the Spirit. And, as Christ said in the gospel: The tree shall be known by its fruits.

26

SHAKESPEARE AND RELIGION

This essay, the last Huxley wrote, was published in Show
Magazine in 1964 soon after his death.

A name that is a household word, and a word that is on
everybody's lips. How simple and straightforward! But
then the inquiring mind starts to ask questions. Who precisely was Shakespeare? And what are the sorts of phenomena to which we apply the words *religion* and *religious?*

> *Others abide our question. Thou art free.*
> *We ask and ask. Thou smilest and art still.*

True enough, the poet penned no memoirs; he merely
left us Shakespeare's Complete Works. Whatever else he
may have been, the author was a genius-of-all-trades, a
human being who could do practically anything. Lyrics? The plays are full of lyrics. Sonnets? He left a whole
volume of them. Narrative poems? When London was
plague-ridden and the theaters, as hotbeds of contagion,
had been closed, Shakespeare turned out two admirable
specimens, *Venus and Adonis* and *The Rape of Lucrece.* And
then consider his achievements as a dramatist. He could

write realistically in the style of a dispassionate and often amused observer of contemporary life: he could dramatize biographies and historical chronicles; he could invent fairy stories and visionary fantasies; he could create (often out of the most unpromising raw material) huge tragic allegories of good and evil, in which almost superhuman figures live their lives and die their often sickening deaths. He could mingle sublimity with pathos, bitterness with joy and peace and love, intellectual subtlety with delirium and the cryptic utterances of inspired wisdom.

And what about "religion"? The word is used to designate things as different from one another as Satanism and satori, as fetish-worship and the enlightenment of a Buddha, as the vast politico-theologico-financial organizations known as churches and the intensely private visions of an ecstatic. A Quaker silence is religion, so is Verdi's *Requiem*. A sense of the blessed All-Rightness of the Universe is a religious experience and so is the sick soul's sense of self-loathing, of despair, of sin, in a world that is the scene of perpetual perishing and inevitable death.

Our many-faceted Shakespeare commented on religion in almost all its aspects. Here, for example, is what Shakespeare, the detached and amused observer of the Human Comedy, has to say about popular religion— religion as it is apprehended and practiced by the more ignorant and simple-minded members of his society. The passage I have chosen is taken from that marvelous scene from *Henry V* in which the Hostess tells Bardolph of the passing of Sir John Falstaff.

BARDOLPH: Would I were with him, wheresome'er he is, either in heaven or in hell!

HOSTESS: Nay, sure, he's not in hell: he's in Arthur's bosom, if ever man went to Arthur's bosom. 'A made a finer end, and went away, an it had been any christom child; 'a parted ev'n just between twelve and one, ev'n at the turning o' th' tide: for after I saw him fumble with the sheets and play with flowers, and smile upon his fingers' ends, I knew there was but one way; for his nose was as sharp as a pen, and 'a babbled of green fields. "How now, Sir John!" quoth I, "what, man! be o'good cheer." So 'a cried out "God, God, God!" three or four times. Now I, to comfort him, bid him 'a should not think of God; I hoped there was no need to trouble himself with any such thoughts yet.

"There lives more faith in honest doubt, believe me," Lord Tennyson earnestly affirmed, "than in half the creeds." Samuel Butler was more interested in Falstaff, Bardolph, the Hostess, and all the rest of them— they were the products of an Age of Faith. For them, the Christian Scheme of Salvation was a self-evident truth, and in their minds the Last Judgment and Hell-fire were unquestionable realities. So was Abraham's bosom, or was it King Arthur's bosom? After all, what difference did it make? A bosom is a bosom, and both names began with A. Their appetite for faith was omnivorous and could swallow anything. All the same, "I, to comfort him, bid him 'a should not think of God; I hoped there was no need to trouble himself with such thoughts yet." The doubt in honest faith is deep indeed.

Honest faith in God, angels and saints implied a corresponding faith in the Devil, evil spirits and the witches, sorcerers and magicians who collaborated with them. Shakespeare lived in an age when preoccupation with the foul Fiend and his human allies was more than ordinarily intense. Vivid descriptions of witchcraft and rules for its repression had been set forth, in the last decade of the fifteenth century, by two learned Dominicans, Father Kramer and Father Sprenger, whose *Malleus Maleficarum* or *Hammer of Witches,* was to remain a standard textbook for nearly 200 years. During the sixteenth and seventeenth centuries, in Protestant and Catholic countries alike, incredible numbers of witches and sorcerers were arrested, tortured, hanged, or burned alive. Like the overwhelming majority of his contemporaries (including his sovereign lord, King James I, who was the author of a learned work on witchcraft), Shakespeare certainly believed in sorcery and the possibility of collaboration between human hearts and devils. But this faith was tempered by common sense and dispassionate observation. Thus Glendower claims that he can call spirits from "the vasty deep." "Why, so can I," says Hotspur "or so can any man; But will they come when you do call for them?" The vasty deep is alive with spirits, and it is possible to establish communications with them—possible, but, as a matter of observable fact, very difficult. Magic works, but is notoriously unreliable even in the hands of those who have contracted their souls away to the Devil.

Most late medieval and early modern writers are anti-clerical—playfully anti-clerical like Chaucer, who writes of the Friar, "there is none other incubus but he," or else savagely anti-clerical like Ulrich von Hutten or the Franco Sacchetti of the *Trecento Novelle*. Shakespeare, on the contrary, has no constant bias against the clergy. He knew, of course, that established churches and the re-gimes they support are great machines for consolidating power and acquiring wealth; he knew that gold

> *This yellow slave*
> *Will knit and break religions; bless th' accurst;*
> *Make the hoar leprosy adored; place thieves,*
> *And give them title, knee, and approbation,*
> *With senators on the bench . . .*

The fact was obvious and deplorable, but he preferred not to harp on it.

Religion is not merely a complex of behavior-patterns and organizations. It is also a set of beliefs. What were Shakespeare's beliefs? The question is not an easy one to answer; for in the first place Shakespeare was a dra-matist who made his characters express opinions which were appropriate to them, but which may not have been those of the poet. And anyhow did he himself have the same beliefs, without alteration or change or emphasis, throughout his life?

The poet's basic Christianity is very beautifully expressed in *Measure for Measure,* where the genuinely saintly Isabella reminds Angelo, the self-righteous Pillar of Society, of the divine scheme of redemption and of the ethical consequences which ought to flow from its acceptance as an article of faith—ought to flow but, alas, generally do not flow!

> *Alas, alas!*
> *Why, all the souls that were were forfeit once;*
> *And He that might the vantage best have took*
> *Found out the remedy. How would you be,*
> *If He, which is the top of judgement, should*
> *But judge you as you are? O, think on that;*
> *And mercy then will breathe within your lips,*
> *Like man new-made.*

These lines, I would say, express very clearly the essence of Shakespeare's Christianity. But the essence of Christianity can assume a wide variety of denominational forms. The Reverend Richard Davies, a clergyman who flourished toward the end of the seventeenth century, declared categorically that Shakespeare had "died a papist." There is no corroborative evidence of this, and it seems on the face of it unlikely; but almost anything is possible, especially on a death-bed. What is certain is that Shakespeare did not live a papist; for, if he had, he would have found himself in chronic and serious trouble with the law, and vehemently suspected of treason. . . . (The casuists of the Roman curia had let it be known that the assassination of the heretic Queen Elizabeth would not be a sin; on the contrary, it would be registered in the murderer's credit column as a merit.) There is, therefore, every reason to suppose that Shakespeare lived a member of the Church of England. However, the theology which finds expression in his plays is by no means consistently Protestant. Purgatory has no place in the Protestant world-picture, but in *Hamlet* and in *Measure for Measure* the existence of Purgatory is taken for granted.

I am thy father's spirit, says the Ghost to Hamlet,

> *Doom'd for a certain term to walk the night,*
> *And for the day confin'd to fast in fires,*
> *Till the foul crimes done in my days of nature*
> *Are burnt and purg'd away. But that I am forbid*
> *To tell the secrets of my prison-house,*
> *I could a tale unfold, whose lightest word*
> *Would harrow up thy soul;*
> *freeze thy young blood;*
> *Make thy two eyes, like stars, start*
> *from their spheres. . . .*

In *Measure for Measure,* Claudio gives utterance to the same fears. Death is terrible not only in its physical aspects, but also and above all because of the awful menace of Purgatory.

> *Ay, but to die, and go we know not where;*

To lie in cold obstruction, and to rot;
This sensible warm motion to become
A kneaded clod; and the delighted spirit
To bathe in fiery floods, or to reside
In thrilling region of thick-ribbed ice;
To be imprison'd in the viewless winds,
And blown with restless violence round about
The pendent world; or to be worse than worst
Of those that lawless and incertain thoughts
Imagine howling! 'tis too horrible!
The weariest and most loathed worldly life
That age, ache, penury, and imprisonment
Can lay on nature, is a paradise
To what we fear of death.

In *King Lear,* the poet presents us with another world-picture that is neither Catholic nor Protestant. Purgatory exists, but not hereafter. Purgatory is here and now.

    I am bound
Upon a wheel of fire, that mine own tears
Do scald like molten lead. . . .

Whatever else he may have been, Shakespeare was not a precursor of Dr. Norman Vincent Peale. Indeed, during the years of his artistic maturity—the years that witnessed the production of *Hamlet, Troilus and Cressida, Macbeth, Measure for Measure,* and *King Lear,* he would seem to have passed through a spiritual crisis that made any facile kind of positive thinking or positive feeling impossible. Other great writers have passed through similar crises—Dickens, for example, and Leo Tolstoy. Tolstoy's negativism resulted in a religious conversion and a change of life. Dickens cured himself of despondency by plunging into amateur theatricals. How Shakespeare managed his private life we do not know.

All that we know is that if he did indeed go through a dark night of cosmic despair, he was poet enough to be able (in Wordsworth's words) to recollect the emotion in creative tranquility and to use his experience as the raw material of a succession of tragic dramas that were followed, during the last years of his professional career, by a series of romances, in which strange and improbable adventures are acted out in an atmosphere of acceptance, of forgiveness, of a conviction that, in spite of all appearances to the contrary, God's in his heaven and all's right with the world. But on the way to the final serenity of *The Tempest,* what horrors must be faced, what miseries endured. Keats wrote of Shakespearian tragedy as being the record of "the fierce dispute between damnation and impassioned clay." But there is much more in these dramas than the classical battle between instinct and duty, between personal desires and the tradition-hallowed ideals of religion. The Shakespearian hero has to fight his ethical battles in a world that is intrinsically hostile. And this intrinsically hideous universe is shot through with moral evil—evil on the animal level, on the human level, on the supernatural level. Thus the "soiled fitchew" is the bestial caricature of womanhood; for in woman, "but to the girdle do the gods inherit, beneath is all the fiend's."

And men are capable of greater wickedness even than women. "Use every man after his desert, and who would 'scape whipping?" There is, no doubt, some kind of moral order. The good go to Heaven, the evil to Purgatory and Hell. And even here on earth it can sometimes be observed that "the gods are just and of our pleasant vices make instruments to plague us." But divine justice is tempered by divine malignity. "As flies to wanton boys are we to the gods—they kill us for their sport." And to the effects of divine malignity must be added those of man's wickedness and stupidity, and the workings of a blind fate completely indifferent to human ideals and values. Sickness, decrepitude, death lie in wait for everyone.

> To-morrow, and to-morrow, and to-morrow
> Creeps in this petty pace from day to day,
> To the last syllable of recorded time;
> And all our yesterdays have lighted fools
> The way to dusty death. Out, out, brief candle!
> Life's but a walking shadow; a poor player.
> That struts and frets his hour upon the stage,
> And then is heard no more: it is a tale
> Told by an idiot, full of sound and fury,
> Signifying nothing.

The speaker is Macbeth; but Macbeth as we know him is Shakespeare's creation, and it was Shakespeare who put the words of this summing up of the case against human life into Macbeth's mouth. Between the thought of the dramatist and of the *dramatis persona* there must have been if not an identity, at least an affinity.

Unlike Milton or Dante, Shakespeare had no ambition to be a systematic theologian or philosopher. He was not concerned to "justify the ways of God to Man" in terms of a set of metaphysical postulates and a network of logical ideas. He preferred to "hold the mirror up to nature." It was a many-faceted mirror that changed with the passage of time, and the nature it changed, reflected, and recorded was a pluralistic mystery. What he gives us is not a religious system; it is more like an anthology, a collection of different points of view, an assortment of commentaries on the human predicament offered by persons of dissimilar temperament and upbringing. Shakespeare's own religion can be inferred in many cases from hints dropped by his characters.

Interpreters of Shakespeare have divided his career into four sections—first, a time of the workshop during which the young playwright was busily engaged in perfecting his technique. The second, the time in the world when the mature technician was using his powers to dramatize history, assorted fiction, and biography. Third, the time in the depths, which is the period we have just been discussing, when Shakespeare produced the series of black, unhappy allegories from *Hamlet* to *Measure for Measure;* and finally the time on the heights. This time on the heights we must now consider.

In our religious context, what is the significance of these later plays? What are we to make of this description of Shakespeare's career? There is certainly a change of mood, there can be no doubt of this. A greater acceptance, a greater openness to the strange anomalies of life. But exactly what does this correspond to in the general history of religious experience? Let us take the case of *The Tempest,* by far the best known and most popular of these latest plays—what did Shakespeare mean by *The Tempest*? We presume that this was the last of his plays, but we cannot be absolutely sure of this, nor can we be sure of the fact that he himself had intended it to be the last. This makes it very difficult to accept the hypothesis that in *The Tempest* Shakespeare was giving a kind of symbolic account of his own career. For he is Prospero. Prospero is the enchanter, the creator of visionary poetry, and in the end after exercising his enchantment with extraordinary success, he goes back to his dukedom at Milan, resolved to throw his magic wand and his book of charms overboard and to live out the remainder of his life on the ordinary level of human experience. But after all, the return of the successful actor to his native place where he would live out the remainder of his life, a solid pillar of society, and the return of a deposed duke to his sovereignty, where he would have to exercise an almost godlike judgment over the destinies of his subjects—these things do not have much in common.

If indeed *The Tempest* was written as an allegory of Shakespeare's life, it was a far-fetched allegory, one which leaves us wondering why this great master of the art should have been unable to find something more suitable. But at the same time we have to remember that the fact that Prospero was an enchanter is a most disturbing one in relation to religion. Enchantment, the use of magic, has always occupied an ambiguous position in religion. Religion calls for opening up the self, the letting that which is more than the self flow through the organism and direct its activities. Magic, on the other hand, is an attempt to establish the complete mastery of the self over everything. It is a technological device making the self all-powerful and so imitating God. But in no religion has this kind of *hubris* or overweening pride been considered admirable, and although supernormal powers may manifest themselves spontaneously on the way toward enlightenment, yet all the Masters of the spiritual life have insisted that they are not important, and that they must, if the aspirant is to go forward, be abandoned.

Prospero, of course, knows this perfectly well and, in the very end of the play, does abandon these powers. But for the greater part of the play we are shown him as a magician—a white magician it is true, but a white magician capable of considerable malice toward the unfortunate Caliban. A white magician who is capable of using a great deal of ingenuity in the preparation of tricks to catch his enemies. He has had the insight into the ultimate nature of things and knows what must be done and what must be left undone.

Our revels are now ended, these our actors,
As I foretold you, were all spirits, and
Are melted into air, into thin air;
And, like the baseless fabric of this vision,
The cloud-capp'd towers, the gorgeous palaces,
The solemn temples, the great globe itself,
Yea, all which it inherit, shall dissolve,
And, like this insubstantial pageant faded,
Leave not a rack behind. We are such stuff
As dreams are made on; and our little life
Is rounded with a sleep.

Prospero is here enunciating the doctrine of Maya. The world is an illusion, but it is an illusion which we must take seriously, because it is real as far as it goes, and in those aspects of the reality which we are capable of apprehending. Our business is to wake up. We have to find ways in which to detect the whole of reality in the one illusory part which our self-centered consciousness permits us to see. We must not live thoughtlessly, taking our illusion for the complete reality, but at the same time we must not live too thoughtfully in the sense of trying to escape from the dream state. We must continually be on our watch for ways in which we may enlarge our consciousness. We must not attempt to live outside the world, which is given us, but we must somehow learn how to transform it and transfigure it. Too much "wisdom" is as bad as too little wisdom, and there must be no magic tricks. We must learn to come to reality without the enchanter's wand and his book of the words. One must find a way of being in this world while not being of it. A way of living in time without being completely swallowed up in time.

Hotspur, as he is dying, sums up the human predicament with a few memorable words:

> But thought's the slave of life, and life time's fool;
> And time, that takes survey of all the world,
> Must have a stop.

We think we know who we are and what we ought to do about it, and yet our thought is conditioned and determined by the nature of our immediate experience as psychophysical organisms on this particular planet. Thought, in other words, is Life's fool. Thought is the slave of Life, and Life obviously is Time's fool inasmuch as it is changing from instant to instant, changing the outside and the inner world so that we never remain the same two instants together.

Thought is determined by life, and life is determined by passing time. But the dominion of time is not absolute, for "time must have a stop" in two senses, from the Christian point of view in which Shakespeare was writing. It must have a stop in the last judgment, and in the winding up of the universe. But on the way to this general consummation, it must have a stop in the individual mind, which must learn the regular cultivation of a mood of timelessness, of the sense of eternity.

We are all well on the way to an existential religion of mysticism. How many kinds of religion! How many kinds of Shakespeare!

27

THE YELLOW MUSTARD

Cabined beneath low vaults of cloud,
Sultry and still, the fields do lie,
Like one wrapt living in his shroud,
Who stifles silently.

Stripped of all beauty not their own—
The gulfs of shade, the golden bloom—
Grey mountain-heaps of slag and stone
Wall in the silent tomb.

I, through this emblem of a mind
Dark with repinings, slowly went,
Its captive, and myself confined
In like discouragement.

When, at a winding of the way,
A sudden glory met my eye,
As though a single, conquering ray
Had rent the cloudy sky

And touched, transfiguringly bright
In that dull plain, one luminous field;

And there the miracle of light
Lay goldenly revealed.

And yet the reasons for despair
Hung dark, without one rift of blue;
No loophole to the living air
Had let the glory through.

In their own soil those acres found
The sunlight of a flowering weed;
For still there sleeps in every ground
Some grain of mustard seed.

LINES

Sure, there are groves, there are gardens;
    but the cactus
Is never far, the sands are never far,
Even from the cedars and the nightingales,
Even from the marble fauns, the little gazebos,
Where, all in breathing silence, a girl's breasts
Are captive doves, and a ripeness as of grapes
Her nipples—never far; for suddenly
A hot wind blows and, frantic on the wind,
Dust and more dust, swarm on swarm of dust,
Peoples your summer night with the illusion
Of living wings and joy. But all the dance
Is only of powdered flint; and, feel! the doves
Are dead within your hands, and those small
    grapes
Withered up to oak galls, and the nightingales
Choked in mid song, the cedars brown,
    the lawns
Savage with stones and aloes, while the wind
Rattles among the leaves, and the June darkness
Creeps, as it were, with the horny stealth of lice.

But always, through the frenzy of the dust,
Always, above that roaring mindlessness,
That headlong absence of a goal, eclipsed
But still unfailing, the familiar Wain
Circles around a point of steady fire.

About the author

Excerpt

Insights,
Interviews
& More . . .

Read on

Aldous Huxley
A Life of the Mind

Poet, playwright, novelist, short
story writer, travel writer, essayist, critic,
philosopher, mystic, and social prophet,
Aldous Huxley was one of the most
accomplished and influential English
literary figures of the mid-twentieth century.
In the course of an extraordinary prolific
writing career, which began in the early
1920s and continued until his death in 1963,
Huxley underwent a remarkable process of
self-transformation from a derisive satirist
of England's chattering classes to a deeply
religious writer preoccupied with the human
capacity for spiritual transcendence. Yet in
everything Huxley wrote, from the most
frivolous to the most profound, there runs
the common thread of his search to explain
the meaning and possibilities of human life
and perception.

Courtesy of Man Ray/The Granger Collection

Aldous Huxley was born in
Surrey, England, in 1894, the son
of Leonard Huxley, editor of the
prestigious *Cornhill* magazine; and
of Julia Arnold, niece of the poet
and essayist Matthew Arnold, and
sister of Mrs. Humphrey Ward. He
was the grandson of T. H. Huxley,
the scientist. Thus by "birth and
disposition," as one biographer put
it, Huxley belonged to England's
intellectual aristocracy.

As Sybille Bedford writes in her
fascinating biography, *Aldous Huxley*
(Alfred A. Knopf / Harper & Row,
1974): "What we know about him as
a young child is the usual residue of
anecdote and snapshot. During his first years
his head was proportionately enormous, so
that he could not walk till he was two because

he was apt to topple over. 'We put father's hat on him and it fitted.' In another country, at a great distance in time and place, when he lay ill and near his end in southern California, a friend, wanting to distract him, said, 'Aldous, didn't you ever have a nickname when you were small?' and Aldous, who hardly ever talked about his childhood or indeed about himself (possibly because one did not ask) said promptly, 'They called me Ogie. Short for Ogre.'

"The Ogre was a pretty little boy, the photographs . . . show the high forehead, the (then) clear gaze, the tremulous mouth and a sweetness of expression, an alertness beyond that of other angelic little boys looking into a camera. Aldous, his brother, Julian, tells us, sat quietly a good deal of the time 'contemplating the strangeness of things.'

" 'I used to watch him with a pencil,' said his cousin and contemporary Gervas Huxley, 'you see, he was always drawing. . . . My earliest memory of him is sitting— absorbed—to me it was magic, a little boy of my own age drawing so beautifully.'

"He was delicate; he had mischievous moods; he could play. He carried his rag doll about him for company until he was eight. He was fond of grumbling. They gave him a milk mug which bore the inscription: *Oh, isn't the world extremely flat / With nothing whatever to grumble at.*

". . . And Aldous aged six being taken with all the Huxleys to the unveiling of the statue of his grandfather at the Natural History Museum by the Prince of Wales, and his mother trying, in urgent whispers, to persuade Julian, then a young Etonian, to give up his top hat—a very young Etonian and a very new top hat—to Aldous, queasy, overcome, to be sick in."

When Huxley was a sixteen-year-old student at Eton, he contracted a disease ▶

3

Aldous Huxley *(continued)*

that left him almost totally blind for two years and seriously impaired his vision for years to come. The loss of sight was an "event," Huxley later wrote, "which prevented me from becoming a complete public school English-gentleman." It also ended his early dreams of becoming a doctor. Yet, in a curious way, though he abandoned science for literature, Huxley's outlook remained essentially scientific. As his brother, the zoologist Julian Huxley, wrote, science and mysticism were overlapping and complementary realms in Aldous Huxley's mind: "The more [science] discovers and the more comprehension it gives us of the mechanisms of existence, the more clearly does the mystery of existence itself stand out."

Huxley took his undergraduate degree in literature at Balliol College, Oxford, in 1916, and spent several years during World War I working in a government office. After teaching briefly at Eton, he launched his career as a professional writer in 1920 by taking a job as a drama critic for the *Westminster Gazette*, and a staff writer for *House and Garden* and *Vogue*. Possessed of seemingly infinite literary energy, he wrote poetry, essays, and fiction in his spare time, publishing his first novel, *Crome Yellow*, in 1921. This bright, sharp, mildly shocking satire of upper-class artists won Huxley an immediate reputation as a dangerous wit. He swiftly composed several more novels in a similar vein, including *Antic Hay* (1923) and *Those Barren Leaves* (1925).

In *Point Counter Point* (1928), considered by many critics his strongest novel, Huxley broke new ground, both stylistically and thematically. In a narrative that jumps abruptly from scene to scene and character to character, Huxley confronts modern man's disillusionment with religion, art, sex, and politics. The character Philip Quarles, a novelist intent on "transform[ing] a detached intellectual skepticism into a way of harmonious all-round living," is the closest Huxley came to painting his own portrait in fiction. *Brave New World* (1932), though less experimental in style than *Point Counter Point*, is more radical in its pessimistic view of human nature. Huxley's antiutopia, with its eerie combination of totalitarian government and ubiquitous feel-good drugs and sex, disturbed many readers of his day; but it has proven to be his most enduring and influential work.

During the 1930s, Huxley turned increasingly toward an exploration of fundamental questions of philosophy, sociology, politics, and ethics. In his 1936 novel *Eyeless in Gaza* he wrote of a man's transformation from cynic to mystic, and as war threatened Europe once again, he allied himself with the pacifist movement and began lecturing widely on peace and internationalism.

For a number of years Huxley lived in Italy, where he formed a close relationship with D. H. Lawrence, whose letters he edited in 1933. In 1937, Huxley and his Belgian-born wife, Maria Nys, and their son, Matthew, left Europe to live in Southern California for the rest of his life. Maria Huxley died of cancer in 1955, and the following year Huxley married the Italian violinist and psychotherapist Laura Archera.

In the 1940s and 1950s, Huxley changed direction yet again as he became fascinated by the spiritual life, in particular with the possibility of direct communication between people and the divinity. Huxley read widely in the writings of the mystics and assembled an anthology of mystical writing called *The Perennial Philosophy* (1945). Around this time he began experimenting with mind-altering drugs like mescaline and LSD, which he came to believe gave users essentially the same experiences that mystics attained through fasting, prayer, and meditation. *The Doors of Perception* (1954) and *Heaven and Hell* (1956), Huxley's books about the effects of what he termed psychedelic drugs, became essential texts for the counterculture during the 1960s. Yet Huxley's brother Julian cautions against the image of Aldous as a kind of spiritual godfather to hippies: "One of Aldous's major preoccupations was how to achieve self-transcendence while yet remaining a committed social being—how to escape from the prison bars of self and the pressures of here and now into realms of pure goodness and pure enjoyment."

Huxley pursued his quest for "pure goodness and pure enjoyment" right up to the end of his life on November 22, 1963. Today he is remembered as one of the great explorers of twentieth-century literature, a writer who continually reinvented himself as he pushed his way deeper and deeper into the mysteries of human consciousness. ∾

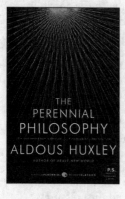

Excerpt

From *The Perennial Philosophy*

CHAPTER I

That Art Thou

IN STUDYING the Perennial Philosophy
we can begin either at the bottom, with
practice and morality; or at the top, with
a consideration of metaphysical truths;
or, finally, in the middle, at the focal point
where mind and matter, action and thought
have their meeting place in human
psychology.

The lower gate is that preferred by strictly
practical teachers—men who, like Gautama
Buddha, have no use for speculation and
whose primary concern is to put out in
men's hearts the hideous fires of greed,
resentment and infatuation. Through the
upper gate go those whose vocation it is to
think and speculate—the born philosophers
and theologians. The middle gate gives
entrance to the exponents of what has
been called "spiritual religion"—the devout
contemplatives of India, the Sufis of Islam,
the Catholic mystics of the later Middle
Ages, and, in the Protestant tradition, such
men as Denk and Franck and Castellio, as
Everard and John Smith and the first
Quakers and William Law.

It is through this central door, and just
because it is central, that we shall make our
entry into the subject matter of this book.
The psychology of the Perennial Philosophy
has its source in metaphysics and issues
logically in a characteristic way of life and
system of ethics. Starting from this midpoint
of doctrine, it is easy for the mind to move
in either direction.

In the present section we shall confine
our attention to but a single feature of
this traditional psychology—the most

important, the most emphatically insisted upon by all exponents of the Perennial Philosophy and, we may add, the least psychological. For the doctrine that is to be illustrated in this section belongs to autology rather than psychology—to the science, not of the personal ego, but of that eternal Self in the depth of particular, individualized selves, and identical with, or at least akin to, the divine Ground. Based upon the direct experience of those who have fulfilled the necessary conditions of such knowledge, this teaching is expressed most succinctly in the Sanskrit formula, *tat tuam asi* ("That art thou"); the Atman, or immanent eternal Self, is one with Brahman, the Absolute Principle of all existence; and the last end of every human being is to discover the fact for himself, to find out Who he really is.

> The more God is in all things, the more He is outside them. The more He is within, the more without.
>
> *Eckhart*

Only the transcendent, the completely other, can be immanent without being modified by the becoming of that in which it dwells. The Perennial Philosophy teaches that it is desirable and indeed necessary to know the spiritual Ground of things, not only within the soul, but also outside in the world and, beyond world and soul, in its transcendent otherness—"in heaven."

> Though GOD is everywhere present, yet He is only present to thee in the deepest and most central part of thy soul. The natural senses cannot possess God or unite thee to Him; nay, thy inward faculties of understanding, will and memory can only reach after God, but cannot be the place of his habitation in thee. But there is a root or depth of thee from ▶

whence all these faculties come forth, as lines from a centre, or as branches from the body of the tree. This depth is called the centre, the fund or bottom of the soul. This depth is the unity, the eternity—I had almost said the infinity—of thy soul; for it is so infinite that nothing can satisfy it or give it rest but the infinity of God.

William Law

This extract seems to contradict what was said above; but the contradiction is not a real one. God within and God without—these are two abstract notions, which can be entertained by the understanding and expressed in words. But the facts to which these notions refer cannot be realized and experienced except in "the deepest and most central part of the soul." And this is true no less of God without than of God within. But though the two abstract notions have to be realized (to use a spatial metaphor) in the same place, the intrinsic nature of the realization of God within is qualitatively different from that of the realization of God without, and each in turn is different from that of the realization of the Ground as simultaneously within and without—as the Self of the perceiver and at the same time (in the words of the Bhagavad Gita) as "That by which all this world is pervaded."

When Svetaketu was twelve years old he was sent to a teacher, with whom he studied until he was twenty-four. After learning all the Vedas, he returned home full of conceit in the belief that he was consummately well educated, and very censorious.

His father said to him, "Svetaketu, my child, you who are so full of your learning and so censorious, have you asked for that knowledge by which we hear the unhearable, by which we perceive what cannot be perceived and know what cannot be known?"

"What is that knowledge, sir?" asked Svetaketu.

His father replied, "As by knowing one lump of clay all that is made of clay is known, the difference being only in name, but the truth being that all is clay—so, my child, is that knowledge, knowing which we know all."

"But surely these venerable teachers of mine are ignorant of this knowledge; for if they possessed it they would have imparted it to me. Do you, sir, therefore give me that knowledge."

"So be it," said the father. . . . And he said, "Bring me a fruit of the nyagrodha tree."

"Here is one, sir."

"Break it."

"It is broken, sir."

"What do you see there?"

"Some seeds, sir, exceedingly small."

"Break one of these."

"It is broken, sir."

"What do you see there?"

"Nothing at all."

The father said, "My son, that subtle essence which you do not perceive there—in that very essence stands the being of the huge nyagrodha tree. In that which is the subtle essence all that exists has its self. That is the True, that is the Self, and thou, Svetaketu, art That."

"Pray, sir," said the son, "tell me more."

"Be it so, my child," the father replied; and he said, "Place this salt in water, and come to me tomorrow morning."

The son did as he was told.

Next morning the father said, "Bring me the salt which you put in the water."

The son looked for it, but could not find it; for the salt, of course, had dissolved.

The father said, "Taste some of the water from the surface of the vessel. How is it?"

"Salty."

"Taste some from the bottom. How is it?"

"Salty."

The father said, "Throw the water away and then come back to me again."

The son did so; but the salt was not lost, for salt exists for ever.

Then the father said, "Here likewise in this body of yours, my son, you do not perceive the True; but there in fact it is. In that which is the subtle essence, all that exists has its self. That is the True, that is the Self, and thou, Svetaketu, art That."

From the Chandogya Upanishad

The man who wishes to know the "That" which is "thou" may set to work in any one of three ways. He may begin by looking inwards into his own particular *thou* and, by a process of "dying to self"—self in reasoning, self in willing, self in feeling—come at last to a knowledge of the Self, the Kingdom of God that is within. Or else he may begin with the *thous* existing outside himself, and may try to realize their essential unity with God and, through God, with one another and ▶

with his own being. Or, finally (and this is doubtless the best way), he may seek to approach the ultimate That both from within and from without, so that he comes to realize God experimentally as at once the principle of his own *thou* and of all other *thous*, animate and inanimate. The completely illuminated human being knows, with Law, that God "is present in the deepest and most central part of his own soul"; but he is also and at the same time one of those who, in the words of Plotinus,

> see all things, not in process of becoming, but in Being, and see themselves in the other. Each being contains in itself the whole intelligible world. Therefore All is everywhere. Each is there All, and All is each. Man as he now is has ceased to be the All. But when he ceases to be an individual, he raises himself again and penetrates the whole world.

It is from the more or less obscure intuition of the oneness that is the ground and principle of all multiplicity that philosophy takes its source.

The Complete Aldous Huxley Bibliography

Dates are the year of first publication.

The Burning Wheel	1916
Jonah	1917
The Defeat of Youth and Other Poems	1918
Leda	1920
Limbo: Notes and Essays	1920
Crome Yellow	1921
Mortal Coils: Five Stories	1922
On the Margin	1923
Antic Hay	1923
Little Mexican	1924
Those Barren Leaves	1925
Along the Road: Notes and Essays	1925
Two or Three Graces: Four Stories	1926
Jesting Pilate: An Intellectual Holiday (The Diary of a Journey)	1926
Essays New and Old (U.S. title: Essays Old and New)	1926
Proper Studies	1927
Point Counter Point	1928
Do What You Will: Essays	1929
Brief Candles	1930
Vulgarity in Literature and Other Essays: Digressions from a Theme	1930
The World of Light	1931
The Cicadas and Other Poems	1931
Music at Night and Other Essays	1931
Brave New World	1932
Texts and Pretexts: An Anthology of Commentaries	1932
Beyond the Mexique Bay	1934

The Complete Aldous Huxley Bibliography
(continued)

Have You Read?
More by Aldous Huxley

**THE DOORS OF PERCEPTION
AND HEAVEN AND HELL**

Two classic complete books in which Huxley
explores, as only he can, the mind's remote
frontiers and the unmapped areas of human
consciousness. These two books became
essential for the counterculture during the
1960s and influenced a generation's
perception of life.

"A challenge is forcibly put, ideas are freshly
and prodigally presented."
— *San Francisco Chronicle*

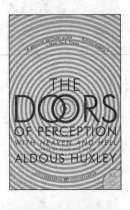

THE PERENNIAL PHILOSOPHY

An astonishing collection of writings
drawn from the world's great religions,
edited and commented upon by Huxley
with characteristic insight, wit, and passion.

"It is the masterpiece of all anthologies. As
Mr. Huxley has proved before, he can find
and frame rare beauty in literature, and here,
long before Freud, writers are quoted who
combine beauty with proud psychology."
— *New York Times*

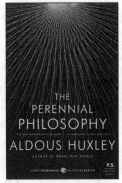

THE DEVILS OF LOUDUN

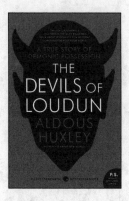

First published in 1952, *The Devils of Loudun* is Aldous Huxley's thrilling account of one of history's most sensational cases of mass demonic possession. The year 1643: When an entire convent is apparently possessed by the devil, a charismatic priest is accused of being in league with Satan and seducing the nuns—both spiritually and sexually. After a celebrated trial, the priest, Urban Grandier, was burnt at the stake for witchcraft. Here is the gripping true history of Grandier and the nuns of Loudun, as told by one of the master storytellers of the twentieth century.

"Huxley's masterpiece and perhaps the most enjoyable book about spirituality ever written. In telling the grotesque, bawdy and true story of a seventeenth-century convent of cloistered French nuns who contrived to have a priest they never met burned alive as a warlock . . . Huxley painlessly conveys a wealth of information about mysticism and the unconscious." —*Washington Post Book World*

BRAVE NEW WORLD

The astonishing novel *Brave New World*, originally published in 1932, presents Aldous Huxley's vision of the future— of a world utterly transformed. Through the most efficient scientific and psychological engineering, people are genetically designed to be passive and therefore consistently useful to the ruling class. This powerful work of speculative fiction sheds a blazing critical light on the present and is considered to be Aldous Huxley's most enduring masterpiece.

"Mr. Huxley is eloquent in his declaration of an artist's faith in man, and it is his eloquence, bitter in attack, noble in defense, that, when one has closed the book, one remembers." —*Saturday Review of Literature*

"Huxley never went out of style. Something about his work seem[s] to tug at our consciousness. . . . There is no escape from anxiety and struggle, and Huxley assists us in attaining this valuable glimpse of the obvious, precisely because it was a conclusion that was in many ways unwelcome to him."
—Christopher Hitchens

THE GENIUS AND THE GODDESS

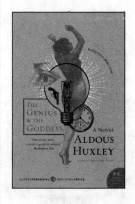

Talking with a friend on Christmas Eve while a small grandson sleeps upstairs, John Rivers is moved to set the record straight about his mentor—the legendary scientific genius in whose home, thirty years before, ecstasy and torment had laid hold of Rivers, shocking him out of "half-baked imbecility into something more nearly resembling the human form." Fatefully, Rivers had an affair with the famous man's young wife, bringing the couple to ruin. Now back in print, *The Genius and the Goddess* is Aldous Huxley's lost novella of the conflict between reason and passion.

"A genius. . . . A writer who spent his life decrying the onward march of the Machine."
—*The New Yorker*

Have You Read? *(continued)*

EYELESS IN GAZA

First published in 1936, *Eyeless in Gaza* is Aldous Huxley's loosely autobiographical novel of one man's search for an alternative to the moral disillusionment of the modern world. Anthony Beavis, a cynical libertine Oxford graduate, comes of age in the vacuum left by World War I. His life, loves, and foreign adventures leave him unfulfilled, until a friend inspires Anthony to become a revolutionary in Mexico. Shattered by the experience, Anthony forges a radical new spiritual understanding. *Eyeless in Gaza* remains one of the finest modern novels, a testament to Huxley's powers as an artist and thinker.

"An important book. . . . Without parallel in our contemporary literature."
—*New York Times Book Review*

BRAVE NEW WORLD REVISITED

When the novel *Brave New World* first appeared in 1932, its shocking analysis of a scientific dictatorship seemed a projection into the remote future. Here, in one of the most important and fascinating books of his career, Aldous Huxley uses his tremendous knowledge of human relations to compare the modern-day world with his prophetic fantasy. He scrutinizes threats to humanity, such as overpopulation, propaganda, and chemical persuasion, and explains why we have found it virtually impossible to avoid them. *Brave New World Revisited* is a trenchant plea that humankind should educate itself for freedom before it is too late.

"It is a frightening experience . . . to discover how much of his satirical prediction of a distant future became reality in so short a time."   —*New York Times Book Review*

ISLAND

In this, his last novel, Huxley transports us to a Pacific island where, for a hundred and twenty years, an ideal society has flourished. On the island of Pala—as in the *Brave New World*—science has helped to advance the founder's plans. But this time those plans have the goal of freeing each person, not enslaving him. Inevitably this island of bliss attracts the envy and enmity of the surrounding world—not least because of its vast oil reserves. A conspiracy is underway to take over Pala, and events begin to move when an agent of the conspirators, a newspaperman named Faranby, is shipwrecked on the island.

"*Island* is a welcome and in many ways unique addition to the select company of books—from Plato to now—that have presented, in imaginary terms, a coherent view of what society is not but might be."
              —*New York Times Book Review*